Early Court Records
of
Columbia County, Georgia

This volume was reproduced from
an original edition located in the
Publishers's private library
Greenville, South Carolina

Please direct ALL correspondence and book orders to:
Southern Historical Press, Inc.
PO Box 1267
375 West Broad Street
Greenville, SC 29602-1267
www.southernhistoricalpress.com

Originally printed: Albany, GA.
Reprinted by: Southern Historical Press, Inc.
　　　　　　　　　　　Greenvill, SC 29601
ISBN #0-89308-679-7
Printed in the United States of America

Foreward

These records were copied by Mrs. F.F. Baker, Thomson, Georgia, who spent many long hours searching through musty, old, handwritten volumes at the Courthouse in Appling. Not only were the records faded, but the handwritting in many instances was incredibly hard to read. Present day, as well as future generations of descendants of those whose records are contained herein, owe Mrs. Baker a deep debt of graditude for her untiring efforts in gathering these records in order that they may be made permanent before they have entirely faded away.

Columbia was cut off from Richmond County On December 10, 1790. Richmond, an original county, was created by the Act of February 5, 1777, from lands of the Creek cession, May 20, 1733, which was organized as the Parish of St. Paul in 1758.

COLUMBIA COUNTY, GEORGIA - Deeds of Gift - Bills of Sale - Powers of Attorney - Plus other Legal Oddments.

NOTE: Some of the Powers of Attorney are the usual ones, requesting lawyers, or others, to act in business affairs, but many of them are from Revolutionary Soldiers, asking that their bounty lands and pensions in other States be obtained for them.

1792, Nov 10
ROBERT DIXON to BRITTAIN SANDERS, of Wake County, N. C., Power of Attorney. "Being a Soldier in the N. C. State Legion, do appoint said Sanders my lawful attorney. To receive all bounties and pensions due me."

1790 - 1792 Following listed persons give Power of Attorney to JOSHUA GRINAGE, Columbia County:
    JAMES HESTON, of Wilkes County
    CHARLES TAYLOR, of Elbert County
    ROBERT NIXON(DIXON?), listed both ways, Columbia County
    RICHARD BULLOCK, of Columbia County
    SAMUEL POOL, of Columbia County
    WILLIAM DENNIS, of Columbia County
    ISAAC RAZOR, of Columbia County
    LITTLETON YARBOROUGH, of Columbia County

1793, Aug 29th - Book B
PETER THOMAS, late a soldier of the 14th Va. Regt., Col. Lewis, Commanding, afterwards by ANTHONY WHITE, in the Horse Service, do appoint JOSHUA GRINAGE my attorney, to collect all arrearages of pay, bounty land, etc., due me from the U. S. Gov't. or the State of Va.
The following are of same type, and were filed the same day with Joshua Grinage as attorney:
CHARLES TAYLOR, soldier in 1st Va. State Regiment, Col. Chas. GIBSON, Commander
JOHN SUDTHARD, late a soldier in Col. Anthony WHITE'S Company of Horse, in Virginia
JOHN BEALLE, late a soldier in the Virginia Line, commanded by Col. BLUFORD
ROBERT HASTINGS, of Richmond County, a soldier in Delaware Regt., commanded by Col. Vaughn; Capt. Kirkwood
GEORGE DOUGLASS, late of South Carolina
JULIUS HOLLAND, of Lincoln County, N. C., in the Light Dragoons, commanded by Col. White
WILLIAM BELLAMY, of the Continental Army of South Carolina
ALEXANDER JOHNSON, soldier in an Independent Company, Capt. JOHN MOORE. Commander, Served in S. C.
WILLIAM CREEMOR, a soldier in the 15th Va. Regt., commanded by Col. INNES.
JOHN TAYLOR, a soldier in the 3rd Regt., of Light Dragoons, Col. Will. WASHINGTON, Commanding
WILLIAM HALL, a soldier in the 5th Pennsylvania, Col. Francis JOHNSON, Commanding
JOHN MC CARTY, 3rd Regt., of S. C. TROOP, Col. THOMSON, Comn.
PATRICK MAHAN, soldier in 14th Va. Regt., Col. Lewis, Comm.

HENRY MC CARDEL, soldier in the 6th Regt. of S. C., Col. SUMTER, Commanding
ROBERT NIXON, soldier in the N. C. Line, Continental Army
TURNER THOMERSON, late a soldier in the 2nd Va., Col. William STEWART, Commanding, do appoint Peachy BLEDSOE, of Wilkes Co., as my attorney

1794, Mar 25
FRANCIS GRIFFIN, a soldier in the 3rd Regt., S. C. Troops, Col. Thompson, Comm. (Appoints Joshua Grinage)
JOSHUA GRINAGE, to ABRAHAM BALDWIN of Philadelphia, Power of Attorney. Grinnage was "Late a soldier in a detachment commanded by Col. William HETH(?), at the Siege of Charleston, belonging to the Virginia Line."

1794, Feb 3
JULIUS SCRUGGS, to JOSEPH BRADBERRY (BRADBURY), to disannull a judgment against ENOCH GRIGSBY, of Henry County, Ga.

1794, Feb 6
JAMES BURROUGHS to BENNETT BURROUGHS, of Maryland. (James was from St. Mary's County, Maryland), now in Columbia Co., Ga. "Atty. to recover from the administrator of the estate of BENJAMIN WOOD, my right and dower of all negroes, and property of any kind to which I am entitled." On the same date he made out a Bill of Sale, "for all the above," to BENNETT BURROUGHS, for £150 sterling

1793, Oct 19 - Recorded 1794
LEWIS GARDNER to ALEXANDER GARDNER - to sell a certain parcel of land in Bertie County, N. C., "formerly belonging to the Tuscarora Indians."

1794, Sept 29
JOHN VAN DORLINDER, cooper, to THOMAS HYNES, to recover from estate of PETER CULBREATH, dec'd., legacy left to "me and my wife, Mary, by her father's last will."

1794, Sept 24
JANE CULBREATH, widow of Peter, revokes power of attorney given to JOSHUA GRINAGE, and names son, James, to recover her dower rights.

1795, Apr 18
SARAH WEBSTER, of Lancaster County, S. C., to JOHN FLEMING, of Lancaster Co., S. C., to settle title of any purchase of land in Ga.

1795, Oct 16
JOHN SHACKLEFORD, to beloved son, Mordecai, power to dispose and sell a tract of land in Commonwealth of Virginia, in King and Queen County, "within a mile of the crossroads near Mantapike(?), on the waters of Mattapone River," 200 acres. "The land was given to my mother, Isabella, by her father, W. David Wedderburn, and it reverted to me by me being the only male heir."

1790, Dec 4
JAMES GRADY, of Columbia Co., Ga., to JOSEPH RENNOLDS, Spottsylvania County, Va., "to recover debts due me in Virginia."

1796, Mar 8
"I, Martha HOWARD, widow, and sole Adm. of estate of Lemuel HOWARD, do appoint my well beloved sons, Aquilla and Dorsey Howard to recover from the Rev. John COLEMAN, minister of the Protestant Episcopal Church, in Harford Co., State of Maryland, the full amount of the bonds and interest due from the said Coleman to the estate of said Lemuel Howard, dec'd."

1796, May 14
Alexander BEALLE to father James BEALLE, of Montgomery Co., Md., "to recover all debts, sums of money, and legacies due me."

1796, May 18
John WALTON, to Matthew WALTON, of Kentucky, "to make good titles to land I now possess in Kentucky."

1796, Nov 19
Mary RAMSEY to John RAMSEY (husband) and John CULBREATH....
"Whereas, the underwritten Mary Ramsey, and Mary Culbreath, wife of John Culbreath, cannot without manifest inconvenience attend the Court in Mecklenburg Co., Va., to make over our respective moieties of 400 acre tract on the Roanoke River, and waters of Grassy Creek, which we are heirs of as minors of Edward CULBREATH, we have therefore authorized our husbands to act for us."
(Above property sold on Jan. 10, 1797, to Thomas GREENWOOD, (Va.))

1796, Dec 26
Concord HAMILTON to Elias LAZENBERRY(LAZENBY)...to demand or sue for return of negro man "Hope" who has absconded from my possession, wherever he may be found.

1795, July 5
Abraham MARSHALL to Henry CARLETON, of Wilkes Co., to act in the State of Maryland, instead of Thomas SKINNER, of Sommerset Co., Md., "To claims and demand of said Skinner, the amount of all claims and demands of which I am now possessed in law and equity against said Skinner."

1795, Sept 21
Joseph DAVIS, to Jesse HAMLETT, Gentleman, of Prince Edward Co., Va., "To recover from Robert HARDEN and Frances de GRAFFENREID a certain parcel of land lying on both sides Ledbetter's Creek, County and State named. Originally the property of Jonathon and W. DAVIS, containing 785 acres."

1803, May 14
Power of Attorney - James MC BRIDE, Atty., for Samuel WRIGHT, of City of Dublin in United Kingdom of Ireland, Gentleman, to Joseph HABERSHAM, conveying power of attorney.
(Stephen DEANE conveyed certain properties in 1775 to his sister, Penelope DEANE. She afterwards married John WRIGHT, of Dorset St., in Dublin, Gent. They have both since died, and this leaves Samuel Wright the only son and heir. Inherited 500 acres conveyed to Stephen Deane May 12, 1775, by Provost Marshall, Levi Johnston.)

Samuel Wright sells said land to Joseph Habersham for $1,750.00

1795, Feb 10
   Joab WATSON, of Pittsylvania Co., Va., to David HARRIS, power of attorney, to ask and obtain from Waters DUNN, Sr., of Columbia Co., a certain sum of money, formerly obtained in Essex Co., Va.

1795, May 15
   John OLIVER, of Greenville Co., N. C., revokes Power of Atty., given to Joshua GRINAGE, Nov 20, 1791, to collect a debt on the estate of Gilbert CLARKE. Appoints friend Dionysius OLIVER, Edgefield, S. C. (District, not County.)

1801, July 10
   Gray BYNUM, of Stokes Co., N. C., Guardian of heirs and property of John CARMICHAEL, of Columbia Co., dec'd., Power of Atty., to Anderson CRAWFORD, to purchase from the tax-collector, or any other person, 150 acres on Kioka Creek, originally granted to Beverly LOWE, by him to William MADDOX, by him to John MADDOX, by him to Mary CARMICHAEL, widow of dec'd. By her conveyed to her children.

1801, Oct 6
   Richard and Robert RANDOLPH to Dr. Bathurst RANDOLPH, of Amelia Co., Va., to sue for and recover from John RANDOLPH, of Chesterfield Co., Va., all sums owing as a legacy from the estate of their father, Henry RANDOLPH, dec'd., Chesterfield Co., Va., of which John is executor.

1801, Dec 22
   Robert JONES, of Person Co., N. C., to Ambrose JONES, to sue and recover from Jos. TURNBULL, a tract of 690 acres in Greene Co., Ga., on the Oconee River.

1802, July 5
   David ROSS, of Cumberland Co., Va., to George HOLLEMAN of Goochland Co., Va., to act, sue and recover from the estate of Thomas MERIWETHER, the sum of £1,286 18s 1p. To receive slaves stolen or seduced from "The Neck," plantation in 1789, now in possession of Widow CLARKSON, who resides part time in S. C., and part time in Georgia. To recover from Seaborn JONES, atty of Augusta, certificates and securities sent to him for renewal, to the amount of £5,098 3s 11p 1f. To recover from Seaborn Jones all monies received on my account, and a copy of his accounts concerning same. To settle with Col. James HAMILTON for such collections as he has made, and a statement of the present situation of debts. To investigate the title of my lands on the Altamaha, and if taxes are in arrears, to pay them up, fully.

1802, Sept 3
   John GRIFFIN, Esq., of Wilkes Co., Ga., assigns and transfers unto Thomas CARR, a judgment against Benjamin FEW, and Thomas FEW, in Superior Court of Columbia Co., for $288.62 1/2

1803, Jan 11
   William FEW, of New York, to brother Ignatius FEW, of Columbia Co., "to transfer in my name, a tract of land in Jackson Co., on the

North Fork of the Oconee River, 1,024 acres granted to me Oct. 30, 1785." Wishes property conveyed to Buckner HARRIS, and Micajah WILLIAMSON.

1803, Feb 15
Pleasant MOORE, Edgefield Co., S. C., to Richard JOWELL, of Columbia Co., Ga. To collect and recover sums of money due him in Columbia Co. He is about to, "Take a trip to the Mississippi Territory."

1803, Mar 1
John AVERY to son Archer AVERY, "for the purpose of transacting all my business in Virginia."

1803, Mar 21
John JONES to James JONES, of Camden Co., N. C., to recover a tract of land containing 400 acres in Halifax County, N. C.

1803, Mar 21
"We, John JONES; Penelope COPINGER, formerly Jones, and Thomas JONES, sons and daughter of late John Jones, of Halifax Co., N. C., appoint James JONES, of Camden Co., N. C., to recover a 400 acre tract of land in Halifax County, bequeathed to us, the heirs above, and James Jones, by John Jones, dec'd."

1803, May 14
James MC BRIDE, of Savannah, att'y. of Samuel WRIGHT, of Dublin, Ireland, Esq., names James HABERSHAM as Wright's att'y to recover monies due Wright in America.

1816, July 8
Gazaway DAVIS, having intermarried with Nancy, the daughter of Thomas MOON, dec'd, and Martha Moon, the widow of Jesse Moon, dec'd., (Whereas Jesse was one of the heirs of Thomas Moon, dec'd), and William Moon of Clarke County, one of the sons of Thomas Moon, dec'd., have appointed our trusty friend John Moon of Clarke Co., to be our lawful att'y. To recover our equities in the estate of George Moon, Prince Edward County, Va., dec'd. John Mathews, Esq. of Va., Exr.

1798, Dec 6
Charles YOUNG, of Louisa County, Va., to Peter CRAWFORD, of Ga., and S. C., to sell all of my lands in S. C., and collect all monies due in both states.

1799, Apr 23
Thomas MOORE to Joseph YARBOROUGH, to demand, sue and recover from all and sundry persons the property that is my legacy left me by my father, George Moore, dec'd., in Prince Edward County, Va.

1799, June 27
Thomas COBBS, Jr., to Thomas COBBS, Sr., to recover from Michael GILBERT, of Hancock Co., part of estate of Jacob MOON, dec'd., of Buckingham Co., Va., to which I am entitled by law, as one of the heirs of the said Jacob Moon.

1787, Mar - Recorded Aug 7, 1799
   Jonathon SELL to Joel CLOUD, and Camm THOMAS, to act as trustees for Cowpen Land granted Joseph MADDOCKS, and Jonathon SELL, "for use of the People Called Quakers," in 1769.

1799, Dec 17
   Ann SPIERS, to Samuel BOWDRIE. Mrs. Spiers was Admx. of the estate of Harris SPIERS, and appointed Bowdrie, "true and lawfull," att'y, to recover from Col. Benjamin DREW, of South Hampton County, Va., such sums as are due dec'd Harris SPIERS, and any property he may have possessed.

1800, Mar 13
   Abednego WRIGHT to John BURNETT, of Richmond County, to settle, sell, recover and dispose of, of and from James THOMSON, Esq., and William SLIGHT, Charleston, S. C., Exrs. of will of Jesse JONES, dec'd a legacy of £54, 5 s, left to Elizabeth JONES, Dec 8, 1789, she the late wife of said Jesse. Also the interest on said sum to date, left by Jesse Jones to maintain the infant son of Joshua JONES.

1800, May 18
   Ann SPIERS, Admx. of estate of Harris SPIERS, dec'd., names Joshua BUTTS as lawfull attorney, to recover from Benjamin DREW of Southampton County, Va.,"any monies or properties due me, or the estate of Harris SPIERS, dec'd."

1800, Nov 9
   Silas MONK to John MONK, to recover from the Honorable Assembly of N. C., "wages due me for two tours of duty performed by me in the State of N. C., during the late War, as will appear by a discharge given by Gilford DUDLEY, dated Lynche's Creek, May 13, 1781. Also one dated Wake County, July 21, 1781, by Thomas WALTER."

1801, Jan 30
   Daniel DAUGHERTY, of Cabarrus Co., to Robert and Joseph WHITE, to act as arbitrators in any controversy over estate of James WHITE, dec'd.

1801, Feb 9,
   Sarah HARRIS, to James HARRIS, power of att'y. Sarah Harris, Excx., of Last Will and Testament of Benjamin HARRIS, dec'd, appoints James HARRIS to demand, sue for, levy, and recover all such sums of money, debts, rents, lands and goods owing to the estate by Benjamin FORSYTHE, of Virginia.

1801, May 12
   David HODGE to Richard BULLOCK, to demand, sue for and recover from the Land Office of Virginia, a bounty of land due me for a tour of duty performed by me in the said State, in the year 1755, under the command of General Braddock, in Capt. Chumbler's(?) Company.

1801, May 12
   John MC DONALD, SR., Lieut., and Caleb RUSSELL, of Columbia Co., to Richard BULLOCK, of Va., to sue for and recover from Assembly of Va., or Land Office, bounties of land due us for a tour of duty performed in the said State, in defense of our County, in the year

1758, under command of George MONROE, in the 67th Reg., under Archibald MONTGOMERY. The said Russell served in year 1755, in Capt. ARMSTRONG'S, company, under Col. Hanto(?) HAMILTON.

1804, May 10
Mary HAYNIE to Samuel THOMPSON, of Abbeville, S. C. Mrs. Haynie, Excx. to estate of John HAYNIE, dec'd., appoints Sam'l. THOMPSON to recover slaves; Sarah, Harriot, and child Rachel, all of yellow complexion.

1804, May 10
John BRISCOE, to Samuel THOMPSON, of Abbeville, S. C., to recover from Lawyer Wallace of Natchez Territory, or from any person, in whatsoever part of the world she may be found, negro Amy, of yellow complexion, sent to Natchez for sale by my attorney, John HAYNIE, dec'd. Sold to above Lawyer Wallace.

1804, May 10
Mary HAYNIE to Samuel THOMPSON, to recover my negro Gilbert, deformed in his left hand, and of yellow complexion. Also any monies my dec'd husband John HAYNIE had in his possession in the Natchez Territory.

1804, June 5
Joseph ALLEN to Samuel BROOKING, of Woodford Co., Ky., to sell, or otherwise dispose of lands which I hold in said State.

1804, June 28
Benjamin JOHNSTON, of Halifax Co., Va., to John Wynne SMITH, to settle father's estate with Smith JOHNSTON, of Oglethorpe County, exr., of said estate.

1804, Oct 10
Daniel ELAM to Peter CRAWFORD, to collect monies due me, and pay my lawful debts in my absence.

1805, Feb 12
I, John EVANS, of Mecklenburgh Co., do nominate my nephew, Humphrey EVANS, as my attorney, to represent me as if I were personally present.

1804, Apr 19
Sarah BLACKWELL, widow and relict of late George BLACKWELL, and Joseph ALLEN, Adm., of estate of said Blackwell, do appoint General John BLACKWELL, of Fauquier Co., Va., to collect from James WHEATLEY, of said County, all monies owing by him to the estate.

1815, June 1
Elizabeth BARHAM, relict of Charles BARHAM (late of Southampton Co., Va., son of Joel and Sarah BARHAM), and guardian of persons and property of James, Joel, Edmond and Sarah Barham, minors and orphans of said Charles...do appoint my trusty friend, Thomas PARKER, of the aforementioned county and state, to receive all monies, debts, lands, etc., to which I am entitled as guardian. Particularly from Wilkinson CAPEL.

1818, June 8
Susan BARLOW appoints Thomas PARKER (see above) to recover "all properties due me from any person or persons, especially from Matthew PARKER.

1806, Jan 2
Elizabeth Gordon TRUEMAN, widow of James, late of Prince George Co., Va., dec'd., and Ann McGruder DENT, dau. of said James, and her husband George DENT, appoint Capt. James SOMERWELL, of said county and state to convey to John MORAN, of said county and state, 1/2 of a 243 acre tract called "Buttonton," late the property of James TRUEMAN, dec'd. Surveyed by Henry TRUEMAN, Jan 27, 1776.

1806, Jan 22
George DOWNS appoints Notley WHITCOMB, "to receive property to which I may be entitled in behalf of my wife, Lucy DOWNS, from the estate of her late father, William CRITTENDON, dec'd."

1806, Mar 25
Mary CLARK appoints Archibald CLARK, of Mecklinburgh Co., Va., to recover my share of estates of Michael MC NEIL and James MC NEIL, dec'd., of Columbia County, Ga.

1806, July 16
Sarah HARDEN, of Tenn., now in Ga., appoints James ROSS, Esq., to demand, sue for and receive monies, damages, goods, etc., from all persons, particularly John AYRES, and William WILEY, Adms., of estate of Allan WILEY, dec'd., also from John AYRES, William WILEY, and Owen BLADWIN, Adms., of estate of William WILEY, SR., dec'd.

1806, July 22
Thomas JACKSON to brother, William JACKSON, to sue for and recover all my portion of the estate of my late father which is due me.

1775, Mar 21 - Rec. Aug 26, 1805
Seizure, and public vendue .. Lewis JOHNSTON, provost-marshall, to Mordecai HARRIS, laborer. Richard CAPERS obtained a judgment against James BROWN. Provost-marshall levied on property, part of which was a 150 acre tract in St. Paul's Parish, sold to Mordecai Harris, as highest bidder, at public vendue. Price £5, 10 s.

1798, Dec 5, - Rec. Sept 6, 1805
Affidavit - James FEW, for Henry HUGHES. On above date this deponent was at Brownsborough, in Columbia Co., when a dispute took place between Henry HUGHES and John Lewis POAGE, at which time a combat ensued, and said Poage did bite a piece out of the left ear of said Hughes, or so near off that the Doctor (N. Crawford), saw fit to cut the piece off. Said Poage also stabbed Hughes through the left wrist. Deponent never heard of anything derogatory to the character of said Hughes. And further deponent saith not.
s/ James FEW.

1798, Dec 5 - Rec. Sept 6, 1805
Nathan CRAWFORD, Physician for Henry HUGHES...About Dec 6, 1798,

I was called to see a man named Henry HUGHES, said to have been
stabbed by Mr. Poage. I found him bloody and much abused, and in
a state of syncope, but recovering. The principal wound was in the
left wrist, the instrument used, seemingly to have passed right
through the member, and the radial artery had been cut. Upon the
representation to me of his ear being bitten or cut, I cut the pen-
dulous portion off, and dressed the wound. s/ Nathan CRAWFORD, Doctor.

1806, Aug 20
    Dianna CLARK, of Duplin Co., N. C., appoints Elias FAISAN, of
same county, to complete a certain settlement respecting the estates
of John and Rowland GRIFFIN, dec'd., with Thomas MURRELL.

1806, Aug 22
    James OATS, appoints Samuel CLAYTON, to ask, demand, and re-
ceive all the legacy bequeathed to my wife, Sarah OATS, formerly
Clayton, dau. of Alexander and Elizabeth CLAYTON, left to her by
John BEASLEY, dec'd., of Charlotte Co., Va., contains 27 1/2 acres.

1807, Jan 1
    Joshua WHITAKER, of Harford Co., Md., to Darsey HOWARD, of
Columbia Co., Ga. Lemuel HOWARD, at the time of his death, was
possessed of lands in Columbia Co. Whereas, Martha HOWARD, his wid.,
was appointed Admx., and is since dec'd., a certain Peter EVERBY is
now Adm. Joshua WHITAKER, and wife, Ruth., dau. of said Samuel,
appoint her brother Darsey, to recover all the legacy due her.

1807, Jan 17
    Jane BEALLE, of Columbia Co., appoints her son, Thomas, to
recover property in Charles Co., Md., from the estate of her brother,
Francis SHEPHARD. He died intestate, leaving a 200 acre estate on the
Patomack River, inherited by him in the last will and testament of
her father, John SHEPHARD.

1807, Mar 20
    Richard WHITE, to Thomas M. WHITE, to transact all his busi-
ness in states of Ky., and Va., most particularly, to recover debts
due by Edmond HAWKINS, in Kentucky.

1807, Mar 23
    Mary MC NEIL, to John CULBREATH, to transact all business what-
soever.

        (These few P. of A's on last pages of Book N, and dated much
        later than the others.)
1815, Feb 2
    John BORUM, of Prince Edward Co., Va., to George AVARY, of
Amelia Co., Va., to act for me, and settle with Execs., of estate
of John AVARY, of Ga., and recover all monies and debts due me from
said estate, in right of my wife, Ann BORUM, late Avary.

1815, Feb 13
    John MADDIRA, and wife Patsey, and Ezekiel MEADORS, and wife
Polly, of Bedford Co., Va., appoint George AVARY to settle with

Exrs. of John AVARY, dec'd, to receive all monies and property due us, in right of our wives, Patsey and Polly, formerly Avary.

1815, May 23
George DENT, and wife, appoint Benjamin Freeman TINDELL, Esq., of Charles Co., Md., to act in our names in all matters pertaining to our right and title to land in Charles Co., called Indian Town, 1,000 acres formerly property of George (HUCHERSON - HICKERSON?), dec'd., then left to his daughters; Mary Ann m. William HARRISON; Jane m. Theophilus HARGRAVES; and Ann m. George DENT. Also a tract in Hampshire Co., Va., purchased by George Noble LILES from G. McMun, and conveyed by him to George Dent, said to contain 450 acres. Also to settle "accompts" with Capt. William Dent HARRISON, of Charles Co., to which we are entitled. Also to sell all our part of stock of cattle, hogs, horses, crops of corn, wheat, and tobacco, at Indiantown.

1815, May 26
Martha WALTON to George W. MOORE, "To adjust and settle my demand against citizens of Georgia, which I claim as Excx. of the estate of my dec'd husband, of Prince Edward Co., Va., and whose will was duly recorded in the County Court."

Current dates, in Book O.

1807, Nov 22
Heirs of William BAYLISS appoint John BAYLISS to transact all necessary business concerning a tract of land in Richmond Co., now in possession of Isham BAYLESS.

1807, Oct 21
John BENNING to Pleasant BENNING. To sue for and recover from Adms. of last Will and Testament of Joseph BENNING, late of Buckingham Co., Va., all legacy willed to me.

1807, Oct 22
Alexander CAMPBELL to Walter DRANE. To make and execute, in my name, a good and lawful title to John FLEMING, to a tract lying in Wilkinson Co., Ga., #326 in the 4th Dist.

1808, Mar 10
Tarleton CHENNAULT appoints Elijah NELSON, his attorney. Having inherited land in Buckingham Co., Va., 125 acres on waters of Whispering Creek, by last Will and Testament of John NELSON, dec'd., att'y is to sell the land.

1809, Mar 30
James ALLEN, in right of wife, Elizabeth (formerly WHITE), one of heirs of Armistead WHITE, of Culpepper Co., Va., dec'd., appoints trusty friends Presley and John WHITE, att'ys., to sell or otherwise dispose of property assigned to me in right of my wife.

1809, Apr 10
Cader POWELL, of Hancock Co., Ga., to Thomas VICKERS, to recover

my share of estate of John WATSON, of Va. (No county given.)

1809, Apr 13
Sarah BLANCHARD to James BLANCHARD, she being the widow of Reuben BLANCHARD, dec'd; Jeremiah BLANCHARD; Uriah BLANCHARD, Ezekiel REED, (who m. Sarah BLANCHARD); only surviving heirs of said Reuben and Jeremiah Blanchard, who married Mary, only surviving dau. and heir of Robert BLANCHARD; appoint James BLANCHARD, att'y., to recover from Adms., of Noah HINTON, all property to which we are entitled, as heirs and representatives of Robert and Reuben BLANCHARD, who were heirs of Benjamin BLANCHARD, who intermarried with Sarah HINTON, sister of said Noah HINTON.

1809, Apr 20
Garah DAVIS, appoints Richard BEALLE of Montgomery Co., Md., to demand of and bring suit, if necessary, against Solomon DAVIS, Exr., of estate of Solomon SAMPSON, of said County, to recover six negroes for which said Sampson was indebted to me.

1809, June 7
Henry HAMPTON, Exr., of estate of Benjamin ANDREWS, has appointed Austin DAVIS, as my att'y., to recover my share of said Andrews.

1809, Aug 14
Alexander E. BEALLE appoints Alexander R. BEALLE, to sue for and recover from James BEALLE, of Montgomery Co., Md., all sums of monies and debts due me from said Bealle.

1808, Aug 10
James LOVELACE to William LOVELACE (or LOVELESS), power of att'y. James BELL (or BEALLE), late of Montgomery Co., Md., dec'd, did give to his wife, all real and personal estate, and at her death, the same was to be divided between Marguery LOVELACE, wife of William, three bros. and sisters and their heirs. Margaret and Marguery having since departed, James Lovelace, Allen Lovelace, John COLLIER (husband of Mary LOVELACE), James STAPLER, (husband of Elizabeth LOVELACE) Isham FULLER, (husband of Peggy LOVELESS), and William STAPLER, (husband of Patsey LOVELACE), have appointed William Lovelace to recover from Daniel BEALLE, Adm. for estate of late James BEALLE, our shares of said estate.

1810, July 23
WHEREAS, by the death of my father, Jeremiah LAMKIN, I became heir to three negro slaves, be it known that I, Daniel LAMKIN, being resident in the Mississippi Territory, have appointed my sister, Elizabeth NORMENT, my atty., to take charge of said negroes, if any survive, take them into her possession, or sell them, if she wishes.

1806, June 13
Sally GIBSON to Dexter GIBSON, to transact all business in State of N. C., to ask and demand and receive of Joseph SANDERSON, Exr., of estate of Micajah FRAZER, dec'd., any property left me by my grandfather, the said Micajah Frazier.

1807, Aug 5

William SEWALL, of Lincoln County, to John LUCKEY, to recover all legacy left to my wife, Joanna, by her father, Charles DUNHAM, dec'd., also property in Ky., left to her under the name Joannah ENGLEMANN.

1811, Oct 2
Obedience LOWE, of Baldwin Co., Ga., appoints Peter CRAWFORD her lawful att'y., "Whereby Beverly LOWE, my late husband, by his last Will and Testament, made such provisions for me, as his widow, that I cannot accept them, I wish to relinquish the legacy, and take dower rights instead."

1812, Feb 1
John SCOTT, and wife, Catherine, formerly COBBS, of District of Ste. Genevieve, State of La., appoint Josiah ELLIS att'y., to receive any property due me, in right of my wife, from estate of Thomas COBBS, and William Beckham, Exrs. of estate of John COBBS.

1812, Feb 14
Samuel WILSON, being legator, in right of my wife, Polly PAYNE WILSON, to a legacy left by her grandfather Samuel PAYNE, SR., dec'd., appoint William JAMERSON, of Twiggs Co. Ga., to collect same.

1812, Feb 21
Obadiah LOWE, and wife, Judath, of Baldwin Co., Ga., disputing a legacy of late father, Beverly LOWE, leaving all rest and residue of estate (after few specified legacies), to James CULBREATH. Whereas, my two daughters, Elizabeth and Obedience, are infants and incapable of acting for themselves, and, Whereas, I live at a distance, have appointed Peter CRAWFORD to recover legacy of $430.00.

1812, Mar 4
Elizabeth WALKER to Jamerson ANDREWS, power of attorney, to sue for and recover all monies due to me from Columbia Co., or elsewhere. Also to sell tract of land, 350 acres, whereon David WALKER formerly lived. (Elizabeth was widow of David WALKER, SR.)

1812, Dec 1
Peter CRAWFORD, guardian of James CARY, a minor of John CARY, dec'd., of Frederick Co., Md., appoints George CARY, of Fredericktown, Md., to ask, demand, and sue for all monies, legacies, etc., due said James CARY, minor, from estate of Robert TURNER, dec'd. (Relationship of James and Robert Turner not given.)

1813, Apr 20
George Washington DENT appoints Benjamin TINDALL, of Charles Co., Md., to obtain in my name, a deed for a tract of land in Va., sold by my brother, Dr. Patrick DENT, to a certain Major WAGGONER, and to recover my share of estate of my late brother.

1813, Oct 29
John KENDRICK, to Thomas NUNN, of Henry Co., Va., to sue for and recover a tract of land on Smith's River, by an obligation and execution on Elizabeth SIMMONS, by Wm. DILLON. This revokes all former powers of attorney.

1814, Feb 24
    Elizabeth ALLEN appoints Anderson CRAWFORD att'y to act for and recover her share of estate of Joseph ALLEN, dec'd.

1814, Mar 11
    William LINVILLE, of Lincoln Co., appoints John LUCKEY, trustee for all legacy left to my wife, Joannah, by her father, Chas. DENHAM, dec'd., under name of Joannah ENGLEMANN. Also appoints Luckey as his attorney.

1814, Nov 7
    Joseph MILLER appoints William LOWE, of Preble Co., Ohio, as his lawful attorney, to sell "my quarter-section in Montgomery, Ohio, on Stillwater River."

1814, June 6
    James GOODWIN, of Amelia Co., Va., and Nathan AVERY, appoint Barrington AVERY, of Brunswick Co., Va., to receive our share of estate of John AVERY, dec'd., in Columbia Co., Ga.

1814, June 6
    Hannah and Sally AVERY, Admxs., of estate of Joel AVERY, dec'd, of Amelia Co., Va., appoint Barrington AVERY, to recover their just proportion of estate of John AVERY, brother of Joel, dec'd.

1814, June 6
    Augustus NAPIER to Washington W. STONE, to recover "my share of estate of Robert RANDOLPH, Esq."

1814, Sept 25
    Thomas Jenkins MOORE, of Butler Co., Ohio, appoints Joseph MILLER, attorney, to recover from Thomas HAMILTON, a debt of $115., with lawful interest.

1816, Feb 5
    George FAWCETT to Robert FAWCETT, of Orange Co., N. C., to dispose of 164 acres, part of 640 acre tract granted Geo. FAWCETT, SR., in Orange Co.

1816, July 5
    Peter COLLINS and others, to James STEWART and Jacob MC GAHEE; Peter H., John; Cornelius, Robert MARTIN (in right of wife Frances, formerly Collins), and Hendley BOSWELL, (in right of wife, Mary, formerly Collins), heirs and representatives of Martha and William COLLINS, dec'd., appoint James STEWART and Jacob MC GAHEE, of Prince Edward Co., Va., to obtain our rights to a 240 acre tract willed by Jacob McGahee, Sr., to Martha and William Collins, dec'd., on Bush River and Mountain Creek. Attys are to sell the land.

1816, July 8
    Amasa JACKSON, of New York, Adm. of estate of Stephen MEARS, dec'd., to William HOBBY, of Augusta, to recover all property due said Amasa from any person, whatsoever, whether in his own right, or as Adm., of any person, dec'd. Also to make title to William

MICON(?), of Augusta, to a house and lot on corner of Reynolds and Washington Streets.

1816, Sept 9
    Drewry GOOLSBY, SR., to James GOOLSBY, of Oglethorpe Co., to transact all business in Tenn., as if I were present, respecting the estate of John Curby GOOLSBY.

1817, Jan 27
    Jonathon ARMSTRONG, of Lincoln Co., to William PASCHALL, Lincoln Co., to sue for and recover payment on certain notes and bonds due me from several men throughout the state.

1817, Jan 27
    Joseph BENNING to Robert or William MERIWETHER, to sell tract of land on Lloyd's Creek, known as Shaw's land.

1817, Jan 27
    Legatees of Nicholas MERIWETHER to Thomas MERIWETHER, Whereas, there is now pending a certain appeal at the instance of Joshua GRINAGE, assignee of Micah Evans, woman of color, against Exrs of Thos. MERIWETHER, dec'd., and, Whereas, it is desirable to settle amicably: know ye, that we, William, Robert and Francis MERIWETHER; Thomas WHITE; Nicholas WHITE; Pleasant BENNING; Joseph BENNING, and Marshall MIMS, heirs of dec'd Nicholas, do authorize said Thomas Meriwether, Exr., of last Will and Testament of Nicholas Meriwether, who was Exr., of estate of Thomas, Sr., dec'd., as our trusty attorney, to pay off and settle said legacy, as best as they can agree upon.

1817, Oct 28
    Martha BROOKS, of Rutherford Co., Tenn., to William PACE, to sue for and recover all monies and properties due me from estate of father, Luke DEVORIE(?), of Edgefield Co., S. C., from hands of John LYON, Adm. Also to adjust title to a dower of land in Edgefield Dist., 500 acres from estate of Joseph ROBINSON, which belongs to me.

1818, Jan 19
    John SKINNER to Augustus SKINNER, to trade or sell my part of mother's estate in Columbia County.

1818, Mar 5,
    Sarah YOUNG to Benjamin FLINT, of Ky., to recover from Nathan HARRIS, of Ky., Exr., of estate of Thomas HARRIS, dec'd., of Maryland, bequeathed to me by Harris' last Will and Testament.

1818, Mar 24
    John FOSTER, Guardian of person and property of Mathew WALTON, minor of John WALTON, dec'd., appoints friend John W. WALTON, att'y, to demand and recover all legacies due said Matthew in state of Va., from estate of grandfather, Sherwood WALTON, in Amelia Co Va., dec'd.

1818, Apr 3
    Patrick NAPIER, of Fluvanna Co., Va., appoints Seaborn JONES, of Augusta, Richmond Co., att'y, "in my name, for benefit of David ROSS, Esq., of Richmond Co., to receive of Peter CRAWFORD, Esq.,

Clerk of Columbia Co., the sum of $500., deposited in his hands by.. ......(name not given.)

1819, Mar 16
William JONES, of Rapide Co., (La?), to James JONES.."Before me, Thomas Scott, Parish Judge in Rapide Co., appeared William Jones, and appointed his brother James Jones, of Columbia Co., Ga., to be his legal att'y, and to recover his legacy from estate of father, Thomas JONES, dec'd., Town of Alexandria, Sept 25, 1818."

1819, June 28
Elizabeth WHITE, widow of Presley WHITE, of Culpepper Co., Va., dec'd, appoints Stanton SLAUGHTER, of said county, for me, and in my name, and as guardian of minor children of said Presley White, viz: Elizabeth and Presley, Jr., to ask for, sue and demand from William BROADUS, of said Co., Adm., of estate of late husband, all monies and properties due me or the minor children. And to sue for and recover from Adms., of the late Elizabeth, widow of James ALLEN, dec'd., all monies or property due me or minor children.

1819, July 9
Thomas MYERS, of Lancaster Co., Va., to son William MYERS, to recover from Juriah HARRIS, following sums of money due me for sale of two parcels of land, of 202 1/2 acres each, lying in what was known then as the "New Purchase." $550. due Jan 1, 1817, with interest; $550. due Jan 1, 1818.

1819, Aug 30
Elisha BOWDRE to Collier FOSTER, to act for me, sue for and recover all sums due me from any person whatsoever.

1819, Dec 7
Elizabeth NEAL and Juriah HARRISS, appoint Thomas MYERS, of Lancaster Co., Va., to transact our business concerning estates of Rodham NEAL, and William NEAL, of Lancaster Co., Va., dec'd.

1820, Oct 17
Susan A. G. MC INTOSH, of Savannah, widow of Lachlan MC INTOSH, to Robert RAIFORD, of Savannah, broker, to ask for, sue for and recover all monies and property, debts, and notes due me, as heir and Admx., of my husband, dec'd. Especially to recover from Ignatius A. FEW, certain notes, negroes, etc., and to remove same from any part of the state, they being under his care.

1820, Oct 29
Rene STONE appoints Walter STONE, "to act for me, as Admx., of estate of father, Marble STONE, dec'd., as if I wer personally present."

1821, Mar 21
Margaret CLARK, of Mecklinburgh Co., Va., to Archer AVERY, Columbia Co., to obtain possession of such parts of estate of Mary McNEAL as I am entitled to as an heir.

1822, Oct 28
    Dredzil PACE appoints George Greene TANKERSLEY his att'y., to receive from James MITCHELL, of Rhea(?) Co., Tenn., negroes, Bender; Jack; Kitt; Harry; Melly, and children: Clarissa and her child; Abram; Frank; Jim; Joe; and Keziah, also such sums of money as are due me from said Mitchell.

1820, Aug 29 - Rec. Nov 26, 1822
    John CARRINGTON, and James and Ann (Carrington) WISHER, appoint William LOVE, att'y to settle accounts with administrator of William CARRINGTON, who died without lineal heirs. John Carrington, half-brother, and Ann Wisher, formerly Carrington, half-sister, of York Dist., S. C., claim a share of estate.

1822, Nov 26
    Samuel CARRINGTON, of York Dist., S. C., appoints John MCELWEE, of Columbia Co., Ga., to recover all rights and claims he has in estate of William CARRINGTON, dec'd., half-brother.

1822, Dec 7
    Caleb EUBANK to James LUKE, Esq., to recover certain negroes who have absconded themselves from my service, and are confined in jail, in Charleston, S. C., viz: Negro man, Ned, 30 years old, of a yellow complexion; negro Peter, about 40, dark complexion, woman Ann, and small girl child, about 35, yellow complexion.

1820, Sept 5 - Rec. Dec 10, 1822
    John WALLACE to James LUKE, to settle all necessary business with Nathan ROBEY, Adm. of estate of William CARRINGTON.

1822, Dec 10
    Affidavit: Personally came Christian MONTGOMERY, of York Dist., S. C., who declares that the bearer, John Wallace, is the lawful husband of Mary WALLACE, formerly Carrington, half-sister of William Carrington, dec'd., late of Columbia County, Ga.
s/ SAMUEL TURNER, Justice, York District, S. C.

1824, June 2
    William MC GEE to Abner MC GEE, of Oglethorpe Co., in my name, and also as guardian of Martha Ann and William A. BERRY, children of my sister, Nancy BERRY, formerly McGee, to recover from brother Archibald McGee, of Wilkinson Co., Miss., Adm., of estate of brother, Nathan, dec'd., 1/5th part of estate for my claim, and 1/5 part for children of sister Nancy.

1824, Feb 5
    George MONROE of Frederick Co., in Va., appoints Henry SLAUGHTER, of Columbia Co., Ga., att'y, to recover "my just claim to the estate of Thomas WROE, dec'd."

1824, Oct 12
    Francis F. ALLEN, guardian of person and property of Moses JOHNSON, only and minor child of Benjamin and Ann JOHNSON, dec'd., appoints Stanton SLAUGHTER, Esq., of Culpepper Co., Va., to ask for

demand, and recover from Newman ALLEN, of Culpepper Co., Exr., of last Will and Testament of Elizabeth C. ALLEN, relict and widow of James ALLEN, of Columbia Co., Ga., all monies and property due me in my own right, and as guardian for a minor child.

1825, Jan 15
Benjamin and Kinchen JELKS, of Southampton Co., Va., appoint Capt. Robert ROCHELLE, as att'y to recover from Arthur FOSTER and Turner CLANTON, of Columbia Co., any monies or property due them from estate of Richard JELKS, dec'd.

1825, Feb 25
John BEALLE, of Tuscaloosa Co., Ala., a legal heir of Edmond ROBERTS, of Columbia Co., appoints Dennis DENT attorney to obtain just share of estate.

1825, Apr 25
Owen WILLIAMS, of Limestone Co., Ala., appoints William Lewis CRAWFORD, att'y to transact all my business of any kind, in Wilkes County, Ga.

1825, May 4
Jennett LOVELACE, to Green DOZIER, being aged and infirm so that I am incapable of attending to my temporal affairs, appoint Green Dozier my attorney to transact all business of any kind, in my behalf.

1825, July 18
George WEISSINGER, of Perry Co., Ala., appoints Leonard WEISSINGER, att'y, to any land "I may possess on Germany's Creek, and convey them to William MC GRUDER.

1825, Sept 9
Philip STUART, of Washington, D. C., to George CARY, to dispose of negro girl, Daphne, bequeathed by George Washington DENT in Last Will and Testament, to dau. Matilda, otherwise known as Eleanor Matilda DENT. I desire a clear Bill of Sale, as Guardian of said Matilda. I have been appointed her legal guardian by the Orphan's Court, of Prince George Co., Md."

1825, Oct 3
Jeremiah SAMPLER to William UPTON, to recover from Morgan MALONE, and all other persons indebted to me, all sums of money due me.

1825, Jan 5
Owen WEST, Sr., Robert FERRALL, and Nancy, his wife, formerly WEST, John FERRALL, and his wife Jane, formerly WEST; Joshua BETTERTON, and Mary, his wife, formerly WEST; Joseph WRIGHT, and Susannah, his wife, formerly WEST; Thomas; James, and Peyton WEST; Ezekiel HAWORTH, and Elizabeth, his wife, formerly WEST; James HAWORTH, and Amelia, his wife, formerly WEST; Rebecca and Owen WEST, Jr., of Clinton Co., and William WEST, of same County, to transact all business on their behalf, and recover from estate of James MARTIN, dec'd, of

Columbia Co., Ga., all such properties and monies rightfully theirs, also power to sell any lands to which said Martin, dec'd., had equity, or any lawful claim.

1826, Sept __
William WILKINS, trustee for Charity BYNUM, appoints John BYNUM trustee in his place, and gives him power of attorney. He is to pay particular attention to the plantation and farm, and to attend to crops of fodder, cotton, wheat, oats, and all crops whereon he now lives.

1827, Feb 27
Benjamin and James REYNOLDS, of Baldwin Co., appoing Larkin REYNOLDS to recover from Turner CLANTON and James BURRIS (BURROUGHS), "our claim to estate of Hannor (Hannah) CLANTON, dec'd., as requested by her will."

1827, Feb 27
"The same to Turner CLANTON, and James BURROUGHS, Exrs., of estate and will of Hannah CLANTON, dec'd., bonded for $1,696.96. Whereas, it is provided in will of Hannah Clanton that money due the estate is to be converted into slaves, and divided equally among heirs. Should any child die without issue, property reverts to remaining children. Larkin Reynolds, intermarried with Eliza CLANTON, rec'd. from Exr., a negro boy, Charles, valued @ $430., and there being a balance of the estate that could not be divided into slaves, he secures an order of the Court to divide remaining money. Demands $377.68, as his share."

1827, Mar 2
Jonathon WOOD appoints wife, Blanche WOOD, as att'y., to ask for, demand and recover from all persons or bodies corporate all sums of money and debts due me in my own right and that of my wife.

1827, Mar 31
William E. CLIFTON, of Richland Dist., S. C., to Thomas BURNSIDE, Power of att'y. Clifton, Exr., of est. of Claiborn CLIFTON, dec'd., gives power to sell and transfer, for sum of $500., negro man, Dick, sold by sheriff of Columbia Co., as property of Dr. David COOPER, but now belonging to estate of C. Clifton.

1827, Apr 12
Jeremiah DUTCH appoints Adam SCOTT to recover from the State of Ga., or other proper authority, all right and title to a claim to property from Lottery, as far as one draw may extend, and to obtain acquittances for same.

1827, Sept 13
John CULBREATH, Adm. of James MC NEIL, and Archer AVERY, agent of Archibald CLANTON, Adm. of late John MC NEIL, appoint Thomas BURNSIDE to collect all sums due by note of hand or otherwise, made by Solomon ELLIS, Charles ELLIS, and Elisha ELLIS, payable to estate of McNeil.

1827, Oct 5
John GUNBY, of Amite Co., Miss., appoints William GUNBY att'y., "to transact all legal business in Ga., and to sell my part of tract in Laurence (Laurens) Co., Ga."

1828, Jan 30
James DEAN, appoints Peter CRAWFORD, to act as att'y. Dean is guardian of person and property of Obedience Lowe, a minor, and wants to recover her claim in the estate of Beverly LOWE, dec'd., formerly of Columbia Co., in right of his wife, Elzabeth DEAN, formerly Lowe.

1828, Feb 27
William HURST, guardian for James SCRUGGS, idiot, appoints Isaac LOWE, to recover from James SMALLEY all sums of money, and property due said James Scruggs.

1828, Mar 31
Solomon FUDGE, Elizabeth, his wife, formerly CARRELL; Jacob FUDGE, and wife, Matilda, formerly CARRELL; and Ann CARRELL, all of Houston Co., appoint Daniel CARRELL to sell 300 acre tract in Columbia Co., originally granted to William CARRELL, dec'd.

1828, Apr 1,
Above named sell the tract to Mary JENKINS, for $416.00

1828, July 21
William YARBOROUGH appoints Gabriel JONES, to collect all debts due him from any person whatsoever.

1828, Dec 25
Thaddeus REES, of Putnam Co., guardian of Ann and William LOWE, orphans of Thomas LOWE, dec'd., appoints Jame CARTLEDGE att'y., to recover from Edmond BLUNT, Exr., of last Will of Fanny (Lowe) CARR, all such property as shall justly belong to said orphans, as children and heirs of Thomas and Fanny (Lowe) Carr, dec'd. (After death of Thomas LOWE, Fanny married Thomas CARR.)

1828, May 10
Patty and Nancy HILL appoint brother, David, to sell land in Columbia County.

1828, May 10
David HILL sells above tract,(1/3 interest) to Hannah SUTHERLAND, Excx., for John SUTHERLAND...31 and 66/100 acres for $91.00.
1828
1828, May 10
James COMPTON appoints brother-in-law, David HILL, to sell his interest in land in Columbia County.

1828, May 10
James HILL appoints David HILL to sell land in Columbia Co., David Hill sells above tract to Hannah SUTHERLAND, for $137.50.

1833, Feb 19
Joel CRAWFORD, appoints Simmons CRAWFORD to sell 300 acres on

Kiokee Creek.

1833, Feb 25
Robert POUNDS appoints Isham FULLER to recover from Thomas BEALLE, Adm. of estate of Jared Pounds, all my share of estate of dec'd father, being principally slaves, Isham; Hiram; Ben; Sam; Lewis; Sarah; Dorcas; Charity; Anderson; Aaron; and Boswell. Permission to sell any or all of them.

1833, Feb 19
Frances ALLEN appoints Archer AVARY to sell negroes Milly, 26; children Lewis, 10; Jim, 8; and Thaddeus, about 8..all dark complected. Also Adam, about 50. With proceeds, he is to pay all Allen's debts.

1833, Mar 20
Charles BEALLE appoints James CARTLEDGE to recover from Nathaniel CRAWFORD, Exr., of Joseph MARSHALL, dec'd., all such sums of money due me, also from any other persons indebted to me.

1833, Apr 8
Kinchen JELKS, of Southampton Co., Va., appoints Tilghman JELKS, of Columbia Co., to recover all property due to me from Turner CLANTON, Exr., of estate of Benjamin JELKS, dec'd.

1834, Jan 14
Robert POUNDS appoints Isham FULLER to recover from Thomas Edmond BEALLE, Adm. of estate of Jared POUNDS, all monies and property due me as heir.

1834, Aug 21
Thomas M. COWLES, Montgomery Co., Ala., John A. COWLES, and Gilbert SHEARER, of Dallas Co., Ala., heirs of William COWLES, dec'd., appoint Samuel HALE, of Augusta, att'y., to sell all Georgia property. (Cowles owned the Old Sweetwater Iron Works). Hale sells Iron Works to John Adkins, Warren Co., for $4,000.00.

1835, Jan 7
Matthew BOLTON, of Monroe Co., Missouri, to Alexander EADY, to dispose of 1/2 a parcel of land in Twiggs Co., formerly Wilkinson, designated as Lot #101, 28th Dist., containing 202 1/2 acres. "I am authorized to sell this land as executor of John TINSLEY, dec'd."

1835, June 15
William B. HAWES appoints James CULBREATH to collect all debts owing me. Also to sell Household and kitchen furniture, corn, fodder, Bacon, stock of all kinds remaining on the plantation, also tools of all kinds. Negro fellows Jim and Tom, and Rilla, a woman. Also permission to sell 205 acres on East Fork of Sullivan's Creek.

1835, Oct 21
Lucinda HILL, of DeKalb Co., to John BUYS; Lucinda being one of the lawful heirs of John HILL, dec'd., appoints Buys to sell all interest in an 18 acre tract. Buys sells above tract to Hannah SUTHERLAND, Excx., of John SUTHERLAND, dec'd., for $45.83..18 acres, a 1/6 share of a 100 acre grant in name of Alexander Johnson.

1835, Dec 23
Elizabeth and Frances HATCHELL, of Mecklinburg Co., Va., to Samuel BUGG. John HATCHELL having died intestate, his heirs app't Bugg to obtain their rightful share of his estate.

1836, May 11
Stephen HATCHELL, father of dec'd John HATCHELL, Mary, Elizabeth, Lucy (wife of Charles THOMAS), Fanny (wife of Samuel BUGG), Franky, Angelina, and minor brothers of Stephen J. Peterson HATCHELL, and William HATCHELL, all heirs at law to estate of dec'd., appoint Samuel WARREN to recover from Turner CLANTON, Exr., all lawful shares.

1836, Nov 4
Alexander DORTCH, guardian of minors of Stephen HATCHELL, appoints Benjamin WARREN, Esq., of Augusta, Ga., to recover from Turner CLANTON, Exr., of John HATCHELL, all sums of money due from estate.

1836, Dec 6, Lucy BENTON to Archibald HEGGIE, to demand, sue for, and recover from Nelson BENTON, Adm., estate of Nathan BENTON, "the legacy due me."

1837, Jan 10
The Reverend James HUCHINGSON revokes Power of Attorney granted to John CARTLEDGE, and appoints Josiah ROBERTS and James CULBREATH, to recover from Cartledge all monies and property due him.

1837, May 25
Isaac WATSON appoints George GUNBY, "my true and lawfull attorney," to recover from Gabriel JONES, Adm., of estate of Robert CULPEPPER, dec'd., all the interest of George and Stephen CULPEPPER in said estate. (Isaac was guardian for the boys.)

1837, May 26
George GUNBY, attorney for Isaac WATSON (Guardian for Stephen CULPEPPER), receives from Gabriel JONES, Adm., of Robert CULPEPPER, estate, Stephen's distributive share, $319.85 1/2. Gunby also receives George CULPEPPER's share of above estate, $215.58, which sum, added to $104.37 1/2, already recovered, totals $319.84 1/2.

1837, June 14
Jane CULPEPPER appoints George GUNBY to recover her share of estate of Robert CULPEPPER, dec'd., also the share of Nathaniel CULPEPPER, which has been assigned to her.

1837, June 14
Jane CULPEPPER signs receipt for share in full; $66.75 1/2, together with $137.95 1/2 already recovered, plus $100.00 previously paid in cash, and a judgment against estate of $300.00, plus $35.00 interest, makes total of $639.71.

1837, Oct 25
George BARKER appoints Elbert MARSHALL attorney to collect any monies due me as distributive share of any estates in Ga., also lands and properties. (Barker was from Pike Co., Ala.)

1837, Oct 25
    Receipt for foregoing, $200.00, in full. Elbert MARSHALL sold all of Barker's interest in estate of Susannah MARSHALL, dec'd., to Daniel L. MARHSALL.

1837, Nov 4
    William LOWE, of Jones Co., appoints Abraham LOWE as his att'y to recover from Daniel L. MARSHALL, "all legacies due me from estate of Susannah MARSHALL, dec'd." (William Lowe m. Charlotte MARSHALL, Feb 8, 1805, Columbia County, Ga.)

1837, Nov 4
    Receipt for above...Abraham LOWE, agent and att'y for William LOWE, sells to D. L. MARSHALL, all of William's claim to estate of Susannah MARSHALL, for $200.00.

1837, Dec 28
    William MONCRIEF, of Lowndes Co., Ala., appoints Wiley MONCRIEF, of Lincoln Co., Ga., his att'y, to make and execute a receipt in full to Henry SPAULDING, of Columbia Co., for all the property he has in his possession in right of his wife, Mary SPAULDING, dec'd., in estate of David MONCRIEF.

1837, Dec 28
    Henry SPAULDING appoints Isaiah STOVALL to represent his interest in above estate. Property in his possession consists of negroes: Betty; Dick; Charlotte; Phereby; Polly; Betsey; young Dick, and two children of Phereby.

1838, Mar 8
    Mary A. HATCHELL, one of children of Stephen HATCHELL, of Mecklenburg Co., Va., appoints Benjamin WARREN, of Augusta, Ga., to recover from Turner CLANTON, Adm., of estate of "my late brother, John HATCHELL, all properties and sums of money now due me."

1838, Oct 4
    Samuel MARSHALL, of Tallapoosa Co., Ala., appoints Joseph G. MARSHALL, to recover from Joseph RAWLS, of Tallapoosa Co., all monies and debts due me.

1839, Jan 20
    Peter MARSHALL appoints William BLUNT att'y to sell two negroes, Harry and Dick, and settle all debts owing in Columbia County.

DEEDS OF GIFT

1791, Feb 24 - Rec. Apr 8, 1795
    Mary ELKINS, to William TAYLOR, "for natural love and affection she hath for her son-in-law, as well as the cost and trouble about the survey of a certain Estate in Va., for the property of my uncle, Jeremiah WHITNEY, and also the sum of £5 paid by said William....all that part of my Uncle Jeremiah Whitney's estate that my lawful attorney may recover."

1791, Aug 6
   Robert BURTON to Caleb BURTON, "my loving and dutiful son, for love and affection: All the tract of land, cont. 300 acres, which was granted to me; also 1 cow, named Lady, 1 named, Blossom, 1 named Motley, and Old Gently's youngest heifer, and all their increase from the year 1782. The above cattle marked with a crop and slit, and underpiece in the right ear, and a crop and overpiece in left ear, branded, C. B; and 1 horse named Harry, 9 years old, branded C. B; also one featherbed and the cloathes thereto belonging, and my six pewter plates; 1 pewter dish; 1 bason; and 1 iron pot."

1791, Nov 23
   Ann LINN, widow of Charles LINN.."for the love and good-will and maternal affection I have for my three youngest children; Jane; Ann; and Charles: 1 negro girl, named Jane, with her issue, now living in my dwelling house in Wrightsborough."

1792, Feb 26
   Thomas NAPIER to Robert RANDOLPH..."for love and affection I bear for my loving son-in-law, Robert RANDOLPH...all that parcel of land cont. 300 acres, lying on the East side of Germany's Creek, originally granted to Jonathan SELL, also 300 acres of North side of Malcom's Creek, sold to me by Robert MC GINTY. My land on West side of Germany Creek, originally granted to Jonathan Sell, also 33 acres originally granted to me, also all that part of 200 acres, originally granted to John JONES, on West side of Germany Creek." (Robert Randolph m. Elizabeth Napier, Jan 10, 1789).

1792, July 13
   Elizabeth BOYD, widow of Edward BOYD, to daughter, Mary Elizabeth, now about to be married, for the good-will she had for her dec'd., husband, her only daughter shall have all the property that was her father's: The tract I now live on, three cows and calves; one black cow with a short tail, marked with a swallowfork in each ear and an underkeel in the right ear, with her calf; 1 brindle cow, with a swallowfork in each ear, and underkeel in left ear; 1 2-year old heifer; 1 black and white bull yearling, and all their future increase.

1793, Jan 24
   George WALTON to Jesse WINFREY, in consequence of love and affection, and the sum of £5: All the Plantation tract near Claibourne's Mill, on Great Kiokee Creek.

1793, Sept 13
   Moses THOMSON to John THOMSON..."For love and affection to my loving and dutiful son, John: 200 acre tract on South side of Briar Creek."

1793, Sept 13
   Moses THOMSON to Joshua; Reuben; William and Mary THOMSON.."For love and affection to my children: 1 brown mare, branded on the near shoulder with "M"; 1 brown mare colt; 20 head of cattle, marked 1/2 crop in left ear, 2 slits in right; also all my household furniture."

1793, Sept 16
David MAXWELL to Daniel BULLOCH, of S. C., .."For love and affection I have for Jane BULLOCH, wife of Daniel, and my loving daughter: 1 negro woman, Moll, and her increase; 1 negro boy, Bobb; 1 mare and colt, and their increase; 1 fetherbed and furniture."

1794, Feb 6
Rachel HOGE, to her children, John and Elinor.."For good-will and affection: My household furniture; 7 head of cattle; 1 "mair".. share and share alike."

1794, July 24
Mary CARMICHAEL, widow, to her four children: Joseph Wade Carmichael; Elizabeth Grey Carmichael; Abner Carmichael, and Peggy Bynum Carhichael..."For good-will and affection: 3 negroes; 5 cows, and calves; 4 head of horses, and 650 acres of land formerly belonging to Beverly LOWE, transferred by deed to William MADDOX, and wife, Ann, and by him sold to me."

1795, July 31
Richard NAPIER, to daughter, Molly Wells NAPIER.."For love and affection" - four negroes.

1795, Mar 25
Stephen COLLINS to Richard SHACKELFORD..."For 5 shillings, and the natural affection I have for my son-in-law: 1 negro woman, Betty, and her increase; land and Plantation whereon I now live; 1 featherbed; 2 pr. sheets; 2 counterpins; 1 boulster; 2 pillows, and 1 blanket; all household and kitchen furniture, whole of my stock of cattle and hogs; 1 sorrel colt."

1795, Apr 20;
William SIMS to Mann SIMMS, for 5 shillings and natural affection..."For my son: 2 negro girls, Bess and Charity, both the daus., of Betty, whom I had of Colonel MARBURY."

1795, June 10
Anthony HAYNES makes a deed of gift of all property to Chaney Reade, mulatto woman, and her eight children by him. (He married her June 13, 1795).

1795, Oct 17
Richard NAPIER to Richard Claiborne NAPIER, my son, for love and affection: 4 negroes.

1796, Mar 16
Ann FLOYD, widow, of S. C., to Winifred JOHNSTON, wife of Thomas JOHNSTON..."For love and affection I do bear to her, my daughter: 1 negro girl, Roze; 1 negro boy, Davy."

1796, Mar 25
Mary MATHIS to William MATHIS..."For natural love and affection I have for my son...both them tracts of land on Briar Creek, one of 100 acres, granted to M. Mathis, Sept 21, 1785, by Sam'l. ELBERT, Esq., Governor, Reg. in Book HHH, folio, 548. Second tract granted to M.

MATHIS by George HANDLEY, Gov., cont. 150 acres, registered in Book QQQ, folio 513. Plus 16 head of cattle, marked with a crop and half-crop in each ear, and a hole in the half crop. Branded "M3". Also 2 featherbeds; 6 basons; 2 dishes; 6 plates; 2 pots; 1 oven; 1 skillet; 1 pair fire-tongs; and a box iron.

1796, July 28
Joshua MORGAN, of Wilkes Co., to Joshua MORGAN, JR., and others: For love and affection I have for my loving grand-children, Joshua; Betsey; Polly; Thomas, and Jeremy(?); 4 cows and calves; 1 three-year old steer; 1 two-year old heifer; 2 bulls and 1 calf, marked with a swollowfork in the right ear, and a poplar-leaf in the left; 26 head of hogs; (three sows marked with a crop of two fingers in each ear). The rest of the hogs are marked the same as the cattle; 1 brown horse, about 11 years old; 14 hands high; a woman's saddle and bridle; 2 featherbeds and furniture; 2 bedsteads; 14 head geese; 3 pewter dishes; 14 plates; 4 basons; 1 earthen dish; 12 earthen plates; 1/2 doz. cups and saucers; 4 bowls; 3 muggs; 2 iron pots; 1 Dutch oven; 1 skillet; 2 pine tables; 4 chairs; 1 spinning-wheel; and 1 candle-mould. Which property is now in the possession of my daughter, Keziah MORGAN, and is to be divided between my children as they come of age or marry.

1797, May 16
Nancy SANDERS to her children-heirs and minors of Ephraim SANDERS, dec'd., viz: Billington McCarthy SANDERS; Betsy Hubbard SANDERS; and Dennis Downman SANDERS, the whole of personal estate of their father.

1797, May 18
Abigail LATHROP, "To my loving children, John DARLING; Benjamin DARLING, and Joseph DARLING, and grandson Timothy JONES, all of my estate of every kind."

1797, July 19
John GERMANY, Planter, to Sarah PHILLIPS, and others. "For goodwill and affection to my loving niece, Sarah Phillips, 1 negro woman, Rosey, and 1/3 of my 744 acre tract on Briar Creek. To Jane GERMANY, my dear daughter, 1 negro girl, 1/3 part of said land, 1/2 household furniture, and 1/2 of all stock of cattle; horses; hogs and sheep that are on the Plantation of my brother, Samuel GERMANY. To Mary GERMANY, daughter of Samuel, 1/3 part of land, and other half of household furniture and stock."

1797, July 28
Patrick BRISCOE, "For love and affection to my wife, Hannah, and seven children: Mary; Andrew; Nancy; James; Jane; Abraham, and Jacob, 1 black mare and mare colt; 12 head of cattle; 26 hogs; 5 featherbeds and furniture; all household and kitchen furniture, all grain of all kinds; all bacon; and the present crop."

1800, Dec 18
Joshua WINN to Joshua WINN, JR., my son, .."For love and affection, three negroes."

1801, Feb 24
Thomas MOORE, "For love and goodwill to my dau., Nancy, negro girl, Nice."

1801, Mar 1
Charles DENHAM to John HOLLINGSWORTH, for paternal affection and good wishes, "the said John's father being dec'd., I feel myself obligated to donate something to said John, a minor. For and in consequence of 100 cents paid by said John, one wench, China, and her child, Poll."

1798, Nov 22
David WALKER to Elizabeth.."in consequence of love and affection I have for my daughter, Elizabeth, one negro girl, Dilsey, and her increase." (Written in Chatham Co., Ga., July 10, 1785. Witnessed by Thomas TILLER, and Isaac LOWE.)

1798, Jan 26
Affidavit for above. "Personally appeared before me Thomas TILLER, who being duly sworn, saith he was present and saw the said David WALKER sign the within instrument, purporting a deed of gift, and that he, the deponent, together with Isaac Lowe....(illegible) deceased, did subscribe their names." Witness thereto signed in presence of Sheftall SHEFTALL, Chatham County.

1794, Oct 12 - Rec. Nov 17, 1797
Martin MELLOWN, to his children. "For love and affection to my sons, William; Morgan; James and Martin, all right and title to all the lands I now possess: 267 acres on White Oak Creek, all goods; cattle; horses; sheep; swine; goats, and every other moveable effect."

1797, Nov 28
Andreson CRAWFORD (m. Rachel SINQUEFIELD), to Zachariah SINQUEFIELD, late of Edgefield Co., S. C., for good-will and affection, all that land I possess on waters of Saluda River, Edgefield Co., S. C., 150 acres, being 1/2 the tract granted to Catherine YOUNGBLOOD, conveyed to Crawford by executors of estate of Francis SINQUEFIELD, dec'd.

1801, June 6
George RAY, for love, goodwill, and affection to son, Benjamin, all tract of land on which said Benjamin now lives, on headwaters of Greenbriar Creek and White Oak Creek, originally granted to Ezekiel OFFUTT, in 1787.

1801, July 10
Edmond CARTLEDGE, of Edgefield Co., S. C., "For love and affection I have for my dutiful son, John CARTLEDGE, Columbia Co., a parcel of land, originally granted to George GALPHIN, by him to Daniel MC-MURPHY, by him to said Edmond Cartledge."

1801, July 18
Waters DUNN,for love and affection for his gr-daughter, Catherine JONES, formerly Catherine DUNN, daughter of my son, Richard, one negro woman.

1802, Mar 10
    Thomas JONES to son, William, "For divers good causes, two tracts of land in Richmond Co., when surveyed, on the Ogeechee River, one tract of 200 acres, the other of 150 acres, granted me, Thomas Jones, Feb 25, 1785."

1797, May 30 - Rec. Jan 9, 1802
    Waters DUNN, Sr., to William DUNN, "For divers good causes, and the sum of 5 shillings, 4 negro slaves. The said William shall let Milly SATTERWHITE, wife of William SATTERWHITE, receive all profits arising from labor of said slaves. Increase of said slaves shall go to Sally; William; Thomas; Betsy; Nancy; and Polly, at the death of said Milly, the children of said William Satterwhite, and Millicent Dunn Satterwhite."

1802, July 8
    George RAY, to William Ray, my son. For love and affection. That tract containing 100 acres on waters of Kiokee Creek, where said William now lives.

1802, July 8
    William SIMS to William HANSON, for good causes, and natural affection I have for my grandson, the said William Hanson, and the sum of $2.00, a negro lad named Isaac, now in the possession of my daughter, Peggy HANSON.

1802, July 24
    Reuben GARNETT, "For the love I bear my wife, Nancy, and my son, Mager, one negro, Tom, two beds and furniture."

1803, Jan 24
    Waters DUNN, to Thomas RICHARDSON, "For love and affection to my son-in-law: one negro girl, Vilet; one negro boy, Lewis; boy James; man, Isaac; women, Winny and Silvey."

1773, Dec 25 - Rec. Apr 9, 1803
    Randel RAMSEY, in the 13th year of the Reign of our Sovereign Lord, George III, husbandman, "For love and affection for my only sons, John and Samuel and Isaac RAMSEY: all tract of land on Little Cyogus (Kiokee?), containing 300 acres, the plantation to be evenly divided; dwelling house; springs; buildings; water courses; timber; gardens; orchards; pastures; plus all goods and chattels now upon said plantation and in the dwelling house. Prior to delivery I have given John, Samuel and Isaac an inventory. Viz: Two negro fellows, Tom and Peter, cows; horses; sheep; swine and household goods."

1803, Sept 22
    William JONES, "For love and affection I bear to my daughter, Nance E. JONES, one negro wench, Rose, and her two children, Betty and Reuben. She is also to have her full share of my estate, at my decease."

1777, Nov 27 - Rec. Mar 21, 1798
    Peter YOUNGBLOOD, SR., of Richmond Co., "For good will and

affection I have for my sons, Abraham and George, 200 acres of land on Whiteoak Creek, where I now do dwell, to be divided as follows: To Abraham, 100 acres on North side of said Creek. To George, 100 acres with the plantation house on South side of Creek."

1800, Dec 25
Joshua WINN, to loving son, John WINN, for love and affection, three negroes.

1799, Mar 22
Jacob BULL, SR., to Jesse BULL. One negro woman, Cate, 23, and two children, Lee, 4 years old, and Gabe 6 mos. old; one negro woman, Took, 21, and her two children, Milla, 3 years, and Hannah, 1 year; one waggon; 1 horse; 3 mares, with gear and chain belonging to the team; 1 clock, with its case; 1 large looking-glass.

1799, Aug 26
Thomas MOORE to Martha Moore BANNING - "For love and affection to my daughter: 1 negro woman named, Sylvey; 1 negro girl, Abby, and their future increase."

1799, Aug 26
David HARRISS, "For love and goodwill to my daughter, Polly, 1 negro boy, Jack; 1 girl, Fanny. To son, Edward HARRISS, 1 male negro child, Tom. To son John HARRISS, 1 negro girl, Jenny."

1800, Apr 1
Sherwood BUGG, Planter, to Susannah BONNER, of Richmond Co., "For natural love and affection to my niece, all title and claim to certain negroes, Jack; Tenor; Mary and Dick."

1800, July 8
Joshua SANDERS, to son, Jeremiah, "For love and affection - 2 negroes, Harry and Peter, which were the property of my beloved wife, Patience, until her death."

1801, Oct 10
Joshua WYNNE, to Jesse H. MOORE, "For goodwill and affection to my son-in-law, three negroes, Sydney; Sarah, and Peter."

1800, Dec 29
Joshua WYNNE, to "my loving son, Williamson WYNNE, for natural affection, and goodwill, three negroes, Sylvey, about 17 years old, purchased from Samuel BOWDRE; Isaac and Anna Booker, children of my house wench." "To Robert WYNNE, for goodwill and affection to my son, three negroes, Mary; Spencer and Billy."

1803, Nov 3
Jesse SANDERS to Levi SANDERS (relationship not stated - assumed to be a son), a 100 acre tract of land in Columbia County.

1804, Jan 2
William TINDILL, Planter, "To Betsey A. TINDILL, my daughter, for love and affection, four negroes: Molly; Selina; Silvey; and George."

1804, Feb 4
James READ, to Ezekiel; James; John and Michael READ, for love I bear my sons, all the land I now hold by purchase, on Kegg Creek, 308 acres, to be divided into equal lots. The N. lot to Ezekiel, the S. lot to John, the W. lot to James, and the E. lot to Michael.

1802, Nov 24 - Rec. Apr 4, 1804
Samuel PAYNE, Planter, "For love and affection to my loving grandchildren: Elizabeth; William; Ann; John; Lewis and Polly LOVELL, a tract of land cont. 70 or 80 acres, more or less; negro woman, named Venus, with her increase; a sorrell mare called, English; 2 cows and calves; 1/2 a crib of corn, supposed to hold 500 bushels; a parcel of cotton, supposed to be about eleven hundred pounds; 2 beds and furniture; 2 potts; working tools; 1 loom and gear; 1 woman's saddle; some pewter; and a note of hand on William PAYNE, for $20.00."

1804, May 14
Joseph MOREHEAD, SR., of Richmond Co., and N. C., to Sarah CATHELL, dau., for love and affection. I lend my daughter a negro boy by name of Tom, to serve my dau., during her life, then to fall to Elizabeth CATHELL, and her heirs." Wit: by John MOREHEAD, JR; Chas. MOREHEAD, and Josiah CARTHIEL.

1804, June 28
John MINOR, "For natural love and affection I hold for my dau., Julia MINOR (so Christened, but now going by the name of Julia Nancy Daniel MINOR); for the advancement of said Julia in marriage, should she arrive at proper age; negroes John and Phoebe, his wife, and their two children, George and Nancy. Also Mary, dau. of my housewench, Luckey."

1804, July 9,
Thomas MOORE, to loving son, Jesse, negro man, Swift and girl, Molly.

1804, July 19
Loveless SAVADGE, and Elizabeth, his wife, to Hardy FOSTER, for divers good reasons, 75 acres of land, part of tract granted to Loveless Savadge, originally cont. 100 acres, by grant from Governor Wright, Mar 7, 1769, including the place whereon I now live.

1804, Feb 23
Stephen COLLINS, to Richard SHACKLEFORD, "My loving and beloved son-in-law: negro Woman, Betty, and her child. Also land and plantation whereon I now live, 54 acres; 1 featherbed and furniture; all household and kitchen goods; my stock of cattle and hogs, to be fully enjoyed by said Richard, after my death and that of my wife."

1804, July 25
Rachel GERMANY, widow, to John HOGG, for love and goodwill, one sorrell horse; 1 featherbed and furniture.

1804, July 26
Michael GRIFFIN to Snowden GRIFFIN, "my son, for love and natura

affection: All tract on waters of Kegg Creek, cont. 200 acres, with barns; houses; stables; gardens, etc., one other 100 acre tract on Kegg Creek; one 220 acre tract on Kegg Creek."

1804, July 27
    Mary PACE, to Mary Ann PACE, "For goodwill and affection to a dear and loving daughter, negroes, Edy; Jacob; Joe; and Agg., to dau., Sarah RAY, negro woman, Lucey., to William PACE, son, negro man, Charles, to David PACE, son, negro girl, Phillis., to Silas PACE, son, negro man, Stephen, called Step."

1805, Feb 12
    Charles CRAWFORD, "For love and goodwill to son, William, negro man, Jerry; 1 bed and furniture; 1 tract of land cont. 150 acres; one of 100 acres on Red's Creek, one tract of pine land, 150 acres, known as Quaker Springs Tract, through which the market road from Washington to Augusta runs, which I have had from Abigail WELLS, wid., of Humphrey WELLS, physician. For love and affection to my son, John CRAWFORD, 1 negro man, Stephen; 2 mares; 1 bed and furniture; 200 acres of land on Uchee Creek; 60 acres in the Old Field, on East side of Watery Branch; 200 acre tract in Washington Co., on Limestone Creek."

1805, Mar 19
    Daniel MC NEIL, the Elder, to grandsons, William RILEY, and Fenel RILEY, for natural affection, all that tract of land on Kiokee Creek.

1803, Mar 5 - Rec. Mar 20, 1805
    David PERIMON(PERRYMAN), "For love and affection to Dixon PERRYMAN, a 267 1/2 acre tract in Halifax Co., Va."

1805, Mar 21
    Quit Claim Deed. Flory PERIMON(PERRYMAN), of Pendleton Co., S. C., widow, and relict of David PERIMON, and we, James; John; Jeremiah; and Vinson, the legal heirs, relinquish all claim to a tract in Halifax Co., Va., deeded to said Dickson, "18 years ago" by David Perimon.

1805, Mar 27
    Quit Claim Deed. Nathaniel COLLINS, and wife, Elizabeth, and Elisha PERRYMAN, legal heirs and representatives of David PERIMON, dec'd., relinquish all claim to above mentioned land.

1805, Mar 27
    John PEEKE, JR., "For love and affection to my loving children, Lurana Lewis PEEKE, and Louisiana Thomas PEEKE, all my goods and chattels; six negroes, Daniel; Ned; Suckey; Monday; Delia; and Priss. Four featherbeds and their furniture; 1 bofat(buffet); 1 sideboard; all the residue of my household furniture; 1 sorrel horse and saddle, and bridle; 2 cows and calves; horses; all personal estate whatsoever. My friend, John LAMKIN, is to be guardian and trustee of the persons and property of my beloved children until they marry, or reach the age of 21."

1805, May 2
    Mary MCGRUDER, for love and affection to son, Archibald, one

negro boy called Jim.

1805, May 3
    John FRALE (FREEL, FRAIL), Farmer, "To John FRALE, JR., for goodwill and affection, the 260 acre tract whereon I now live, one negro man Dick, and negro girl Clary."

1805, June 13
    William BINION, to William BINION, JR., a tract of land containing 290 acres, on both sides of Germany Creek, known as O'Neal's Old Place.

1792, Oct 14 - Rec. Oct 14, 1805
    Jesse WINFREY, and wife, Frances, of Greene Co., to Walter LEIGH, of Mecklinburgh Co., Va., "For 5 shillings and other valuable considerations, all my plantation in Columbia Co., cont. 250 acres."

1805, Sept 20
    Charles CRAWFORD, to Joel CRAWFORD, for goodwill and affection, one negro man, Matt; one featherbed and furniture; all tract of land on East side of Deas'(?) Creek, from the old Mill to the head thereof, then down a branch of Hayes' Mill Creek; one sorrel gelding.

1805, Oct 10
    Charles CRAWFORD, to "beloved son-in-law, Peter CRAWFORD, for goodwill and affection, to Daughter, Mary Ann, in trust with her husband, Peter, one tract of land containing 250 acres adjoining Deas' Old Brick House tract, where said Peter now lives; one negro woman, Wynny; one feather bed and its furniture. To son, Anderson CRAWFORD, for goodwill and affection, two negro men, Abram and Harry; oen featherbed and furniture."

1805, May 17
    John EVANS, "To Humphrey EVANS, in consideration of certain 'servises' rendered, and 'risques run' for and in my account, by said Evans, do convey to him one house and lot in Augusta, known in the city plan as lot #27, on N. side of Broad St., four negroes, Frank; Milly; Abby and Billy."

1790, Feb 19 - Rec. Oct 25, 1805
    Mordecai HARRIS, "To Elizabeth HARRIS, for natural love and affection to my loving dau-in-law, wife of James M. HARRIS, dec'd., and to my grandson, James M., son of J. M. Harris, dec'd., 150 acres."

1805, Dec 10
    Mary GRAVES, gives to Demsey TUSTREE (Indian name?), commonly 'cald' Demsey GRAVES; 3 cows; 2 calves; 2 bulls; 1 heifer yearling; 1 'bead and furnitur' also a small amount of 'citchen furnitur."

1805, Dec 14
    John PITTMAN, farmer, for love, goodwill and affection for a dutiful son, Marshall PITTMAN, 200 acres on waters of Big Kiokee Creek.

1805, Dec 30
   Richard DUNN, for love and friendship, and the ties of nature, do give unto John BURGAMY, son of Nathaniel BURGAMY, of Elbert Co., one negro boy, Spencer.

1806, July 21
   John DURDAN, to beloved son Miles DURDAN, a small bay horse, with a hard lump on the right side of her head, under her right eye, and a star on her forehead; also a bridle and saddle.

1806, Aug 22
   Daniel STURGIS, "To beloved grandson, William, one negro boy, named Gilbert."

1792 - Rec. Aug 23, 1806
   John MARSHALL, to the Trustees of Kiokee Baptist Church, for 5 shillings, 3 and 1/4 acres, surveyed off my place.

1806, Sept 3
   Nathan BENTON, "To son, Nelson BENTON, for love and affection, negro woman, Olive, and her child, Sophia; negro woman, Jane, and her son, Marcus."

1806, Dec 4
   Lewis POWELL, planter, to Polly POWELL, slaves Rachel; Phillis, and Jude; 2 mares, one roan and the other sorrel; 5 head of cattle; 1 ox; 1 plow; 2 hoes; and two beds and furniture.

1807, Mar 11
   Samuel POOLE, to the Trustees of Silver Run Church, for 6 and 1/4 cents, 3 acres, 54 rods, on waters of Silver Run Creek, including the Meeting House.

1806, July 2
   Joshua MONK, to trustees of Silver Run Church, for 6 1/4¢, a tract of land on waters of Silver Run Creek, 3 acres, 54 rods.

1807, Mar 13
   Hadden PARHAM, To daughter, Agnes DOZIER, for love and affection, and $1.00, a negro fellow named, Anderson.

1807, Sept 22
   Elizabeth WALKER, to her children, for love and affection: "All my right and interest in estate of my late husband, Micajah ANDREWS, to my children, Katherine RAY; Elizabeth DIXON; John ANDREWS; Jameson ANDREWS; Sarah GARDNER, and Hannah YOUNG."

1807, Sept 19
   Daniel MARSHALL, to Trustees of Baptist Meeting House, viz: A. MARSHALL; Isham BAYLISS; Samuel CRABB; William BECKHAM; John BOYD, and Elisha PERRYMAN, Trustees of Baptist Incorporated Church, for love and affection, and promotion of the Gospel, 3 1/4 acres, part of tract granted to John MARSHALL, Jan 7, 1786, between Greenbriar and Kiokee Creeks, on the Washington to Augusta Road.

1807, Oct 20
"I, Jonn FREEL, JR., have signed over to my father and mother, John and Elizabeth FREEL, the parcel of land they live on, 264 acres, joining Waters DUNN; also one negro man, Dick, and negro woman, Clary."

1808, Oct 11
James and William STAPLER, to trustees of schoolhouse: William BECKHAM; John GARTRELL, and Andrew STURGIS, for 12 cents, 1/2 acre on which to build a schoolhouse, located on Cane Creek.

1809, Dec 11
Basil WHEAT, "For goodwill and affection to my dear children: to son, Eli, 4 negroes: Will; Polly; Hannibal, and Precious; 1 horse, Jim; 1 mare, Nancee. To dau., Rebeckah O'NEAL, 1 negro boy, John; 1 featherbed, bedstead and furniture; 1 chest; 1 cotton-gin; 1/4 part of 25 hogs; 3 head of cattle; 1 bay mare colt, 2 years old; and $150.00. To son Moses, 100 acre tract, adj., to Pleasant WALTON; J. GRIFFIN, and Little River; 1 black horse, Ball; 1 featherbed, bedstead, and furniture; 1/4 of 25 head of hogs; 2 head cattle; 10 goats; 10 geese. To son, Harrey (Harvey?), 1 negro named, Cook; 1 bed and furniture; 3 cattle; 8 goats; 1 road waggon and gear; 1 negro, Tampet(?); 1/4 of 25 head of hogs; 3 head of cattle; 1 featherbed and furniture; 1 set blacksmith tools; 1 horse, 'Jack.' " To son, Ila, 1/2 of 200 acre tract I now live on; 1 sorrel colt, 1 1/2 years old; 1 roan colt, 5 mos. old; 1 featherbed and furniture, balance of household and kitchen furniture, all plantation utensils; 1 Latin Book."

1810, May 11
James WALKER, of Washington Co., to Commissioners of Republican Grove Meeting House, viz: William ZACHRY; Elisha WALKER, and John ALLEN, for the sum of $1.00, land where said Meeting House stands, adj., lands of David WALKER, dec'd. Part of survey granted to Isaac LOWE, cont. 2 1/2 acres, to be used for a house of worship only.

1810, Aug 28
John HATTAWAY, "For natural love and parental affection for dau., Anne BOSWELL, a negro girl, Jean. For same, to Maria HATTAWAY, dau., three negroes, old Charles, about 52 years old; Phillis, a wench, about 55; a bay horse named, Dublin, 4 years old.. For same, to Robert C. HATTAWAY, two negro fellows, Jacob, 30 years old; Charles, 3 years old."

1810, Aug 30
William BECKHAM, "For love and affection to granddaughter, Polly DIXON, 1 negro girl, Scilla, and her child, Friday. The same shall not be enjoyed by Solomon ELLIS, JR., with whom she now lives, or by any other person with whom she may be hereafter connected, whether by marriage or otherwise. Trustees appointed: Lewis CODDS; John MINOR; and Thomas COBBS."

1810, Oct 13
Martha HARDEN, "For love and affection to children: Dau., Nancy RUTLEDGE, sons John; Erasmus; Thomas; Daniel; William and James HARDEN, I, Martha HARDEN, wid., do give and share and share alike, all

and singular, my goods, chattels, plate, jewells, leases, and all
real and personal estate, including negroes, stocks, and tract of
land whereon I now live, containing 132 1/2 acres. I have put the
children of my body in full possession, by giving them at the time
of sealing, one pewter basin."

1810, Dec 12.
John BEALLE, to trustees of Union Church, viz: Jonathon WOOD;
George TANKERSLEY; John BEALLE; William LOWE; John FOSTER; George
DENT, and William THOMAS, said church to be built by subscription
for all denominations of Christians, Gives 1 and 6/10th acres.
Also free passageway 50 ft. wide, from church to Washington Road.

1810, Dec 11
Lewis POWELL, to John Nelson CHENNAULT, trustee for heirs of
Elizabeth CHENNAULT, 1 negro man, Big Davy; 1 negro woman, Judy; 1
boy, Little Davy; 1 boy Harry, also 4 horses; 10 head of cattle;
2 beds and furniture. (Lewis Powell m. Elizabeth Chennault, Dec.
10, 1810.)

1811, Jan 7
Thomas MARTIN, for love and affection "to my son-in-law,
Valentine AUSTIN, negroes, Dick and Clary."

1810, Jan 26 James (Jane?) SIMMS, "For love and consideration for my
beloved son, Jared POUNDS, give all stock of horses; cows; hogs; and
sheep; also household and kitchen furniture; plantation tools; blacksmith tools; waggon and "geers" also four slaves, Louder; Cezar;
Char, and Furtune."

1811, Feb 24
Thomas HUNT, for love and affection for dau., Constantia, and
son, Henry, negroes: Cuffey; Nancy; Lucy, and Dick; Adaline and
Belinda, children of Nancy; Stephen, the son of Lucy, to be equally
divided.

1811, Mar 20
Lucy LAMAR, "To son, Zachy (Zachariah), for love and affection,
three negro women: Vice, her son Mitchell, and girl Malinda. To be
his when he comes of age. To dau., Martha LAMAR, three negroes,
woman, Beck, and child Accarchy(?), and girl named, Vina. To son,
Harmon, negro women, Hannah and Jane; man, Leander."

1811, Apr 1
Elenor CRAWFORD, wid., of John CRAWFORD, to children, Lewis and
Nancy, "with love and affection, all my right and title and interest
to estate of late husband."

1811, Apr 17
Daniel MC NEIL and wife, Margaret, "for love and affection to
loving children: Archibald; James; Asa; Allen; Anderson; Andrew;
Effie; Lucy; Martha, and Leonore SULLIVAN: 400 acre tract on Kioka
Creek; 200 acre tract on Kioka Creek; 100 acre tract granted to
Philip UPTON, whereon Daniel McNeil now lives, and upon which he
reserves the right to live for natural life."

1811, Apr 17
   Nathan BENTON, to Permelia Frances BENTON, and James Tinsley BENTON, for live and affection: 1 negro woman, Lilly, and her three children, Will; Mary and Lady.

1811, Oct 30
   Robert WALTON, and wife, Sarah: "For natural love and affection to Jeremiah; Talbot, and Albert Rees, children of said Sarah, and Benjamin REES, dec'd., all the goods and chattels, and personal estate that may fall to Robert Walton, in right of his wife, Sarah, wid., of said Benjamin, from estate of Benjamin REES."

1811, Aug 13
   John MOORE, and William LAURENCE, claimants to a negro girl, Charity, 12 or 13 years old, give said girl to Eliza Moon LAURENCE, and Martha Emeline LAURENCE, daus., of Sally LAURENCE, dec'd., and said William; grand-daughters of John Moore.

1811, Sept 19
   William MERIWETHER, "For love and affection of son, Thomas: Negroes, Betty; Franky; Letty; Jincy; Caesar; Mason and Cate. Same to Jane BENNING, wife of Joseph BENNING, negroes, Sally; Billy; Randal; and Marshall."

1811, Oct 17
   James OATES, "For love and affection to children, William; Alexander and Nancy: 1 sorrey horse, 14 hands high, 5 years old, an and a small white spot on his forehead; 1 'sque ball' (skew bald), or pied colored horse, 14 hands high; 1 man's saddle and bridle; 3 cows and a calf; 2 heifers, poplar leaf in right ear, small crop in left; 2 two-year old barrows; 13 year-old hogs; 3 sows, one with 7 pigs, marked with poplar leaf in right ear, smooth crop in left. My present crop of cotton and corn, all household and kitchen furniture."

1812, Jan 6
   Philip SANDERS, to son, Madison M. SANDERS, negro wench, Lucy, and her child, Randolph.

1812, Feb 12
   Hugh LESLY, to children for goodwill and natural affection. To Moses and Mary LESLY, 1 negro girl, Dinah.

1812, Feb 19
   Daniel MC NEIL, For natural love and parental affection to children Anda and Martha: 25 head of cattle; 25 head of hogs; 2 chests; 5 featherbeds and furnishings, bedsteads; 1 cupboard and furnishings; 1 loom, 250 yards of homespun; 3 spinning wheels; 2 p pair of cards; all rest of household and kitchen furniture.

1812, Jan 27
   Willoughby SLATON, to Elisha and David WALKER, Jr., Slaves: Zach; Guy; Dilcy; Nelly; Moses and two children, David and Sarah. 2 featherbeds and furniture; 1 large black chest; 1 white trunk; 1 slab; 1 pine table; 7 chairs; 2 pots; 1 Dutch oven; 1 skillet; also cooking ware, and glass-ware; 2 pails; 2 piggins; 1 wash tub; 1 bu-

cket; 1 doz. knives and forks; 3 hoes; 2 mattocks; 1 grub-hoe; 2 spitoons. (Willoughby Slaton m. Elizabeth (Walker) LOWE, wid., and daughter of David WALKER, Sr. He was Adm. of Walker's estate.)

1812, June 8
    John W. SMITH, to Anderson CRAWFORD; George MC GRUDER; Johathon CLIETT; Thomas PARKER, and James BROWN, Commissioners of the Republican Grove Meeting House, for 1 cent: 2 1/2 acres of land adjoining said Meeting House, for a house of worship for the Almighty God, forever. No other Church but Baptist shall be constituted at said Meeting House.

1813, Mar 24
    Benjamin GRUBBS, to Mary GRUBBS, with love and affection to my beloved wife: 50 acres of land at mouth of Stephen's Creek; 3 boxes; 1 cotton-wheel; 1 ladies saddle; 1 ditto; 2 iron pots; 1 iron kettle; 1 spider; 1 pot-rack and hooks; 1 iron spice-mortar; 3 smoothing-irons; 1 pair fire-dogs; 1 cupboard; 2 tables; 2 pails; 1 wash-tub; 1 piggin; 1 powdering-tub (this was used for salting meat); 5 basons; 1 dish; 2 jars; 1 jug; 3 beds and hides, and furniture; 1 bedstead; 1 trunk; 1 sugar cannister; 2 tea cannisters; 10 plates; 1 pitcher; 1 tin tray and waiter; 6 chairs; 1 loom and gear; 1 looking glass; 1 axe; 1 drawing-knife; 1 grub-hoe; 1 iron wedge; 2 hammers; 3 bed-quilts; 1 rug; 4 blankets; 4 sheets; 10 plates; 4 bowls; 3 tea-pots; 1 butter-boat; 10 saucers; 11 cups; 1 pepper-box; 2 Glass China bowls; 1 milk pot; 1 tumbler; 5 tea-spoons; 6 knives and forks; 6 chairs; 6 bottles; 1 salt cellar; 14 head of cattle; 1 bed, bedstead and furniture, called, "Sarah Bullman's," and 215 acre tract whereon I now live.

1813, Mar 24
    Frances GRUBBS, to sister-in-law, Mary GRUBBS, for love and affection: 1 cupboard and furnishings; 2 bedsteads; 3 pots; 2 tables; 1 clock-reel (a sort of primitive timer used when roasting meat on a spit - regulated the turning); fire-tongs; spinning-wheel; 1 Dutch oven.

1813, Mar 24
    Aletha DRANE, for love and affection to children, Walter; Polly and Effy DRANE, 1 negro woman, Rachel, and child Levina. To son, Walter, and right or title I have to real estate of Walter DRANE, dec'd.

1814, May 16
    James OLIVE, for love and affection for dau. Frances BUTT, and son-in-law, John BUTT, negro girl, Charity, 7 years old; negro girl, Priscilla, 5 years old, both the children of my negro wench, Road.

1814, May 18
    Thomas HUNT, with love and goodwill for, "my son Henry HUNT, 1/2 of my 700 acre tract called, 'Vinemount'; negroes, Cuffey; Lucy, and her two children. Stephen and Madison.

1814, May 20
Gerard MORRISS, to John Marshall MORRIS, and Abraham Rittenhouse MORRISS, my infant sons; negro girl, Betty. If either of the children dies in nonage, property to go to the other.

1814, June 10
Sarah GARRETT, to Madison SANDERS, "my loving grandson: One bay horse, Dragon; 2 cows and calves; 14 head of hogs; 2oo bushels of corn; 2 stacks of fodder; 6 chairs; 2 trunks; 2 pots, and one oven; 1 chest; 2 tables; 1 man's saddle and bridle; and one lady's saddle and bridle."

1814, July 20
Edward BUGG, "For love and affection to children, Jeremiah; Benjamin; Charles; Tilbon; and William, and children of dau., Elizabeth HATTAWAY: Negroes, Cyrus, son of Dinah; Peter, son of Dilly, to Jeremiah, and to Molly, daughter of Peggy. To Benjamin, Ned, son of Peggy; Hannah, daughter of Dilly. To William, Arthur, son of Peggy; David, son of Dilly, Mary, daughter of Sarah. To children of Elizabeth Hattaway: One negro named Frank; 11 head of cattle, 7 marked with crop in left ear, and a slit in right; 2 marked with a slit in each ear, 2 not marked."

1815, May 12
David WILLIAMS, blacksmith, "Being subject to diseases, maladies, and uncertain of my time of departure, when my dear wife, Winnyford, will be deprived and left destitute of a husband and guardian, leave the following in a deed of gift: One negro boy named, Tobe; one negro girl named, Dorcas; 1 featherbed and furniture, $450.00 in the hands of John BOYD, of Edgefield, S. C., who has agreed to act as trustee."

1815, July 15
Daniel STURGIS to Benjamin Hicks STURGIS, for goodwill and affection: All landed property conveyed to me by my dec'd brother, William STURGIS, in state of South Carolina.

1815, June 2
Rebecca COCKE, to beloved children: Polly and Augustus COCKE, for two dollars earnest money, Joe; Ned; Isabell; Sally; Boston; Henry; Toby and Charley.

1815, Nov 30
Fitz Maurice HUNT, to Eleanor DANIEL, "For love and affection to my daughter, 1 tract of land on Germany Creek, 250 acres."

1810, Feb 24 - Rec. Jan 1, 1816
Fitz Maurice HUNT, for love and affection to my dau., Elizabeth HUNT, a negro girl, Elmina.

1810, Apr 15- Rec. Apr 2, 1816
Edward SHORT, to Harriot JONES, negro child, Rose. (Harriot relinquishes all claim to Rose, to father, Richard Jones, Apr 20, 1810

1816, May 8
    William WILKINS, Sheriff, levied upon property of Richard JONES and Thomas JONES, sells negro, Rose, 12 years old, at auction, to John BACON, for $436.00.

1816, May 15
    John LEITH, for love and affection to John SEARGEANT, and Thomas SEARGEANT, heirs of John SEARGEANT, dec'd, and Sarah ROBERTS, formerly Seargeant, 1 negro man, Adam.

1816, May 15
    John LEITH, for love and affection to John ROBERTS, son-in-law, negro man Will. To William MEGAR (MC GAR), negro boy, Little Matt. To Hannah LEITH, daughter, negroes, Pollidore; Betty; Jack, and Jacob.

1816, Sept 25
    Owen SULLIVAN, to son-in-law, John KENNADEY, for love and affection, and better maintenance, support and livelihood, 100 acres granted to Owen Sullivan on Little River and Sullivan's Creek.

1816, Oct 9
    Dorothy SHORT, to John LEE, with love and affection to son-in-law, nine negroes, to-wit: Barbara; Davis; Aaron; Levi; Alethea; Ratsy; James and Hawes. Also chest of drawers; 2 beds and furniture; 1 bedstead and curtains.

1816, Nov 11
    William EUBANK, to beloved son, William EUBANK, JR., at death of myself and wife, Mary, $700.00, to be levied out of estate.

1817, July 1
    Henry SPAULDING, for love, goodwill and affection, to my cousin, William PAGE, on Little River, farmer: A negro named Martha, about two years old. To Elizabeth SPAULDING, dau-in-law, widow, and to heirs of her body. If no heirs, to William Page, her brother, a tract of land whereon she now lives, 200 acres more or less.

1817, Oct 28
    Joseph MARSHALL, for love and affection to children, Mary; Daniel, and Santitena Martha James Marshall, motherless children: Mary to have 2 negro women, Jena and Chaney. Daniel, 2 negro boys, Will and Joshua. Santitena, 2 girls, Chloe and Mariah. Also they are to have 1 tract, 200 acres near Brownsborough, 100 acres adj. the same, conveyed to me by my brother, Samuel MARSHALL.

1818, Feb 23
    Fitz HUNT, to beloved daughter, Eleanor DANIEL, 1 negro girl, named Gincey.

1818, July 4
    John Tyler ALLEN, for love and affection for my four daughters, Alice Ann; Mercy Ruth; Mary Hariot, and Sarah L. Allen, eight negroes: Bob; Wash; Jack; George; Fanny; Milly; Diner, and Luce.

1818, Sept 29
   John BYRD, for love of children, John Irea BYRD, and Eliza BYRD, offspring of Elizabette BYRD, formerly NEAL, negroes, Biddy, a woman, and Jim, a boy.

1818, Sept 30
   Elizabeth SAVAGE, to John and Rebekah SAVAGE, for love of my two dear little children, negro slaves, Sam and Lewis.

1818, Nov 12
   Alice ALLEN, to beloved daughter, Elizabeth WHITE, a negro man, Jerry, and a small bay horse.

1818, Dec 21
   John WILLINGHAM, for goodwill and affection for four sons, William; Cash; John, and Isaac, the tract whereon I now live, and where Cash and John reside, 550 acres on Sullivan's Creek.

1819, Jan 1
   William UNDERWOOD, for love and natural affection of my sister, Nancy, nagroes: Winny, 15, and George, her brother, 11.

1819, Jan 2
   Ann DORSETT, for natural love for Martha Ann and Susannah Eleanor, WISEMAN, daus., of Robert and Eleanor WISEMAN, and my nieces, a negro girl, Sophia.

1819, Jan 14
   John TERRILL, to Mary BONNER, and her five children, Grief Grammer; Tabitha Davis; Jemima; Samuel and John BONNER, for divers good reasons, all my goods, chattels, household and kitchen furniture, and my share of my father's estate. (John TERRILL, of Prince George Co., Va.)

1819, July 7
   John YOUNGBLOOD, to Isham and Polly PHILLIPS, a negro boy, James, and a negro girl, Phillis.

1819, July 7
   Jeremiah GRIFFIN, to "beloved son, John GRIFFIN, the whole of my interest in mill on Little River, and the two acres where the two mills now stand, also a 1 1/2 acre tract in Wilkes Co., across the river, containing the Mill Dam."

1819, July 8
   Thomas HUNT, "For love and affection to son-in-law, Green DOZIER, and dau. Constantia, his wife, 294 acres originally granted to Leonard CLAIBORNE, in 1776, conveyed to Henry HUNT, SR., and by him willed to two sons, William and Thomas, also 1 tract of 100 acres, adj. the last mentioned tract."

1819, Aug 2
   Ann MC FARLAND, "For love of my grandson, John COLEMAN, of Wilkes Co., 1 negro girl, Minny, aged 8 or 10, very light complexion."

1819, Aug 2
    Ann MC FARLAND, "To John MC FARLAND, for parental affection, 1 mulatto girl, Minna, about 6 years old."

1819, Sept 1
    Pleasant TINDELL, "To sons, William; John B., and Thomas, 3 negroes: Dave; Charlotte, and Maria, with all my stock of horses; cattle; sheep, and hogs, also plantation utensils."

1819, Sept 7
    John LING, to John LING, JR., "all my property, real and personal, to my eldest son."

1820, Apr 23
    Jared POUNDS, to "Christiannature SIMS, for natural love and affection to my mother, all stock of horses; cows; hogs; and sheep; household and kitchen furniture; plantation tools; waggon and gears; also slaves, Lowder; Caesar; Charles; and Fortune, deeded to me by James SIMS, in 1808. Also Gilbert, the increase of Furtune."

1820, Sept 11
    John MC FARLAND, to Daniel MC FARLAND, for parental love, 85 acres on waters of Maddock's Creek, in Wrightsborough.

1820, Nov 18
    Elizabeth (Denham) WALTON, to her son, Charles DENHAM, a negro boy, Jim.

1820, Dec 19
    John MC FARLAND, "For natural love and affection to my son-in-law, William STARKE, a mulatto slave girl, Minna."

1821, Mar 22
    Thomas CARR, "For love and affection to son, Thomas CARR, JR., all my lands on Germany's Creek, to take effect after my death."

1821, Oct 15
    James ROSS, to Benjamin Franklin GERALD, and Nancy GERALD, children of James and Polly GERALD, a negro boy for Benjamin, named Chance, and a negro girl, named Dye, for Nancy. (They were grandchildren, Mary (Polly) ROSS m. James GERALD, Feb. 23, 1807).

1821, Oct 22
    Beverly SPIVY, to the Commissioners of Franklin Academy, to-wit: Thomas DOOLY; Mark P. DAVIS; Billington SANDERS; Beverly SPIVY, and William SCOTT. Spivy gives for use of school, 2 acres originally granted to William STANFORD, adj., lands of Robert FLOURNOY, (known as DEVEREAUX'S Old Tract) Adam SCOTT, and Thomas DOOLY. (From names and locations given, this is believed to have been in Wrightsborough.)

1820, Jan 7 - Rec. Jan 5, 1822
    Ignatius FEW, SR., "to loving son, Crapus FEW, 925 acres on both sides of Rocky Comfort Creek, whereon is now a grist and sawmill, and a cotton machine. Also, 40 acres opposite to the mill, 500 acres lying 3 miles below; 500 acres in Warren Co., on Joe's Creek;

1,000 acres in same county, on Fort's Creek; and 200 acres on Sweetwater Creek, granted to John MC DUFFIE. Also negroes, Rose, and her son; Flora, sister to Rose; young negro man, Jack, son of Dulce; Daphne and Isaac, children of August's wife, and 2 children of Bob, named Mark, and _____."

1810, Jan 7 - Rec Jan 5, 1822
      IGNATIUS FEW, SR., "for love and affection to sons: Camillus FEW, 287 1/2 acres in Washington Co., on Ogeechy River, granted to Lewis DAVIS; 287 1/2 acres adj., granted to Ezekiel MILLER, both tracts part of 700 acre tract of low ground, in bend of River; 400 acres of pine land, adj., to above, granted to John COBB, 250 acres adj., above, granted to Eli CUNNINGHAM, 2/3 of a 287 1/2 acre tract on Oconee River, (in Washington Co., near Buffalo Creek, granted to George WAINWRIGHT.); 287 1/2 acres on main Buffalo Creek, granted to John SUTTON. Also negroes, Betty Hamilton and her four children, David; Maria; Limus; and Simon; Lucinda, Peter, Dulce, and Lucy. To Alfred FEW, for love and affection to my son, 3,900 acres on the Walnut Fork of Broad River, also negroes, Fan, and her six children, Edie; Millie; Edmond; Ned; Farm; and William. Also Dick's two sons, Emanuel and Arlington. To my son, Leonidas, 1,760 acres on Walnut Fork; also 2/3 of a 1,000 acre tract in Franklin Co., purchased from heirs of Greenberry LEE; 2/3 of a 287 1/2 acre tract in same county, granted to James CARTLEDGE; 2/3 of 287 1/2 acre tract, same county, granted to Cornelius MC CARDLE. Negroes, Betty, wife of Cyrus, and five children, Eleanor; Rachel; Mary; Anderson, and Sarah, also Cudjoe and Moses."

1823, _____
      John CRABB, for love and affection to Nancy RAY, my grand-daughter, 1 sorrell horse named, Charles.

1822, Dec 25 - Rec. _____(?)
      James TOOLE, "To my loving grandchildren, James and Harriot TOOLE, children of my son, George, 2 negro girls, Silly and Sally."

1823, Aug 22
      Sarah MOORE, "For love and affection to grandson, William BLADWIN, son of Owen BALDWIN, all my right and interest in presently contemplated Land Lottery, on land between Ocmulgee and Chattahoochee Rivers. If I draw land, he is to assume ownership, and register it in his own name."

1820, Nov 23 - Rec. _____1823
      Martha ALBRITTON, "To Ansel Mitton, and Nancy Lee ALBRITTON, my beloved children, all right and title to estate of late husband, Jesse ALBRITTON, dec'd., providing the property shall not be taken out of my possession in my lifetime, unless they give bond for $10,000.

1824, Jan 31
      Stanton PORTER, for love and affection for nephews, John W. BETTS; B. P. BETTS; William O. BETTS, and nieces, Martha and Marion BETTS, negro girl, Hannah, 9 or 10; 2 beds; bedsteads and furniture; 3 cows and calves; 3 yearlings; 2 sows, and seven pigs; 14 shoats; 1 horse colt; 2 pots and 1 oven.

1819, Nov 13 - Rec. Mar 1, 1824
    Mark SULLIVAN, "For love and affection for grandchildren, Elenor and Malinda JONES; James Madison and Arabella SULLIVAN, children of son, Samuel, plantation tract whereon I now live; 131 acres; negroes, Gilbert; Abraham, and Lucy; stock of all kinds, viz: 2 geldings, 1 mare; 1 colt; 20 head of cattle; 7 sheep; 70 hogs; all household and kitchen furniture; and farm utensils." (Note: Elenor and Malinda were children of Henry Jones & Mary Sullivan, m. Jan 1, 1807).

1824, Mar 31
    Thomas O. MARTIN, for love, goodwill, and affection, to wife, Rebecca, and daughters, Elinor; Sarah, and Eliza: 202 1/2 acre tract in 8th Dist., Henry Co., #136; 250 acres in 11th Dist., of Early County; $136.00.

1824, May 15
    William WILKINS, to Agnes PEARRE, wife of William PEARRE, during her life; Negro woman, Lucy, and two children, Dave, and Carmeler(?), after her death, to her heirs.

1824, Jan 27
    Thomas MURRELL, for love and affection to William COBB (stepson), all rights to a tract of 325 acres on Greenbriar Creek.

1824, Nov 20
    Elizabeth BAYLESS, to grand-daughter, July Hubbard BAYLESS, 1 negro man, Isaac.

1825, May 25
    Warrenton HAYNIE, for natural love and affection to sons, A. Melius (Emilius?), and Augustin HAYNIE, 2 negro girls, Nelly and Phillis.

1825, May 9
    James SHAW, for love and affection to daughters: Louisa B. SHAW, negro girl, Mariah; Matilda B. Shaw, negro girl, Martha; Ann M. SPIERS, negro girl, Kissie; Emily C. Shaw, negro girl, Leah; Rachel E. Shaw, negro girl, Phillis.

1801, Nov 17 - Rec. May 24, 1825
    John WINFIELD, to Commissioners of Whiteoak Meeting House; William JONES; John TABOR, JR; James ALLEN; and Samuel MANES, for $4.00 earnest money; a tract consisting of 10 1/2 acres at head of Whiteoak Creek.

1826, Jan 4
    Mary LLOYD, to William WILKINS, in trust for beloved niece, Charity BYNUM, 1 gig and harness.

1826, May 3
    Hugh REESE, "For love and goodwill I have for my son, Vincent, I do give him a piece of land containing 100 acres, formerly purchased from Mercer BROWN, with all appurtenances thereon."

1826, June 2
   Archibald HENDERSON, "For love I bear to my children, Alta Ann and Eliza Jane: 202 1/2 acres in Fayette Co., 7th Dist., Lot #70; 1 gray mare; 1 red cow; 1 red calf with some white on back and belly; 2 featherbeds; bedsteads and furniture; 3 pine tables; 6 sitting chairs; 1 pine chest; 1 pine slab; 1 loom; 2 pots; 1 Dutch oven; 1 set cups and saucers; 6 earthen plates; 1 earthen dish; 6 teaspoons; 6 tablespoons; 1 set of knives and forks; carving knife and fork; 1 coffee-pot; 2 spinning-wheels; 3 pairs of cotton cards; 1 clock reel; 1 safe; 1 pair flatirons; 1 iron potrack; 1 washtub; 2 water pails; 1 piggin; 2 sow shoats."

1826, _____
   Betsey HARRISON, with natural love and affection for grandson, Benoni HARRISON, a tract of land in Monroe Co., Dist., #3, Lot #35, 202 1/2 acres.

1827, Mar 16
   John CULBREATH, for love and affection for daughter, Elizabeth, three negroes: John; Betty, and Jenny.

1827, Mar 9
   Martha BULL, with love and affection for daughter, Amanda, 2 slaves: Dick and his wife Linda.

1827, Mar 21
   Sarah WALTON, with natural love and affection for daughter, Blanche WOOD, of Alabama, give and grant to Jonathon WOOD, in trust for his wife, Blanche, negro man, Lewis, with a blemish in his eyes, about 25 years old.

1827, May 1
   George MAGRUDER, to daughter, Mary BATTEY, wife of Cephas BATTEY, gives in trust with George MAGRUDER, JR., negroes, Jim; Brister and wife, Pat; Ned; Jerry; Chaney; Ephraim; Brister, Jr., an and   ...(name scratched out.)

1827, May 11
   James ROSS, of Franklin Co., N. C., to children of Edward ROSS, negroes: Hannah; Sam; Sue; Orrin, and Larcy.

1827, Sept 18
   Catherine CLANTON, to son-in-law, Harmong LAMAR, negroes: Sarah; Betty, and her two children, Simon and Mary; Molly, and her three children, Dick; Ned and Randal; Hardy and her five children, Sophia; Chloe; Sylvy; Mary and Louisa; also Big Sylvy; Ben, and Kitty. Said negroes were bequeathed to me by the last will of my mother, Mary FOX, of Edgefield Dist., S. C., for my natural life.

1828, Jan 28
   Margery BEALLE, for love and affection to Thomas E. BEALLE, son, a negro man, Jeffrey.

1828, Mar 31
    Isaac VAUGHN, with love, goodwill and affection to beloved children: Armnella; Fanney; Wyatt; Caroline, and Irving VAUGHN; 1 negro man, William,45; 1 gray horse; 1 sorrell horse; 1 small Jersey wagon; 3 beds and furniture; 23 hogs; 1 lot of land in Early Co., #61, 22nd Dist., 250 acres.

1828, June 16
    Elizabeth BAYLISS, for love and affection to grand-daughter, Emily BAYLISS, dau. of son, Thomas: 2 horses; 2 cows and calves; 2 trunks; 1 bed and bedstead, and mattrass; 1 bolster, and pillows; 2 blankets; 2 quilts; 4 sheets; 2 chairs; 4 counterpains; 1 walnut table; 3 sows; 1 pot, and 1 oven.

1828, June 23
    John SMITH, of Houston Co., to niece Elizabeth Harriet SMITH, negro girl named Price Anderson. To niece, Eudosha SMITH, negro girl, Eliza. To Gazaway Davis SMITH, nephew, boy Jordan.

1829, Jan 8
    Sarah WALTON, with love and affection to daughter, Blanche WOOD, (in trust with husband, Jonathon WOOD), and her children, John; Sarah F. C; Willis H; Blanche M; Naomi Ann, and Jesse S., 1 tract of land containing 307 acres, on Big Kiokee Creek, known as Tulloss(?) tract; 198 acre tract known as the Harden Place; 125 acres known as the Ganby (or Gunby) Mountain tract. Said tracts described in deed from Adm. of William WALTON estate to me.

1829, Jan 8
    Jesse WALTON, to Blanche WOOD, of Franklin Co., Ala., with love and affection for sister, gives same to be held for her children, a 344 acre tract on Washington Road, Columbia Co., Ga., on Big Kiokee Creek, formerly owned by William BOOKER.

1829, Feb 4
    John CULBREATH, to dau. Martha HUCHINGSON, negro girl, Ginny, about 10 years old. To grandson, John HUCHINGSON, negro boy, Early.

1829, Feb 18
    Martha HUCHINGSON, with natural love to children, Susan Evaline; Caroline Elizabeth, and Seaborn Payne W. D. Huchingson: Negro woman, Edy, about 22, dark complexion, negro boy, Abraham, 13, dark complexion; negro girl, Fanny, about 11, dark complexion.

1829, Mar 27
    Robert JONES, for love of grand-children, William; Martha Ann; Robert; Mary, and Susan POWELL, property as follows: William, 1 bay colt; 1 red headed heifer and calf; 1 sow and pigs; Martha Ann, 1 cow and calf; Robert, 2 cows and calves; Mary, 1 no-horned cow and her calf. To William and Robert, jointly, 1 yoke of oxen and cart. To Martha and Susan, 2 sows and pigs.

1829, June 1
    William STAPLER, to beloved daughter, Martha, negro girl, Lucy.

1829, June 1
    Nancy STANFORD, widow, for love and affection to grand-daughter, Elizabeth SPIVEY, 1 white cow with red speckles, together with two other cow kine, a white heifer with a red head, and a white yearling with a speckled head.

1829, Aug 4
    Elizabeth BAYLISS, to beloved son, William BAYLISS, a 50 acre tract, part of a tract granted to George DIVINE. To grandchildren, Ann Eliza; Julia Hubbard; Georgianna Troup, and Elizabeth Jane Bayliss, children of my son, John: All the tract whereon John now lives, 350 acres on Germany Creek, conveyed to my son, Thomas BAYLESS, by my husband, Isham BAYLESS, dec'd.

1831, Mar 2
    John COCHRAN, with love and affection to his children, Jefferson Berrian; Louisa Marian and William Benjamin, negroes: Moses; Jenny, and their children, Anderson; Henry, and Harriot.

1831, July 6
    Thomas AYRES, to son Abraham AYRES, a tract of land in Appling Co., Lot #212, Dist., 19, consisting of 490 acres.

1831, Dec 22
    Elizabeth FULLER, with natural love for daughter, Elizabeth, and son, Wade, all and singular my personal estate: 2 beds and furniture, 1 white and red pieded cow; 8 hogs; 1 table; 2 chests; 2 pots.

1832, Aug 3
    Jeremiah GRIFFIN, with love and affection for son, Richard, 241 acres on North prong of Upton's Creek, and Germany's Creek, originally granted to Thomas MOORE; also 6 acres adj. above. (This was in the Goldmine area.)

1833, Jan 7
    David DU BOSE, to H. SMITH, nephew by marriage, 50 acres on the N. W. side of my estate, adj., Marshall KEITH, including the Graveyard purchased from Sarah BLACKWELL, with dwelling house, gin-house, and all other improvements.

1833, Jan 18
    Jemima BLAIR, to grand-daughter, Ann DAWSON, 300 acres of land on North side of Greenbriar Creek, where I now reside; also negro slave named Little John. And also: Peter; Allen; Little Joe; Patience and her children, Betsy and Selina; all my stock of horses; cattle; sheep and hogs, and property of every description.

1833, Mar 5
    Jemima BLAIR, for love and affection to Robert BROWN (kinship not shown), a negro boy, Little Joe.

1829, Sept 7 - Rec. _____ 1833
    Waters BRISCOE, to the Methodist Episcopal Meeting House, called "Shiloh,". by its commissioners, Patrick DOUGHERTY; Basil NEAL;

Ralph BRISCOE, and Green DOZIER, a portion of land including the Spring, now made use of by the meeting house.

1829, Sept 7 - Rec. _____1833
Green DOZIER, to above named commissioners of Methodist Episcopal Meeting House called "Shiloh" land where the meeting house now stands, 164 yards by 202 yards.

1833, Dec 24
Henry GIBSON, with love and affection to Lycurgus Gustavus REES, a negro man, Derry, about 30.

1833, Dec 28
Archibald MAGRUDER, to loving niece, Martha MILLER, dau. of John OLIVE, wife of Andrew MILLER, of Richmond Co., Ga., a negro woman, Hess, about 25, and her two children, John and Sofy.

1833, Dec 28
Archibald MAGRUDER, with love and affection to niece, Ann B. ANDERSON, dau. of John Olive, and wife of John ANDERSON, of Richmond Co., negro slaves, Kit, 27; her children, Suky; Ann; Gilbert; Abram; and Elizabeth.

1834, Mar 29
John FOX, for love and affection to great niece, Martha Ann Fox LAMAR, wife of Harmong LAMAR, in trust with Simmons CRAWFORD: Fortune, a small negro man, black complexion, between 45 and 50; Delia, his wife, a large dark complected woman, about same age; Rosetta, dark-complected, about medium size for a woman, 35 years, and her five children; Kingston (commonly called, King), dark, medium size, 22 years old; Nancy, dark complected, medium size, 18 or 19; Dolly, dark complected, 16 or 17; Prince, dark complected, 14 years old; William (or Will), dark, about 10; Anderson, 18 mos. old, child of Nancy and John Smart, commonly called, John; child of Dolly, about 2 years old; also 351 acres of land on Uchee Creek, to be held in trust by Simmons Crawford. Harmong Lamar is to cultivate said land, "without molestation."

1834, Apr 4
William BEALLE, and wife, Betsey Ann, to dau., Evalina W. WILLIAMS, a 232 acre tract on waters of Uchee Creek. (On same date, Evalina and her husband, William M. WILLIAMS, sell same land to Littleberry LEWIS, for $1,000.00).

1834, Apr 4
Susannah TOOLE, for natural love and affection to son, James TOOLE, and his seven children, viz: Mary Lucinda; John; James; Alexander; George; Isabelle, and Ann Hasseltine Judson TOOLE, five negroes, to wit: Dublin and Annett, and three children, Betty; Jude, and Milly.

1835, July 8
Elizabeth JONES, with love and affection to son, Samuel JONES, of Columbia Co., son-in-law, William SKINNER, of Richmond Co., son-in-

law, John SKINNER, of Columbia Co., and Robert CLEVELAND, of Franklin Co., the following property: Negroes Jincey; John; Frank; Cashel; Milly; Matilda; Eliza; Jerry; Kate; Poll; Phebe; Jerry; James; Henry; Luke; Amos; Lucy; Scott; Lett; Chloe; Nancy; Bill; Leonard; Pug; Peter; Bob; Patience; Fanny, and Edmond. Also my cattle; horses; stock; furniture, and every other article of personal property belonging to me; also 300 acre tract on Savannah River, in Columbia Co., to be equally divided.

1835, Aug 4
Rebecca PERRYMAN, to Jefferson S. BRISCOE, with natural love for my grandson, a negro woman, Minder, at present hired out to William S. DUNN.

1835, Oct 22
Ann L. COLVARD, wid., of Thomas COLVARD, "In consequence of the disability of my dearly beloved sister, Mary Frances COLVARD, (prob. a sister-in-law), and the fact that I am about to enter into matrimonial contract with Mr. Daniel MAHONEY, I do hereby give and convey a negro woman, Jenny, about 30, black complexion, a pair of looking glasses, and 1/2 doz. silver dessert spoons."

1836, May 11
John DAY, for love and affection I have for Martha E(?) DAY, wid., of my son, Nathan, dec'd., the following negroes: A boy, Tarver, 2 yrs old. To my grandchildren, Sarah Margaret DAY, and Joseph William DAY, negroes Esther and her children, George; Robert; and Frank.

1836, June 27
William SHEFFIELD, of Hancock Co., and Sary JOHNSON, of Jasper Co., for love and affection, give to William SATTERWHITE, of Greene Co., all rights to a 100 acre tract in Columbia Co., as legator of estate of Mille and Mary SATTERWHITE.

1836, Dec 10
Frederick BROWN, to Phebe BROWN, and others: Although I have made a will, I do not wish it altered, so leave in a deed of gift to my belove wife, two horses; one a sorrel called, Westley, the other a gray called Sealum(?); also a 117 acre tract of pine land, three sets of ploughs and gear. To my daughter, Concord WHITE, a mare, Pegga, dark Bay. To my grandson, Frederick WHITE, Peggy, my youngest colt.

1837, Mar 25
John OLIVE, to beloved dau., Ann ANDERSON, of Richmond Co., wife of John ANDERSON, 2 tracts of land, containing in all 194 acres. To be held in trust by John Anderson.

1837m Mar 28
John LAMAR, to dau., Caroline R. A. LAMAR, negro boy, Edmond, 14, and girl, Charity.

1837, May 26
Henry GRAY, for love and affection to step-sons, Thomas WALL, a negro child, Amy, 18 mos. old; and Wesly WALL, negro girl, Jane 8.

Sons of my beloved wife, Frances. (Henry and Frances were married, Aug 13, 1833)

1837, June 14
　　William BARNETT, for love and affection to wife, Elizabeth, and the children gotten during our coverture, in trust, with Harmong LAMAR: Falby, negro woman of 32, and her children, Jenny 7; Billy 5; Martha 3; Romulus, 1; and Caty, a young negro woman, about 18, sister to Falby.

1837, Nov 4
　　Isaac LOWE, for natural love, goodwill and affection to dau., Selina Thomas ROBERTS, 101 acre tract of land known as the Quisenberry Place.

1838, Jan 27
　　Daniel L. MARSHALL, for regard I have for my sons: To Joseph G. MARSHALL, negroes, Axim, 20, and Amos, 7 or 8. To William A. H. MARSHALL, Nat, 20, and Anderson, 10. To Daniel MARSHALL, Golding, 20, and Louisa, 13. And to daughter, Emily, Jack, 20, and Maria, 15. To daughter, Martha A. MARSHALL, Willis, 16, and Lucinda, 20.

1838, Mar 24
　　Elizabeth MAGRUDER, for divers causes, and $10., to Henry SMITH, tract about ten miles fron Augusta, on Fury's Ferry Road, 865 acres.

1838, May 16
　　Mahala JORDAN, with love and affection to three children: Frances; John, and Amanda, a parcel of land in 7th Dist., Lot #165, in Monroe County, Georgia, 202 1/2 acres.

1838, May 29
　　Isaac LOWE, for love and aff., to beloved daus., Delaney GARRET, negro girl Chaney; to Hepsey VAUGHN, negro girl, Mary 13. (Delaney m. Absolom Garrett, Nov 15, 1832).

1838, Sept 25
　　Thomas WILKINS, with love for dau., Elizabeth OLIVE, negroes, Aggy, and her children, Cyrus and Sam. At her death, to go to grandson, Thomas OLIVE. Not to be subject to control or debts of Elizabeth's husband. (Elizabeth m. Berry OLIVE, May 1, 1813).

1839, Jan 2
　　David STANFORD, in trust with George A. P. WHITEFIELD, for love of dau., Sarah WHITEFIELD, sells to said George, for $1.00, a 217 acre tract where David Stanford now lives, on Greenbrier Creek. (Sarah and George m. Aug 31, 1837).

1839, Feb 8
　　Michael DAUGHERTY, to dau., Matilda, for love and affection, two negroes, Frances, a yellow girl, 5 years old, and Rhoda, a black, 2 years old.

1839, Oct 9
　　Samuel MARSHALL, of Tallapoosa Co., to Joseph G. MARSHALL; Wil-

liam A. MARSHALL, and Daniel MARSHALL, "I do give to my beloved nephews, three negro men, Semore; Kit, and Abram."

1839, Nov 11
  Frederick BROWN, with love, goodwill, and affection to James WILSON, son of Elias WILSON, and Temperance WILSON, 103 acre tract on Upton's Creek, formerly property of Seaborn IVEY. (Temperance SAXON and Elias Wilson m. July 7, 1823.)

1839, Dec 3
  Nicholas FOX, for love and affection to dau., Sarah Elizabeth EVANS, wife of William EVANS, slaves, Nancy, and children, Jack; Diannah, and Peter Parker, also girl, Anne, commonly called Priss.

1840, Jan 28
  Pierson PETTIT, with love for dau., Nancy Kennon PETTIT, "For and in consideration of her obedient and dutiful conduct to me at all times," a negro girl, Eliza.

BILLS OF SALE

1791, Oct 14
  Susannah COLEMAN, to William SHIELDS, as guardian of Elizabeth ROSBOROUGH, 1 negro woman, Judy; 1 negro woman, Sal; negro man, Bobb; negro man, Ben; negro girl, Lidda; negro girl, Patience; negro boy, John, and negro boy Ralph; 2 horses; 3 cows and calves; 2 heifers; 1 steer; 2 beds and furniture; 1 woman's saddle and bridle; 2 tables; 8 chairs; 2 potts; 1 Dutch oven; 1 skillet; 1 coffee mill; 2 flat-irons; 1 dish; 11 plates; 1 case, and 9 bottles; 2 plows; 1 pair traces; 1 looking-glass; 5 teacups and saucers; 3 drinking glasses, and decanter; 6 spoons; 1 tea-kettle; 6 knives and forks; 2 weeding hoes; 1 bason, and 7 hoggs, for the consideration of £191, 10 s, 4 p, sterling.

1791, Aug 30
  Sherwood BUGG, Adm. of estate of Peter PARRIS, to Thomas WATKINS, negroes: Quash; Sander; Jamy; Tom; Dinah; Black; Nancy; Phoebe; Sambo; Robin.

1793, Jan 28
  Joseph MORTON, to Gerard BANKS, of Wilkes Co., for the sum of £94, 1 good, new, well-built waggon and gear, with a team, to-wit: A sorrel gelding, 12 years old, with but one eye; a sorrel mare, with a blazed face; a sorrel mare, 5 years old, well-bred; a chestnut-sorrel Gelding, by the name of Pontius; a well-bred black mare, by name of Kitty Fisher.

1792, Nov 5
  Robert DIXON, Planter, to Jacob DUCKWORTH, Planter, for £50: 1 sorrel mare @ £10; 1 gray horse @ £5; 1 bay horse @ £5; one brindle cow and calf @ £2; 1 brown cow and calf @ £2; 1 featherbed, and furniture @ £6; all household furniture @ £5; Riding saddle, £2; 200 bu. of corn @ £10; 5 hogs @ £1.

1792, Dec 14
    James HAMILTON, Sheriff, to Thomas JONES (The estate of Lewis JONES was indebted for £54, 5 s), following items from the estate sold at Sheriff's sale: Negroes, Janus (or James); Tim and Hannah. Capt. Thomas Jones was highest bidder, for £77.

1793, July 10
    William WATKINS, to Sarah UPTON: 1 sorrel horse; 1 bay horse; 2 bay mares; 1 negro man, named Amos; 5 head of cattle; 2 feather-beds, with their furnishings; 2 shot-guns; all household and kitchen furniture...£150, sterling.

1793, July 23
    Gilbert CLARKE, to Absolom FARRER, Milly and Absolom Farrer, Adms., of estate of Gilbert Clark, exposed whole estate to public sale, July 19, 1793. Absolom was highest bidder, at £50.

1793, Aug 14
    John RAMSEY, to John CULBREATH, one negro boy named, James, about 11 years of age, £15.

1793, Aug 20
    William WILKINS, to William MC LAUGHLIN, JR., "a certain negro girl named Alice, about 8 years old, for £30."

1793, Sept 20
    Thomas MOORE, to Godfrey TIMMERMAN, a negro woman, named Lucy, 26 years old, with child, Abiah, 1 year old, for £65.

1793, Aug 20
    William WILKINS, to William WILKINS, JR., one negro man named Dick, about 30 years old, £18, 2 s.

1793, Oct 4
    Sheriff, to Thomas JONES, the goods; chattels; lands and tenements of Lewellin JONES, dec'd., being indebted to Benjamin FEW, for the sum of £363, property sold at public outcry. Negroes, Tom; Lucy; Sylvia; Clarissa; Tubby; Petty; Peter; Isham; Sarah; Rachel; Fanny; Upsey; June; Isaac; Plato; Matthew and Prudence. Capt. Jones, highest bidder, at £358, 15 s.

1795, Sept 30
    Thomas MERIWETHER, to Robert WARE, 8 negroes, for the price of 45,000 lbs. of inspected tobacco.

1795, Apr 20
    Jeremiah LAMKIN, to John LAMKIN, 6 negroes, for £250, sterling.

1795, Apr 20
    Thomas MERIWETHER, to Nicholas MERIWETHER, 38 negroes, at a price of 90,000 lbs., of inspected tobacco, and £1 sterling.

1795, Oct 11
    Elijah BRAGG, to Benjamin REES, for £30, 2 horse creatures, one a black mare, 10 yrs., old, 14 hands high, branded on the left

thigh, thus "EE" a star on her forehead, a natural trotter. The other a bay mare, 2 yrs. old, 14 1/2 hands high, branded on near shoulder, "BR," trots natural.

1796, Mar 16
    David HARRIS, to Benjamin BLEDSOE, for £5, a negro boy named, Caesar, going on 3 years old.

1797, Mar 28
    William APPLING, to Zachariah SINQUEFIELD, one negro man, Isham, for $280.00, now in possession of Basil LAMAR, JR., until 12 months, from November last.

1797, Mar 31
    James HAMILTON, Sheriff, to John MARCUS, nine negroes sold at "public outcry on the Courthouse steps, at Columbia County Courthouse," as result of a judgment against the estate of Col. Horatio MARBURY, by Leonard FIELD, and Richard WYLEY. Marcus highest bidder for £202 ster.

1797, Apr 20
    Joseph GILL, of Oglethorpe Co., to Joshua GRINAGE, for $600.00, two negroes, Sam and Mary, with their increase from Jan 1, 1791, now in possession of William HOPSON, Rutherford Co., N. C.

1797, May 16
    Nancy SANDERS, to self.."I, Nancy SANDERS, sole Excx., of estate of Ephraim SANDERS, dec'd., have exposed to sale the whole of the personal estate of the dec'd., and according, it has been struck off to me for sum of $2,078.00."

1797, Apr 28
    Thomas LOCKLIN, to William WILKINS, one negro girl, 8 yrs. old, named Alsy, for £30, sterling. (Sold Aug 27, 1792).

1797, June 14
    William SIMMS, to Mann SIMMS, for £100, 2 negroes.

1797, July 14
    Randal RAMSEY, to Isaac RAMSEY, the whole of my personal property: 10 negroes; 3 head of horses; all my stock of cattle and hogs; the sheep flock; household furniture; plantation tools, with every other specie of personal property. Sum $1,712.75

1800, Nov 27
    James GRADY and wife, to Benjamin REYNOLDS..rec'd $100.00, as payment in full, for all right and title I may have to estate of late Benjamin REYNOLDS, of Orange Co., Va., in right of my wife.
    s/ James Grady, and Elizabeth Grady, formerly Reynolds.

1800, Dec 25
    Joshua WYNNE (or WINN), to Williamson WINN, for $300.00, one negro boy, about 13 years old.

1801, Feb 27
Samuel BOWDRE, to James STEWART, for $400.00, a negro wench, named Suky, and her child Katy.

1801, Feb 27
Frances SHACKLEFORD, of Fayetteville, N. C., to James STEWART, for $350.00, to be paid by John WILSON & CO., of Augusta, on the account of James STEWART, Planter, of Columbia Co., Ga., a slave I sold to said Stewart, a negro woman named Dina.

1798, Feb 14
Thomas HAYNES, to George FEE, for $300.00, a negro wench, at this time run away, with any issue she may have had since her elopement.

1798, Mar 16
Benjamin FINNEY, to John TINDALL, 1 negro man, Dave, $320.

1798, Mar 16
Rhesa HOWARD, to William TINDILL, SR., 1 negro man Jeffrey, £60.

1798, Mar 16
Absolom JACKSON, to William TINDILL, SR., one negro woman, Moll, and child, Hany, £70, sterling.

1798, Mar 16
John MOORE, to William TINDILL, Sr., 2 negro boys, George and Tony, $400.00.

1798, Feb 16
Richard, Robert and Randolph, to Collin REID & CO., of Augusta, 1 negro girl, Hester, about 20 years old, $300.00.

1796, Jan 25
William SIMS, to Abner SIMS, in consequence of sum of £40, and for keeping and maintaining my daughter, Aggy SIMS, and her child, Martin SIMS, have sold Jinny, a negro woman and her four children: Betty; Billy; Peter, and John, and one negro fellow called, George.

1801, Oct 6
Solomon ELLIS, to Zachariah SINQUEFIELD, 1 negro woman, Dinah; 1 lad, Jim; 1 featherbed and furniture, $400.00. Zachariah Sinquefield is named as trustee for my wife, Mary ELLIS, and my infant dau., Roanna ELLIS. Negroes to be worked for their benefit.

1801, Oct 6
William TYLER, to Isham BAYLISS, Planter, for $900.00, negroes, Sally and her five children: Lydia; Fancy; Bob; Jerry and Humphrey.

1802, Mar 17
James CONE, to William SHIELDS, for $500., a negro woman, named, Jude, about 40 years old, and a girl named Ellinder, about 3.

1802, Sept 18
Richard and Waters DUNN, to Elizabeth UPTON, for £70, one

negro girl named, Letty.

1803, Feb 7
Thomas FLETCHER, to John REEVES, for the sum of $400., one negro woman by the name of Fann, now in Reeve's possession.

1802, Dec 8 - Rec. Feb 9, 1803
Joel MC LENDON, of Hancock Co., to Thomas FLETCHER, for $400., one negro woman by name of, Fann.

1803, May 11
George MOORE, to Thomas HAYNES, for $300., one negro woman, named Juno.

1798, July 26
Thomas MERIWETHER, to Anderson SMITH, for $225., one negro girl, 13 years old, named Dinah.

1799, Apr 9
Richard WHITE and Nicholas MERIWETHER, to Collins REID, Merchant of Augusta, one negro man, Billy, 19 years old, $475.00.

1799, Apr 9
Richard WHITE and Nicholas MERIWETHER, to James WALKER, Merchang of Augusta, one negro girl, Anna, 14 years old, for $400.00.

1799, Apr 17
Thomas HOBDAY, of Currituck Co., Va., to Joseph COTTON, for £116, sterling money, one negro man, Lewis.

1787, Dec 1 - Rec. Aug 6, 1799
John LAMAR, of Richmond Co., to Daniel MAXWELL, one negro girl, Winny, 13 years old, for the sum of $500.00.

1798, Jan 28 - Rec. Jan 4, 1800
Chesley DANIEL, of Granville Co., N. C., to Joshua GRINAGE, of Columbia Co., Ga., for £34, one negro slave, named Glauster.

1800, Feb 5
Coonrad (Conrad) WALL, to John NIDAY, for and in consequence of the sum of £50, do sell: 7 head of cattle; 1 pott; 1 dutch oven; 1 featherbed and furniture; 3 pewter dishes; 1 pr. trace chains; 1 grubbing hoe; 2 iron wedges; 1 piggin; 1 coulter; 2 bill-hooks; 1 iron pot-rack; 1 pr. double-traces; 1 clevis; 1 adze; 1 hand-saw; 1 frow; 1 Bible; 1 hymn book.

1800, July 8
Joshua SANDERS, to Jeremiah SANDERS, for $500., negroes: Peter; Jenny and her four children; Dick; June; Isham, and John, and one British Still, of 60 gallons capacity.

1795, Oct 3 - Rec. _____ 1801
William APPLING, to Commissioners of Columbia County Academy, (William FEW; Abraham BALDWIN; James MC NEIL; Abraham MARSHALL) for

5 shillings, 25 acres of land.

1795, Oct 3 - Rec. _____1801
James HAMILTON, and Ann, his wife, to Commissioners of Columbia County Academy, for 5 shillings, 40 acre tract of land.

1801, May 13
James MOSSMAN, of Chatham Co., Exr., of estate of James MC KAY, dec'd., by virtue of an order by the Inferior Court of Chatham Co., July 6, 1799, sells certain tracts of land belonging to estate. Auction authorized, and total of 500 acres on Kiokee Creek sond to Peter CRAWFORD.

1804, Feb 25
William SILVA, to Peter WATSON, a black mare 8 or 9 years old, 14 hands high. (No price given).

1804, July 24
James ROSS, Esq., to Hon. Edward TELFAIR, for $1,071.54, one negro woman, Elsa, and child Sam; Maria; Will; Delia; Lucy & Rachel.

1804, July 24
Thomas FLINT, to John PRIOR, for $350.00, one negro woman, named Susannah, about 20 years old, black complexion, warranted to be healthy and honest.

1804, Aug 18
Stephen COLLINS, to William and John, and Nathaniel COLLINS, for $1,000.00, one negro man, Cuffee; one boy Jim; 1 waggon, with gear; 10 head of cattle; 13 hogs; 2 mares; 1 colt; all crop of corn and cotton now growing on plantation.

1804, Aug 31
Thomas MOORE, Esq., to Robert WALTON, and Robert WATKINS, of Richmond Co., negroes Jenny, 23 years old, and her two children, Evelina and Nancy, property held in trust for Polly JENKINS, wife of Edward B. JENKINS, for $500.00.

1805, July 4
George TWITTY, to William LOWE, negro wench and child, to have when called for. (No price given).

1803, Sept 23
Eilzabeth and John FLORANCE, Adms., of estate of William FLORANCE, sell to Richard BOWDRE, and Edmond BOWDRE, a 200 acre tract, sold at auction, pursuant to an order by Inferior Court, and published in the Augusta Gazette.

1804, Mar 22
Francis FARRER, Sheriff, to Thomas CARR, Esq., on a writ against Reuben BRUNSON; Isaac WILLINGHAM, late the Sheriff of Columbia Co., now dec'd., seized lands of above Brunson, on a suit brought by Abraham JONES, Indorsee, of Miller & Whitney, of Augusta. Said lands sold at public outcry, on Courthouse steps, knocked off to said Carr for $150.00.

1804, Mar 27
    Robert MILLHOUSE, Exr., estate of James VERNON, in lieu of dec'd., Daniel WILLIAMS, sold at public outcry, 27 acres of said est. of Vernon, dec'd., to Mercer BROWN, highest bidder at $40.50.

1804, May 18
    John HAYNIE, sells to John BRISCOE, a mulatto girl, Amy.

1804, June 29
    Isaac WILLINGHAM, Sheriff, to Peter CRAWFORD, highest bidder on lands of Richard JONES, seized on a suit brought by John GARRETT. Price, $250.00 for 525 1/2 acres.

1804, July 18
    Valentine ATKINSON, Adm., estate of Charles ATKINSON, by order of Inferior Court, sells at auction to Josias BOSWELL, 100 acres on Uchee Creek for $525.00.

1804, Francis FERRAR, Tax Collector, sells to Richard JOWELL, for unpaid taxes, 300 acres in Columbia Co., for $25.00.

1785, Sept 17 - Rec. July 19, 1804
    Commissioners of Confiscated Lands (Hugh LAWSON; Hepworth CARTER, and Abraham RAVOT), sell 700 acres in Kiokee Creek, at auction, formerly the property of John HUME. John FLEMING highest bidder at £90, 8 s, 4 p.

1804, July 24
    Elisha BOSWELL, to Thomas JONES, one negro boy, about 18 or 20, named Prince, for $315.00.

1804, July 24
    Francis FARRER, Sheriff, in obedience to a writ issued in a suit of Jeremiah LAMKIN, dec'd., auctioned 31 acres to John LAMKIN, for $12.00.

1805, Feb 15
    Francis FARRER, Sheriff, at public vendue sells 20 acres of land for $80.00, to Jane BRISON, highest bidder.

1805, Feb 15
    Francis FARRER, Sheriff, sells to Sarah ANDERSON, Admx., of estate of John ANDERSON, dec'd., 3,245 1/2 a., belonging to Anderson estate. Public sale ordered and advertised in Augusta Gazette, "for protection of orphans." Bought in for Sarah for $1,350.00

1810, Mar 22
    Duncan MC NAIR, to Samuel MC NAIR, for $1,800.00, 7 negroes, viz: Chloe, about 30 years old, and her six children, Ben; Hannah; Lucy; Will; Selah, and Aggy.

1818, June 15
    Solomon MARSHALL, to Peter CRAWFORD, for $1,200., slaves as follows: Isaac, 26 years old, stout, well-made, of Black complexion, and Boston, 22, rather small, of dark complexion.

1805, Dec 20
   William THOMPSON, to William JONES, for $400., a negro man, Jacob, his wife, Amy, daughter, Beck, and son, Marcus.

1805, Dec 12
   William WILSON, by note of hand for $706., payable Apr 6th, next, purchases negroes Joe; Pinder and Sarah, part of estate of Martin STEWART, sold at auction, Aug 3, 1805.

1806, William OLIVE, to James OLIVE, for $600., two negro girls, Ginny 13 years old, and Nina, about 11.

1806, July 16
   Francis FARRER, Sheriff, sells at auction, property of James STALLINGS, viz: negroes, Fortune; Sylvey; Nancy; Peggy; Wally; Mary; Judah; Christian, and her child, Harriot. 1 riding-chair, and harness; 1 sulky without harness; 1 waggon; 5 cows and calves; 4 young steers; 3 sows; 10 shoats; 10 pigs; 1 sorrell gelding; 1 bay mare; 1 dark bay filly; 1 sorrell filly; 1 large bay gelding; 4 featherbeds and furniture; 1 mahogany table, with circular ends; a broken set of china; 2 pair of fire-dogs; tongs and shovel; 10 chairs; 3 pine tables; 2 old trunks; 3 demijohns; kitchen furniture. Richard WAYNE, SR., of Chatham Co., highest bidder at $1,231.43 3/4.

1806, July 16
   Francis FARRER, to Richard WAYNE, at auction, mulatto woman, named Judith; man, Jack; crop of cotton and corn; 2 stacks of wheat; 1 of rye; property of above named Stallings. Wayne, highest bidder, at $1,397.00

1806, Aug 20
   Sally BLACKWELL, to John SMITH; Marshall KEITH, and John COLLIER: 27 negroes, property of late husband, George BLACKWELL, for $5,521.27 1/2.

1807, Mar 14
   Dorothy SHORT, to Edward SHORT, 4 negroes, John; Moll; Edd, and Ephraim, for $1,200.00.

1807, Apr 24
   John BARHAM, of Southampton Co., Va., to Abner SIMMS, 1 negro woman, named Tener, and her two children, Louisa and Edmond.

1807, June 15
   Jonathon STEVENSON, and Nancy, his wife, to William PERRIAN and Robert WOOLDRIDGE, for $100.00, two negroes, Jenny, now in possession of Wiley OLIVE, and Sue, in possession of James OLIVE.

1807, June 30
   Thomas MACOMB, to Joseph DARSEY, for $800., negroes, as follows: woman Beck, 30 years; Kitty, her daughter, 12; Sally, a girl about of age; Sam, 4 years; Jim 18 mos., and an infant girl child named Jenny, about 2 months old.

1802, Mar 1
   CONTRACT: Joshua GRINAGE, Planter, leases his plantation to James BAYARD, called Shady Grove, with all the cleared land, and as much timber as will be needed for fencing, inclusive, with gin-house and wheel, for term of three years for $1,800. Terms as follows: $500. worth of good cotton, at price of 20¢ a pound, or $450., in cash, on or before April 1, next. $300., or value thereof, on Jan. 1, 1803. $500., on Jan. 1, 1804, and $500., on Jan. 1, 1805.

1808, Apr 24
   BILL OF SALE, James BAYARD, and wife, Sophia, merchant of Augusta, sells to Joshua GRINAGE, for $360., 1 50-saw gin; 3 horses, now on plantation; 3 beds and furniture; 4 tables; 2 looking-glasses; 4 cup boards; 10 chairs; 2 guns; all household and kitchen furniture; 2 trunks; plantation tools.

1809, Feb 2
   Zachariah RAY, to Allen JOHNSON, negro woman, Phillis, and child, Jenny, for $200.

1809, Feb 2
   William WILKINS, to Samuel WILKINS, for $200., negro slave, Caty, about 45 years old.

1809, Feb 21
   William FEW, to Dorothy SHORT, for $150., negro girl, Ester, and to Edward SHORT, negro boy, Turner, for $200.

1809, June 6
   Zadock MAGRUDER, to A. MAGRUDER, for $6,000., negroes, James; Moses; Hagar, and her children, Minty; Patience; Fan; Washington; and Milly. Sylvey, and her children, Bun, and Mason. Jude, and her family, Daniel and Handy; Hannah, and her child, Jesse; Monday; Jock; Dice; Morris; Peter; Philip, and James; 1 stud horse; 5 head of work horses; 4 colts; 50 head of hogs; 40 head of cattle; 6 feather beds, with furniture; 1 dish; 1 dozen chairs; 2 chests of drawers, with hardware; 1 coach; 1 riding-chair; 2 stills, one holding 75 gallons, the other 35 gallons; 2 waggons, with geers and harness; 1 set of blacksmith's tools, together with every other specie of property I now have.

1809, June 7
   William PACE, Adm., of Mary PACE, to John PACE, for $380., negro woman slave called, Battis.

1809, Nov 5
   William FLEMING, to Basil NEAL, negro boy, Nero, $330., said slave seized from estate of James WOOD, to satisfy an execution in favor of William BIBB, dec'd.

1818, Oct 15
   William THOMPSON, to John L. DOYAL, negro girl, Maria, for $1.00(?).

1809, Feb 18
1809, Martin WINSETT, of Warren Co., to Robert JONES, 3 negro slaves, Beck, and her 2 children, Ester and Lewis; which negroes are remaining with said Jones, late in the employment of Winsett, $550.

179_, Oct 18 - Rec. Mar 7, 1810
    Martha HOWARD, to David MURRY, JR., negroes Hannah and her child, Buckey, @ £52, 4 s, 8 p.

1810, Mar 17
    Ignatius FEW, to Sukey ANDERSON, an African-born negro man named Sambo, purchased at Constable's sale, $50.00.

1810, Aug 21
    Jesse SANDERS, to James BURROUGHS, and Isham BAYLISS, three negro boys, Simon; Surry, and Brutus. (No price shown).

1809, Feb 10
    Received of William STARKE, $237., for a certain negro woman named Ceil, of yellow complexion, about 30 years of age.
    s/ L. WOODWARD

1807, Nov 7
    Josiah BRINSON sells to Thomas MOORE, for $800., 4 hegroes: Agnes; Jerry (or Jeremiah); Daniel, and Thomas.

1811, Jan 1
    Elizabeth FREEL, to Thomas MARTIN, for $800., negroes Dick and Clary.

1811, Feb 14
    John LUCKEY, to Thomas EDMONDSON, for $700., negroes: Negro woman, Chaney, 24 years old; her child, Mary, 2 years old.

1812, Feb 12
    Reuben WILLIAMS, to Obediah LOWE, for $350., negro man, James, about 19 years of age, dark complexion.

1812, Mar 14
    Thomas COLEMAN, of Wilkes Co., to Charles PORTER, for $336., negro girl, Lucy, 14 years old, yellow complexion.

1812, Aug 18
    William BEALLE, to Rebecca COCKE, Excx., of Nathan COCKE, for $303., negro boy, Collin, at auction.

1812, Aug 28
    William BEALLE, to Edmond BOWDRE, for $190., negro boy, Joe.

1813, Feb 19
    William PACE, to John PACE, for $380., negro man, Battis.

1813, Aug 4
    Sarah UNDERWOOD, to William UNDERWOOD, for $300., a negro girl, Phillis, 15 or 16 years old.

1813, Aug 27
   Rebecca COCKE, to Polly and Augustus COCKE, for $300., a negro boy, Collin, 20 years old.

1815, Jan 12
   William TINDALL, to Benjamin JOHNSON, for...(price not given) negro boy, Wyley.

1815, Mar 1
   Edmond BOWDRE, to Hugh SMITH, for.....(?), negro girl, Diannah, 15.

1815, Mar 1
   Berry OLIVE, to Hugh SMITH, $250., negro boy, John, 12 years.

1815, Mar 1
   Berry OLIVE, to Hugh SMITH, for $370., negro woman, Jude, about 22.

1815, May 3
   Elizabeth FREEL, to Zachariah MC DANIEL, for $400., boy, Valentine, 18.

1815, May 4
   David STANFORD, to Anderson CRAWFORD, for $400., negro, George, late the property of James ALLEN, dec'd.

1815, June 12
   Edward PRATHER, to Mary SMITH, for $500., negroes, Letty, and child, Liddy, about 3 years old.

1815, June 12
   Hugh SMITH, to John SMITH, for $500., negro wench, Jude, and child, Mary, about 13 mos. old.

1815, Oct 2
   Thomas HOWARD, to Elias WILSON, for $250., negro girl, Amy.

1815, Nov 20
   John BARNES, to Richard TUBMAN, of Augusta, for $1,500.
   1 large bay gelding; 1 large gray gelding; 1 brown gelding; 1 chestnut gelding; 1 chestnut horse, blind; 1 roan mare; 1 chestnut mare, bay horse colt; 5 mules; 80 head of black cattle; 100 head of hogs; 1 set of blacksmith tools; all plantation utensils (plows, hoes, axes, trace chains, etc.); collars and bridles; 2 waggons; 1 horse cart; 1 ox cart; 1 top chaise and harness; 1 featherbed and furniture; 2 mahogany bedsteads; 2 stained pine bedsteads; 1 doz. blankets; 1 doz. pairs of sheets; 1 doz bed covers, or coverlids; 2 mahogany wash-stands; Basons and ewers; 1 mahogany sideboard, with contents; Plate and plated ware; Cut glass decanters; Tumblers, wineglasses; goblets, etc., 1 set large mahogany dining tables; 1 set small mahogany tables; 1 set tea tables; 1 set card tables; 1 old

round tea table; 1 mahogany easy chair; 1 mahogany desk; 1 mahogany
chest of drawers; 1 portable mahogany writing desk; 2 mahogany
framed looking glasses; 1 large mahogany framed mirror; 1 satinwood
wine cooler; 1 doz. fancy rush-bottomed chairs; 1 pair of settees
to match; 14 Windsor chairs; 1 dozen common chairs; 1 eight-day clock;
1 silver watch; 1 oil painting of Washington; 1 print of Hamilton; 1
print of Wayne; 6 other prints; 1 dozen japanned waiters; 1 dozen
japanned boxes and cannisters; 2 Wedgewood pitchers; 1 elegant set of,
tea china, with silver tea-pot, and stand, and cream pitcher; 1 set
of common china; 1 fowling piece; 1 common fowling piece; 1 tutenag(?)
barrel blunderbuss, with spring bayonet; 1 pr. holsters and pistols;
1 sword belt; 2 carpets, and all other household and kitchen furniture.

1815, Nov 27
    John BARNES, to Richard TUBMAN, for $1,700., negroes, Jacob;
Stephen; Charles and Frank.

1816, May 15
    Rebecca COCKE, to Hannah LEITH, for $250., (Rebecca acting as
Admx., for estate of Dr. William COCKE), negro girl, Sally.

1816, June 1
    John FARRER, of Lincoln Co., to William MC GAR, for $350.,
negro woman, Hannah.

1816, June 1
    John FARRER, of Lincoln Co., to William MC GAR, negro man,
Kitt, for $450.

1816, June 5
    John COLLINS, to Joseph MARSHALL, JR., Esq., negro man, Abram,
from estate of Vincent PERRYMAN, for $1,126.00.

1816, June 6
    Joseph COTTON, to Ferdinand PHINIZY, for $2,200., negroes:
Lewis; Sam, the hostler; Little Sam; Mincey; Willis; Moly; Peggy;
and Fanny.

1816, Oct 22
    Elizabeth JOHNS (or JONES?), to Williams JACKSON, a negro girl,
Rachel, $395.

1817, July 13
    Walter JONES, to Williams JACKSON, negro woman, Mary, and child,
Betty, $600.

1805, Nov 5 - Rec. Oct 27, 1817
    Francis FARRER, Sheriff, to John BERRIEN, at auction, 4 negroes,
property of Solomon ELLIS: Johnny; Jennet; Bob, and George. John
Collins was high bidder @ $1,272., bur relinquished purchase to
John Berrien.

1817, Oct 28
　　Samuel KING, to Richard SKINNER, for $450., in full consideration of my share of legacy in right of my wife, Elizabeth KING, formerly Skinner, dau., and legatee of Isaac SKINNER, dec'd: Slaves, Cate; Nan; Milly; Anthony; Judah; Chloe; Betty; Ellender; and Lucinda.

1819, Apr 27
　　John MC DONALD, to William WILKINS, for $700., a negro boy, 14 years old, name of Gun.

1819, Sept 29
　　Randol NEWSOME, to Amos NEWSOME, for $1,000., all property, real and personal, including negro woman, Phillis; 2 horses, all cows; hogs; stock of all kinds; all household and kitchen furniture; plows; hoes; and guns.

1819, Oct 16
　　George WALKER, to John C. WALKER, for $145.12 1/2: 1 saddle and bridle, val. @ $20., 1 bedstead, $12.00; 1 bed and furnishings $25.00; 1 folding table $20.00; 3 trunks $9.00; 2 Windsor chairs $4.00; 1 set rawhide bottomed chairs $6.00; 1 small pine table $2.00; Crockery and glassware $15.00; Toilet table $3.00; Dressing glass $3.00; Large chest $2.00; 1 Dutch oven, 2 pots, 1 tea-kettle $7.00; 2 pails, 1 piggin, and wash tub $4.00; 1 half-stock shot gun $10.00; 1 gun $2.00; 3 bonnet-boxes $1.12 1/2.

1819, Nov 10
　　William PEARRE, to Jesse OFFUTT, for $1,500., six negroes: Lucy, 27; Jim, 21; Jude, 20; Rachel, 7; Hannah, 2; and Sidney 9 mos.

1819, Dec 29 - Rec. Apr. 13, 1820
　　James BURROUGHS, to Marshall KEITH, for $1,900., negroes Jack, 20; Lewis, 14; Malinda, 21; and her two children, Aggy and Mildred.

1819, Dec 28 - Rec. Apr 19, 1820
　　Marshall KEITH, Adm., of property of Peter KEITH, dec'd., sells slaves at auction, to James BURROUGHS, for $1,900; Jack; Lewis; Malinda; Aggy; and Mildred.

1820, Dec 7
　　John HARRIS, to Moses WRIGHT, for $1,500., the following property: Negro man, Caesar, 44; girl Rachel, 18; 6 featherbeds; cherry bureau; 2 pine tables; 1 walnut table and slab; all my library of·books; 8 chairs; 1 yoke of oxen; 5 cows; 10 yearlings; all kitchen furniture, 1 stage waggon and gear.

1821(?), _____
　　John KESSLER, to John WATSON and Willis COBBS, for $2,000., negro slaves: Nemshire; Judah; Peter; Fanny; Albert; Elly; Betsy; and Fernanda.

1821, Sept 28
　　Tabitha SMITH, to John SMITH: Negro girl, Diannah, 23; negro

girl, Prissy Anderson, 4; 1 cutor(?); all cattle; hogs; and household furniture, for $600.

1821, Dec 22
    Gerard MORRISS, to James BLACKSTONE, for $320., negro boy Daniel.

1822, Jan 28
    William WILKINS, Sheriff, sells at auction, Lucy and her child, Dave, formerly property of William PEARRE. Jesse OFFUTT highest bidder, @ $751.

1822, May 7
    Sarah FLINT, Excx., estate of dec'd., husband, John FLINT, sells at auction, to James KNIGHT, for $70., negro girl, Burrilla.

1823, Mar 4
    Leonard PECK, to James LAMKIN, all claim and title to 5 negroes, (No names, nor price shown).

1823, Apr 1
    Stephen DRANE to William DRANE, for $250., 1 blind bay horse; 1 bay mare, with an eye out, and with a young colt; 12 head of cattle, marked with a swallowfork and an underslit in each ear; 24 hogs, 23 with the same marks as the horses; 2 curtained bedsteads; 2 sets of bed-curtains; 2 beds (feather); and bed furnishings; 1 bed mattrass, household and kitchen furniture, as follows: 1 teapot; 1 coffee pot; 5 dishes; 2 dozen plates; 2 sets of cups and saucers; 1 sugar dish; 1 cream pot; 2 sets knives and forks; 1 tea-kettle; 3 pots; 2 bakers; 1 frying-pan; 1 slab; glassware; 1 small walnut dressing table; 1 cupboard; 1 desk; 1 leaf table; 1 loom and spinning wheel; 1 pair brass candlesticks; shovel and tongs; scythe and cradle; 1 broad-axe; 3 club axes; 1 hand hatchet; 2 bee-hives; 1 churn; 1 pair flatirons; 3 trunks; 8 sitting chairs; looking-glass; 4 tin pans; 1 bason; 2 pair of cotton, and 2 pair of wool cards; 2 plowstocks; 3 sets of plow irons; 1 set spontoons; 1 of shovels; 1 of scrapers; 1 cutter plow; 3 swivel-trees, and clevises; 1 man's and 1 woman's saddle; 2 powdering tubs; 2 wheat stands; 1 washtub; 2 pails; 1 wheat riddle; 1 cutting knife and box; 1 foot adz; 1 drawing knife; 1 dozen chisels; 4 heading chisels; 1 iron square; 1 tenor and 1 hand saw; 1 carry log(?), cash, set of books; 4 bridles; 4 band-boxes; 1 grindstone; 3 hoes; and 2 mattocks. (They were father and son).

1823, Aug 14
    Richard TARVER, to Harrison TARVER, for $360., sells a negro girl, Lucy.
1823, Oct 25
    Mark SULLIVAN, to Cornelius SULLIVAN, for $800., a negro man, Abram, about 25 years old.

1824, Feb 14
    James COOK, sells to Edmond BUGG, of Richmond Co., in trust for "beloved wife, Ann COOK," for $100.00, all household goods; implements of household; all stock of horses; cattle and hogs; all debts

and credits; all other personal estate. Negroes: Rhiner and her child, Dianna; Mary Ann, and child Nancy; Fanny; Isaac; Daniel; and Jerry.

1824, Mar 18
   William WILKINS, Sheriff, to John GRIFFIN, for $33., negro woman, Pat, seized by Constable Joseph MOON, as part of estate of William COVINGTON, and sold at auction. Griffin was high bidder.

1824, Mar 19
   Eugene FENNILL, to Guilford ALFORD, for $400., a negro slave, Henry, about 17.

1824, May 13
   Ganaway MARTIN, to Thomas DOOLY, for $200., negro boy, Jacob, 10 years old; and for $750., Rachel, 20 years old, and her two young children, Randal and Suckey.

1824, June 27
   Simmons CRAWFORD, for $177., sells to Thomas BUGG, negro slave, Hannah, about 43 years old, which said Crawford rec'd., in division of estate of mother, Rachel CRAWFORD.

1824, Aug 16
   Edward BOWERS, sells to Mary ENGLETT, for $400., a negro woman, Sylvia, and her child, Jefferson.

1824, Oct 20
   Charles BEALLE, to Walter LEIGH, of Richmond Co., for $1,650., negroes: London; Charles; Claiborne; and William.

1825, Jan 5
   Stephen BURNLEY, to Jesse EVANS, for $325., a negro girl, Rilly.

1825, Feb 12
   William BASTON, sells to Thomas WATKINS, for $450., a negro woman, Aggy, and 2 children, Sam and Cyrus.

1825, Nov 30
   George CARY, Att'y., of Philip STUART, of Washington, D. C., sells to James BURROUGHS, Exr., of Will of G. W. DENT, a negro girl, Daphne, for $200.

1826, Jan 4
   Col. William WILKINS, paid $330., for a negro girl, Esther, shortly before his death, to Edward HICKS. On date shown, Hicks delivered said girl to heirs of the Colonel.

1826, Jan 14
   Freeman KILLINGSWORTH, sells to William F. WILKINS, guardian of James D. GREENE, for $400., 2 negroes, Chaney and Jack.

1826, Mar 20
   William DRANE, Adm., estate of Chloe NEWSOM, sells to Samuel

MC NAIR, guardian of Nancy and James MILLER, negroes sold at auction by order of the Court, for benefit of Nancy and James MILLER, heirs of estate of Chloe NEWSOM, in right of their mother, Martha MILLER, formerly NEWSOM. McNair high bidder. Hannah, $400; boy Abraham, $281; boy, Ellick $290.

1827, Jan 19
    Thomas CARR, Sheriff, seizes certain property of Thomas LUKE, on writ of fi fa, and sells at auction: 2 negroes, Henry and Caty. John LUKE high bidder @ $291.

1827, Mar 7
    George TANKERSLEY, sells at auction, the interest of James YOUNG, in five negroes: Dave; Charlotte; Maria; Sam; and Priss. John B. TINDALL, high bidder @ $81.

1827, Apr 12
    Elizabeth SCRUGGS, guardian for James SCRUGGS, idiot, sells to Sarah BUGG, for $200., 1 moiety of 61 acre tract on Greenbriar Creek, conveyed by Prudence STORY, jointly to James and Richard Scruggs, on May 10, 1795; part of a 400 acre tract granted to Robert STORY. Also 1/6th part of 30 acre tract, part of above 400 a.

1827, Sept 5
    Thomas WHITE, Daniel MASSENGALE; Thomas BOWDRE; John DAVIS; and David COOPER, Trustees of Town of Wrightsborough, sell to Mark Price DAVIS, for $113.75, three lots within town limits, shown on plat as lots #134; #135, and #137, on South side of James Street.

1828, Jan 14
    William DOZIER, to Robert JOHNS, for $400., slaves, Fanny, 19; and her boy-child, about 2.

1828, Jan 23
    Thomas WILLINGHAM, to Isaac WILLINGHAM, for $700., negroes, Chaney, and her two children, Lewis and Anthony.

1828, May 17
    Mary GRAVES, to William MC GRUDER............

1828, Apr 1
    Samuel HICKS, to Preston BOWDREE, for $150., all my interest in estate of Samuel BOWDREE, except for the following slaves: Barna; Joe; Johnson; Tom; Big Jim; Little Jim; Peter; Dennis; Rachel and Amanda. Also my interest in Lot #113, Dist., 15, in Houston Co., and my interest in Lot #144, Dist., 26, Early County.

1828, May 12
    Jonathon WOODS, Franklin Co., Ala., and wife, Blanche, to Jesse WALTON, and James CARTLEDGE, for $1,333., all our interest in negroes: Lucy; Betty; Tom; Isabel; Young Lucy; Matilda; Banister; Old Sally; Nancy; Lewis; Mansfield; Hannah; Balaam; Elvina; Wally; Dick, and Sandy.

1828, June 19
Isaac RAMSEY, to Martin REYNOLDS, at auction, property of Leonard THOMPSON, negro girl, Mary, @ $130.

1828, Nov 10
William GARTRELL, to Elizabeth GARTRELL, for $500., 2 negroes, Charlotte, and her son, Jerry.

1829, Mar 10
David MAGAHEE, and wife, Mary, to Jesse EVANS, for $300., negro boy, Jesse.

1829, Sept 20
Hillery MURRAY, to Robert STARKE, for $400., negro man, Cato.

1829, Sept 20
James CULBREATH, to Lewis CULBREATH, for $400., boy, Peter, about 20 years old.

1829, Nov 24
Bowling STARKE, to John NESBIT, for $320., negro boy, Abraham, 8 years old.

1830, July 11
John KING, to John BAYLISS, Trustee for his wife, and children, for $1,000., four negroes: Jack; Tidy; and their children, Lucy and Peggy.

1831, Apr 25
John NEILSON, of Richmond Co., to Marshall KEITH, for $341., a negro boy, Jack, about 15. And to Leonard SMITH, for $420., a female slave, Dinah, about 25, and her child, a girl of 4.

1831, Apr 25
Leonard SMITH, to Marshall KEITH, mortgages the above slaves for $91.

1831, Apr 25
John NEILSON, to Marshall KEITH, for $1,700., negroes: Matilda, and her four children, Tom; Stephne; Elizabeth and Amanda; Nelly, and her son, Davy.

1832, July 23
Ansel ALBRITTON, to John CLIETT, Adm., estate of Henry CLIETT, dec'd., for $500., negro man, Stephen, about 25.

1833, Jan 18
William CULBREATH, to Obediah CULBREATH, of Meriwether Co., for $900., four slaves: Austin; Sam; Wiley and Seasor; 10 head of cattle; milch cows; heifers; yearlings and calves; 1 roan Horse; 1 Dearborn Wagon; 2 featherbeds and furniture; 1 mahogany bureau; 1 eight-day-clock; and 2 looking-glasses.

1829, July 2
Edmond HICKS, to Edmond BOWDRIE, for $380., negro girl, Milly.

1829, Sept 4
William and Nancy YARBOROUGH, Adms., of estate of James YARBOROUGH, dec'd., having adm. property as provided by law, sell at auction, 117 acres on Uchee Creek to William ZACHRY, high bidder, $450.

1829, Sept 19
William A. BALDWIN, surviving Adm., of estate of Owen BALDWIN, has permission of Court to sell land assigned to Owen Baldwin's widow, as dower, 183 acres on Upton's Creek, bounded by William WILEY; Sarah WINFREY, and James SHIELDS. Property sold at auction to Wiley, for $601.

1829, Nov 7
Legatees of Isaac WINFREY, dec'd., to-wit: Samuel Winfrey; John Winfrey; Henry Winfrey; Thomas SEAY; John C. BALDWIN; Charles STRONG; William F. WYATT, and Randolph DAVIS, in consideration of $1,000., paid by Reuben Winfrey, do sell 400 acres, being pointed out in Will of dec'd., whereon he lived and died, adj., Felix PRIOR; William WILEY, and John SHIELDS.

1829, Dec 3
Isaac WILLINGHAM, of Lincoln Co., guardian of minors of William D. JONES, dec'd., sells 70 acres of land on Sullivan's Creek, Advertised in the Public Gazettes, and sold at auction. Daniel L. MARSHALL, high bidder, at $661.

1829, Dec 4
Peter SHORT, and William SCOTT, Adms., estate of Terrill HARRISON, dec'd., sells at auction to Guilford ALFORD, for $1,310., land on Germany Creek, amounting to 320 acres.

1830, Jan 15
Mary P. PRIOR, Admx., of Robert ALLEN, sells at auction to David STANFORD, 150 acres on Big Kiokee Creek, high bid $350.

1830, Feb 5
Mary P. PRIOR, to Willian DRANE, at auction, 130 acres, part of a tract granted to Joshua FULLER, high bid, $100.

1830, Mar 12
William COLLINS, to Martin BURRISS, Edgefield Co., S. C. for $1,200., four slaves: Dorcas and her 3 children, Bob; Abram; Mariah.

1830, Mar 31
Joseph GRANT, and William GRANT, of Richmond Co., to George HARGRAVES, for $2,345., negro slaves: Charles, 25; Paris, 25; Peter, 22; John, 18; and Sam, 18. Also Romeo, 18; Dick, 6.

1830, May 23
Richard JONES, Sheriff, to Thomas HAMILTON...Sheriff levied on property of Richard SHACKLEFORD, dec'd., and his Exr., Slaves sold at auction, purchased by Hamilton, high bidder, @ $1,106. Negroes, Tabby, a woman, 25, and her children, Abram, 10; Augustus, 7; Martha Ann, 3; and Jane, 4 mos.

1830, June 3
Richard JONES, Sheriff, sells property of Isaac BOWEN, at auction, and Gabriel JONES is high bidder, @ $732.50. Purchases 16 3/4 acres and dwelling house on Big Kiokee Creek, adj., village of Appling.

1830, Sept 21
Nancy PORTER, and James SHIELDS, Adms., of estate of Stanton PORTER, dec'd., to James KENDRICK, in obedience to an order of Court, sell at auction, for $200. 70 acres on Little River.

1830, Sept 25
Peter LAMAR, Exr., of Thomas COBB, dec'd., sells at auction, after due advertisement in the Augusta Chronicle, 530 acres on headwaters of Greenbriar and Briar Creeks; highest bidder, Green DOZIER, for John W. DOZIER.

1835, Apr 17
Commissioners of Columbia County Academy, viz: Juriah HARRIS; Nathan CRAWFORD, James CARTLEDGE, agreeable to an Act of Legislature, sell to William JONES, 40 acres of Academy land, on North side of Appling, to the Wrightsborough Road, for $324; also for $200., all lot or parcel of land known in the plan of the Academy lots as Nos. 11 and 12, bounded by Main Road, and Academy Street, each lot containing 1/2 acre in town of Appling.

1835, Apr 23
Commissioners of Columbia Academy sell to William ADAMS, and Nathaniel BAILEY, Trustees of Methodist Episcopal Church, for $100., one lot containing 1/2 acre, it being Lot #14 in the plan of lots laid off, lying West of the street which separates the first and second tier of lots.

1835, Nov 6
Franklin C. HEARD, Exr., of Abraham HEARD, dec'd., to Abraham HEARD, JR., for $400., all tract of land in Columbia Co., on Town Creek, adj., Wrightsboro Commons, containing 100 acres.

1835, Oct 27
Mrs. Mary GRAVES, Excx., of late Dr. George GRAVES, sells to John GRAVES, negroes, Isaac; Baldwin, and Nelly.

1835, Oct 27
John GRAVES sells to Mrs. Mary GRAVES, three slaves, Isaac; Baldwin, and Nelly, also 2 gold watches, chain, seals, and keys, for $1,200.

1836, Jan 22
John ROSCOE, of Chatham Co., sells to Archer AVARY, for $420., a negro girl, Wrinah, of yellow complexion, 26 or 27 years old.

1836, Jan 22
Jesse BULL, to heirs of Joseph BARNES, for $900., paid by Gabriel JONES, Adm., of estate of said Barnes, delivered, to and

for the use of Matilda BARNES, widow of dec'd., William BARNES, and Camilla BARNES, child of dec'd., in common, 1 negro man Tom, 23.

1836, Feb 18
    William L. CRAWFORD, Adm., of estate of David VINSON, sells at auction negroes belonging to estate of said Vinson: Rina, dark complexion, 18 years old, bought by Gabriel JONES, high bidder @ $950.

1836, Mar 15
    Abraham HEARD, sells to Luke LANSDELL, for $200., one house with 10 feet of land attached, (house 10 ft., in width), in village of Wrightsboro, lying on North side of Broad St., opposite residence of Dr. Edward JONES. Said house being built by Henry GIBSON, and occupied by him as a store, afterwards known as Bailey's Schoolhouse, recently held by William DRIVER, as a store.

1836, July 19
    Benjamin MOSELEY, guardian for William LOWE, and agent for Thomas T. WILKINS, who intermarried with William's sister, Ann LOWE, orphans of Thomas LOWE, sells to Michael DIXON, for $800., negro man, Cyrus, aged 40.

1837, Jan 3
    Harris SPEIRS, to Benjamin COXE, for $700., three negroes: Clary, 40; Dicy, 11; and girl, Bickel, 3.

1837, Feb 10
    ADMINISTRATOR'S SALE: Gabriel JONES, Adm., estate of Joseph BARNES, dec'd., to Louisa Matilda Rees BARNES, relict, sells real estate of dec'd., at auction, by permission of Court. Henry MASSENGALE, Trustee for Mrs. Barnes, high bidder, at $150., on lots on North side of Broad (or James Street), in Town of Wrightsboro, in all 10 acres.

1837, Mar 29
    Gabriel JONES, Adm., estate of late Robert CULPEPPER, to William STANFORD, after due process of law, and advertising in the Georgia Constitutionalist and Augusta Chronicle, sells 181 1/2 acres at auction, Stanford high bidder, at $176.50, property located on Sweetwater Creek.

1837, Mar 31
    EXECUTOR'S SALE: James LAMKIN, Exr., estate of Thomas CULBREATH, dec'd., sells at auction 317 acres, "known as land where Isaac LUCAS lives." James ALEXANDER high bidder, at $835.

1837, Apr 11
    ADMINISTRATOR'S SALE. By order of Court, Archer AVARY, Adm., estate and Will of Mrs. Frances (Fanny Lowe) CARR, sells at auction, 408 acres on Big and Little Kiokee Creek, Benjamin PERRY high bidder, at $4,005.

1837, May 18
    John TOMKINS, of Edgefield Dist., S. C., buys from Frank

TOMKINS, for $12,000., following property: 5 mules; 2 wagons; 9 horses; 1 yoke oxen; 12 head cattle; 75 hogs; slaves: Alfred, 38; Little Alfred, 20; Jerry, 22; Isaac,25; Joseph, 24; Peter, 45; Squire, 30; July, 23; Ralph, 65; Jenny, 60; Sarah, 50; Amy, 35; Esther, 36; Hannah, 25; Leanor, 25; Darthula, 12; Lucy, 12; Vicey, 2; Little Amy, 8; Mary, 6; Sam, 4; James, 7; Stephen, 5; Amanda, 4; Hamp, 3; Sandy, 6 months.

1837, May 18
John TOMKINS, sells to Sarah TOMKINS, for $12,000., 303 acres of land known as the Quaker Springs tract, conveyed by John LINES to Francis TOMKINS, and by him to me. Also all negroes (above); stock, household and kitchen furniture.

1837, Aug
John GUEDRON, sells to Thomas WALTON, for $8,000., one-half interest in 100 acre tract known as The Lafayette Racecourse, bounded N. E., by Turknett Springs Road; E. by Savannah Road, S. W., by Milledgeville Road, and on all other sides by lands of Gilbert LONGSTREET. (Not known why this listed in Columbia County, property is now inside city limits of Augusta).

1837, Aug 2
Thomas WALTON, sells above listed property to James LAMKIN, of Columbia Co., for $8,000.

1838, Jan 27
ADMINISTRATOR'S SALE. Harmong LAMAR, Adm., of Thomas COLVARD, sells property at auction. John MESSER high bidder at $30., on a 100 acre tract on Boggy Gut Creek.

1838, Mar 8
Trustees of White Oak Campground, to-wit: Thomas BOWDRE; Thomas DAWSON; Edward WOODING; William ADAMS; Harmong LAMAR; and George GUNBY, sell to Anderson WILSON, for $35.00, a tract containing 35 acres, to be taken out of the North corner of the Camp Ground tract.

1838, Nov 10
Richard JONES, Sheriff, sells at auction, 1 acre lot in village of Wrightsboro, on North side of Broad, (or James Street), adj., the property of Mrs. Louisa Rees Barnes EMERSON, and now occupied by Luke LANDSDELL. William SCOTT, high bidder, at $150.

1839, Dec 16
ADMINISTRATOR'S SALE: Irby HUDSON, Adm., estate of Jabez P. MARSHALL, dec'd., to Trustees of Kiokee Baptist Church: The PUTNAM County Inferior Court having passed and approved an order for sale of estate of Jabez P. Marshall, Hudson sells at auction to said Trustees: Juriah HARRIS; Cornelius COLLINS; Archibald HEGGIE; William JONES; James CARTLEDGE, and David STANFORD, high bidders, at $1.00, 7 3/4 acres of land on waters of Greenbriar Creek, adj., lands where said church stands, bounded on all other sides by lands of said Marshall estate.

1840, Jan 21
   Commissioners and Trustees of Town and Commons of Wrightsboro, viz: Sherwood ROBERTS; Edward W. JONES; C. H. WILSON; James BURNSIDE, and Theo. MASSENGALE, having passed in Council an order for the sale of all unsold Commons, to be sold in lots hereafter, sell at auction before the door of Thomas WHITE & Company, Lot #4, cont., 42 4/10th acres to Mrs. L. M. R. EMERSON, for $296.80, and Lot #3, containing 38 acres, at $211.18 3/4.

1840, Sept 15
   John D. GIBSON, sells to Benjamin REES, for $200., a one acre lot and house in Town of Wrightsboro, on North side of Broad, adj., Tho. WHITE & Co., on East, vacant lot on N., Jones St., on W., and James or Broad Street on South.

1840, Sept 15
   John D. GIBSON, to W. O. and Benjamin REES, for $200., a lot situated on N. side of Broad St., known as Thomas DOOLY'S white storehouse, cont., 1/2 acre, recently occupied by Ganaway MARTIN, and more recently by G. W. PERSONS, as a store, and now by said Gibson as a store. Conveyed by Martin to Peter BENNOCK, of Augusta, and by Bennock to Mrs. Nancy AYRES, by her to Gibson.

1840, Sept 15
   W. O. REES sells his half-interest in above to brother, Benjamin, for $100.

ODDS & ENDS

1791, July 2
   BOND- Marriage Settlement. Whereas, a marriage is shortly to be solemnized between Sarah GERMANY, widow, and Paul CALDWELL, and said Sarah being desirous to secure such part of land or negroes she may receive from estate of her late husband, William GERMANY, unto her children, James; Mary; William; John; Jean (or Jane); and Stephen. Since Sarah Germany and Paul Caldwell are bound unto Stephen HEARD of Wilkes Co., for £3,000 sterling, the above Sarah and Paul do make over all land and negroes they are entitled to, unto Stephen Heard and James Germany, eldest son of Sarah and William Germany, dec'd.

1791, Aug 23
   GIFT IN TRUST - Thomas HAMILTON to Isaiah WRIGHT, Trustee for Mrs. Hamilton, for "love, goodwill and affection I have for my loving wife, Concord, all my goods and chattels, lands and tenements, which are innumerated in my dwelling-house. Also Dr. Edmond DILLON's bond and mortgage, dated Feb 26, 1789, and Robert MONTGOMERY's dated Jan. 18, 1791 .. Also a negro fellow named Hercules; a negro fellow, of a yellow complexion, and named Hope, 18 years old. A negro woman, named Rinch, about 17 years of age, and her child, born Mar. 14, last; also a negro girl, named Sue, about 12 years old; also 800 acres of land on both sides of the trading road, and 700 acres on waters of Little Kioka Creek; 1 large brown bay sorrel gelding,

about 16 hands high; a yellow bay horse, with a bald face, branded N55; one other gelding, black, with all my stock of hogs and cattle.

1791, Aug 30
Thomas WATKINS, received of Sherwood BUGG, Adm. estate of Peter PARRIS, deeds to following negroes, viz: Quash; Sander; Jamy; Tom; Dinah; Black; Nancy; Phoebe; Sambo; Robin; Jack; George; Miny; Hannah; Bet and Fanny; also 2 horses; 1 bedstead and furniture; 1 lot of silver spoons, being the unsold part of the estate.

1792, Nov 23
AFFIDAVIT. William HOZICK, of the County of Greenbriar, in Va., being duly sworn, says that David COURSON made title to him of 200 acres in Columbia Co. (then St. Paul's Parrish), in Sept. 9, 1774. Believes from the best information he is able to collect, that he, the deponent, is of full age, and over 21. "Further deponent saith not."

1778, July 11 - Rec. Feb 28, 1793
Holland MIDDLETON, of Wilkes Co., received of Jesse HAWKINS, £300, clear of all demands, for Plantation on Kiokee Creek, joining Coleman's land, in Columbia Co. "Sir, be pleased to let James HAWKINS have possession of the place, likewise the 1/3 part of what wheat is made, as he has purchased the whole concern." Given under my hand, July 11, 1778. s/ Holland MIDDLETON

1792, Dec 7
AFFIDAVIT - Robert MIDDLETON made oath that the above handwriting signed Holly MIDDLETON, is signed by Holly Middleton, to the best of his knowledge. s/ Robert MIDDLETON.

1793, Mar 1
AFFIDAVIT - By Margaret COOLIDGE, (or COOLAGE), of Columbia Co., late of Prince George Co., Va. In the year 1785, she "lent a negro named Providence to Thomas CARNES, Esq., then an attorney at law in above State and County, living at Upper Marlborough, within a mile or two of her residence. When about to leave Maryland, said Carnes sent the said negro to his father's place, in St. Mary's Co., Md., with directions to send him to his mistress." There must have been some misunderstanding with Carnes, Sr., but she goes on, "I am of the opinion that Thomas Carnes was not actuated by any fraudulent motives. I always considered him a Gentleman of Honor and Integrity." Further the deponent saith not.

1793, Mar 21
RELINQUISHMENT - Robert FLOURNOY, of Greene Co., "for divers good considerations, do fully relinquish all my right, title and claim to a parcel of land, cont. 43 acres, to the only proper use and behoof of the SOCIETY OF THE PEOPLE CALLED FRIENDS, or QUAKERS, being part of a tract originally granted to James WRIGHT, known as the QUAKER MEETING-HOUSE site."

_____ Rec. Dec 9, 1793
ASSIGNMENT - Made 23 August, in the 32nd year of the Reign of

Our Sovereign Lord, King George the Third, by the Grace of God, of Britain, France, and Ireland, defender of the Faith: Between George HUNT; James STALLINGS; Ezekiel STALLINGS, of the State of Augusta, in the Province of Georgia, in North America, merchants and co-partners....(George Hunt and James Stallings being at present in London)..with 12 calendar months, to Chamberlain, Burch and Charles Ouvry, of Fleet St., in London. (The indebted sign over everything they own, except their own wearing apparel.)

1795, Apr 20
EMANCIPATION PAPERS - Thomas MERIWETHER, to Micah Coley (Evans) known as Quash, fully emancipated, with her offspring, for £65. (When Thomas made his will, he left Micah his whole estate, 1808).

1795, July 15
DEED OF TRUST - Anthony HAYNES leaves property in trust with brother, Thomas, and David MAXWELL, for Chaney Reade (a mulatto), and her children. Also wishes trustees to petition next legislature to pass an Act to liberate and emancipate the above. (When Anthony wrote his will, he left all his property to Chaney, and her eight children, and just before his death, went through a marriage ceremony with her.)

1795, Oct 13
EMANCIPATION PAPERS - Ezekiell HUDNALL, to Bridget and her children. For the "goodwill I bear to my slaves Bridget, and her children, Leviny Waters; Nancy Waters; and Daniel Waters, I give them their absolute and entire freedom."

1795, Nov 13
RECEIPT - Reuben BROWNSON, is indebted to Ambrose HOLLIDAY, for 9,900 lbs. weight of inspected tobacco, sent him in 1792.

1801, Jan 21
EMANCIPATION PAPERS - Richard MERIWETHER, to Sucky Barrett. "For consequences of faithful services to me rendered by a certain negro woman, named Sucky Barrett, and two of her children, Lucy and Betty, I desire that immediately after my decease, my Executors shall see that they are forever set free."

1797, Mar 27
RELINQUISHMENT - Thomas WATSON, to Peter ZACHRY, all interest in two tracts of land, one on Uchee Creek, and one other tract adjoining, for one peppercorn, in hand paid.

1797, Apr 11
DEED OF TRUST - Priscilla HORN, widow of Jesse HORN, to John EADS, JR. "My lands; slaves; goods and chattels, to hold said properties in trust for me. If I die intestate, whole of my property to be equally divided between my children."

_____ Rec. Jan 19, 1797
ARTICLES OF AGREEMENT - Between Rowland STONE, and Mary STURGES, in consequence of a marriage to be held between himself

and Mary Sturges, doth confirm upon said Mary, "a full, compleate right and title to the property hereafter named, to-wit: 3 negroes; 1 sorrel mare; 1 cow; and their increase; 2 featherbeds, and furnishings." (They were married Feb. 7, 1797).

1797, Oct 11
TRUSTEE'S PURCHASE - Levin WAILES, to Theodore BRIGHTWELL, and Polydore NAYLOR, Trustees for Mrs. Henrietta NAYLOR, wife of George NAYLOR, for $1.00, the three hundred acres on which Major George NAYLOR now lives, and was sold by the Tax Collector of Richmond Co., for taxes of the year 1794.

1796, Oct 26 - Rec. Mar 12, 1798
MARRIAGE SETTLEMENT - And establishment of trust: Nathaniel TWINING, Esq., to Margaret STUBBLEFIELD, and Evans LONG, of Wilkes Co., Planter. Whereas, a marriage, by God's permission, is shortly to be solemnized between Nathaniel and Margaret, it was agreed between them that all the estate, real and personal, of the said Margaret, should be made over and assigned to Evans Long, for the uses and purposes herein described. For the sum of $1.00, Margaret, with the consent of Nathaniel Twining, her intended husband, assigns all lands; negroes; horses; and stock, named in the attached schedule, inherited by her from her late husband, Peter STUBBLEFIELD, Esq., dec'd., to be held in trust for said Margaret, and her heirs. After the marriage, Margaret and Nathaniel Twining shall be allowed to take negroes and stock into their custody, work the land, and hire out, use and employ said negroes and stock. If Nathaniel outlives Margaret, the property is to go to her niece, Margaret LONG. (The clauses and provisions run to seven pages) Schedule: 600 acres land on Uchee Creek; 12 negroes, viz: Jacob; Harry; Henry; Billy; Lewis; Miranda; Betty; Milly; Mina; Milly, a small girl, and Maria; 5 head of horses; 40 head of cattle; 60 hogs; 15 sheep; one ridingchair and harness; 1 waggon, and geer; plantation tools; household and kitchen furniture; 4 bonds, dated Nov. 15, 1792, given by Nathaniel DURKEE, to Peter Stubblefield, each for £112, 15 s, sterling, bearing 5% interest, and a mortgage on a tract of land near the Town of Washington.

1798, Apr 13
MORTGAGE BOND - Joseph RAY, Planter, bound unto Chamberlain BIRCH, and Charles OUVRAY, for sum of $5,507.18, in order to secure said debt, mortgages 10 acres on Little River, in Wilkes Co., "opposite to my present residence," (Now where Raysville Bridge is located); 1 other tract of 37 acres on Little River, in Columbia Co., originally granted to Joseph Ray, and whereon he now lives, also 750 acres on Little River, formerly the property of James GRIERSON, and purchased at sale of confiscated lands by Joseph Ray, with all mills, the bridge over said River, etc. (The bridge mentioned was a toll bridge, built by Nathaniel DURKEE, a tanner from Wrightsboro, in 1796. He charged 25¢ for loaded wagons, empty, 12 1/2¢; four-wheeled chariots, 25¢; man and horse, 6 1/4¢; rolling tobacco hogsheads, 12 1/2¢; cattle; hogs; sheep and goats, 1¢ apiece.)

1803, May 4
RECEIPT - Received of Hugh BLAIR, 5 shillings in full of accounts, bonds, notes and judgments, "from the beginning of the world to this day." s/ John HENDERSON - Feb 20, 1796

1799, May 18
SHERIFF'S RECEIPT - Anderson CRAWFORD, Sheriff, to David LANGSTON, for land sold at auction, Apr 2, 1799, for sum of $200., 200 acres on both sides of Germany's Creek, originally granted to Timothy RICKETSON, and including plantation known as "Dunn's Old Place."

1801, Oct 6
RECEIPT - George NAYLOR, to Elinor Dorsett NAYLOR, rec'd., sum of £40, sterling, for a "Sola Phaeton, and silver-plated harness."

1802, Feb 23
MORTGAGE BOND - Chappel BONNER, to Dr. Michael BURKE, Physician of City of Savannah, to secure debt of $2,400., mortgages Mount Hope Plantation, Columbia Co., containing 550 acres, also tract by name of Larimore's Old Field, on the Savannah River.

1801, Nov 20 - Rec. Mar. 4, 1802
AGREEMENT TO SELL - Ann, (or Nancy) REED; Elesa MAYS; Elizabeth MC CORMICK (called Elizabeth KILLGORE); Nancy MC CORMICK, and Polly MC CORMICK, agree to sell to James BOYD, for $300., a plantation containing 100 acres, part of 600 acre tract formerly granted to Elizabeth CRITTENDON, on Savahhan River. Elizabeth McCormick, called Killgore, now residing in Abbeville, S. C.

1802, Mar 15
RELINQUISHMENT - John CASTLE; John DAVIES; Jacob GREATHOUSE, and William HOLDEN, of Columbia Co., and Catherine JONES, of Warren Co., heirs and distributees of estate of Jacob GREATHOUSE, dec'd., do release and Quit Claim unto Abraham PERKINS, of Warren Co., one of heirs of above dec'd., Greathouse, 45 acres of tract orig. granted said Greathouse, on waters of Germany's Creek, known in distribution as Lot #2.

1802, Mar 26
"DEED OF BARGAIN" (So called in Deed Book) - John ROBERTS to James and Thomas GARDNER, bound for sum of $417.46, secures above debt with a 200 acre tract of land.

1802, May 30
SHERIFF'S SALE - Sheriff Isaac WILLINGHAM, to Gazaway DAVIS, merchant, and John E. ANDERSON, Richmond Co., Clementius DAVIS, having died intestate, possessed of 3,119 1/2 acres, Gazaway Davis and John Anderson, Adms., a public sale ordered by Inferior Court, for benefit of orphans, and advertised in Augusta Herald. Sale set for Apr. 6, 1802, all lands, and estate, both real and personal (8 pages for description), sold to Gazaway Davis and John Anderson, for $8,000.

1802, Aug 20, 25, & 26
 HEIRS' AGREEMENT AND PARTITION OF ESTATE: Heirs of Jacob GREATHOUSE, John CASTLE, 50 acres (Lot #1); William HOLDEN, 45 acres; John DAVIS, 45 acres.

1803, Jan 30
 EMANCIPATION - William FEW, of New York, for good causes and consideration, have granted unto my negro man, Simon, his freedom and manumission.

1793, _____ - Rec. Mar 15, 1803
 ASSIGNMENT - Robert CHAMBERLAIN, and Mary, his wife, of Baltimore Co., Md., she the only child and heir of Charles CROOKSHANKS, of Baltimore Town, sign over to Robert GILMOR; William PATTERSON; and James DALL, the following lands. The estate owed a debt, dated May 4, 1792: A tract of land called Heworth, in Talbot Co., Md., 205 acres; A tract called Long Point, in Talbot Co., Md., 52 acres; A tract called Fentry, in Talbot Co., Md., 100 acres; A tract called Dawson's Neck, Queen Anne Co., Md., 142 acres; A tract called Hawkin's Thersalia, Queen Ann Co., Md., 600 acres; A tract called Margaret s Hill, Quenn Anne Co., Md., 130 acres; A parcel of ground #40, 36 acres and 68 perches, lying in Baltimore Co., called Orange, purchased May 1, 1786, by Crookshanks, from Charles CARROLL, of Carrollton and Co; All tract of land on South side of Rocky Creek, in Wilkes Co., Ga., 1,000 acres; A tract called "Fruit Hill," in Columbia Co., 350 acres (Wm. FEW); One other tract in the county, containing 200 acres (A. CRAWFORD); One other tract in same County containing 200 acres, originally granted to Alexander DOUGLASS, by him to John CARMICHAEL, by him to Benjamin PORTER and Patsey, his wife, by him to said Crookshanks, on waters of Greenbriar Creek. PROVISION: If Charles CROOKSHANKS, should pay as follows: Robert GILMORE, the sum of £2,791, on or before Jan 1, 1794; William PATTERSON, the sum of £1,301, 17 s, 10 p, before Jan 1, 1794; HEATHECOTE & DALL, the sum of £1,091, on or before Jan 1, 1794; OLIVE & CO., the sum of £154, 5 s, 8 p, on or before Jan 1, 1794; ANDREW, SKINNER & ENNOLDS CO., the sum of £243, 2 s, 4 p, on or before Jan 1, 1794; Ebenezer MACKIE, the sum of £26, 18 s, 9 p, on or before Jan. 1, 1794; All of the above of Baltimore Co., Md. Thomas FITZSIMMONS, of Philadelphia, £2,503; George MEADE, of Philadelphia, £315, 11 s, 5 p; Exrs. of estate of Robert PEACOCK, £252, 1 s, 10 p, 3 f. If the said Crookshanks should pay, on date, the indenture will be void. Crookshanks died intestate, without paying his debts, and left as his only heir, Mary Chamberlain. Upon receipt of five shillings, above properties were conveyed to creditors, with the agreement that if there were "any surplus monies over and above the amount of the debts, when said lands were sold," it was to be given to Robert and Mary Chamberlain.

1803, May 12
 SETTLEMENT - Thomas MC MURRELL; John and Elias LAZENBY, Adms., estate of Alexander LAZENBY, for the settlement of a $400., debt against the estate, convey to the Lazenbys 1/2 acre in village of Applington, adj., Academy and Courthouse lots.

1803, May 19
 SHERIFF'S SALE- Holland MC TYRE, Sheriff, of Richmond Co., to

Jane CARTLEDGE, and her children; James Alexander; John; Polly;
Betsey and Sally, the highest bidders on property of Thomas COLE,
sold at public outcry, Oct. 5, 1801, for $123., 200 acres on Keg Creek.

1797, Nov 23
    APPRENTICESHIP PAPERS, Wm. Anner SMITH hath put her two children,
Elizabeth and William, to apprentice, to Peter WATSON, rarmer, to be
bred up by him. The boy in the business of a Farm, and the girl in
the business commonly followed by females in the house. To serve him,
the boy during a term of 15 years, and the girl for a full term of
10 years. They shall faithfully serve their master, and gladly obey
his lawful commands. They shall not do damage to their lawful master,
or see it done, without giving notice. They shall not waste their
master's goods, nor lend them to others. They shall not contract
marriage, play at cards, or dice. They shall not buy nor sell. They
shall not absent themselves day or night from their master's service,
without leave. They shall not haunt taverns, but shall in all ways
behave as faithfull apprentices. Their master shall provide sufficient
meat, drink, washing, lodging, and apparel. Also 6 months schooling.
s/ William Anna SMITH. (These children were evidently white, otherwise they would have been purchased. Not an enviable life...white
servants, in a household with negro slaves.)

1799, Jan 9
    RECEIPT - To: Peter CRAWFORD, Please pay Dudley HARGROVE, £157,
sterling, out of the monies lodged in your hands, to discharge a bond
against Harris COLEMAN, Exr., of Paul COLEMAN. s/ Susannah Roseborough COLEMAN, and her son, William ROSEBOROUGH.

1799, Feb 22
    SETTLEMENT OF ESTATE - William JOHNSON, and Mary, his wife,
formerly DAVIS; William BALLARD, and Susan, his wife, dau. of Mary
JOHNSON, and the late Theophilus DAVIS, husband of Mary, of County
of Washington: To, Zachariah ATHEY, for $100., 100 acres, bounded
by lands of Zachariah LAMAR; Redmon; John Shackleford; John Wood,
and Walter Maddox. Originally granted to Theophilus Davis, in Parish
of St. Paul (now Columbia Co.), in 1774.

1790, Sept 3 - Rec. Feb 23, 1799
    APPRENTICESHIP INDENTURE - William WATKINS, of Richmond Co.,
Planter, doth bind his son John, as apprentice to William MILES,
Farmer, to serve him for a full term of 16 years. (This follows the
regular form for such an agreement). The master shall, to the utmost
of his endeavors, teach him in reading, writing, and farming, in all
its branches.

1799, Mar 13
    Anderson CRAWFORD, Sheriff, of Columbia Co., to satisfy a debt
of Thomas CUMMING & Co., of Augusta, against Josias SHAW, sells at
public outcry, on the Courthouse steps, 3 featherbeds; 3 checked
counterpains; 2 pine tables; 8 old chairs; one Bald Eagle Mare; 1
bay filly; 1 90 gallon still. Knocked off to George CONN, for
$159.37 1/2

1799, July 18
　　MORTGAGE BOND - John WALTON, of St. Paul's Parish, is indebted to Edward TELFAIR, merchant of Savannah, for £2,440.

1799, Aug 24
　　ASSIGNMENT - In the Inferior Court, August Term 1799, George NAYLOR, vs. Patrick CROOKSHANKS, Attachment. Jurors: Benjamin KING; Elias LAZENBY; Hugh BLAIR; David & Thomas STANFORD; John SUTHERLAND; Solomon ELLIS; James WRIGHT; John BEALLE; John DORSETT; Theodore DORSETT; and Theodore BRIGHTWELL. Jury found for Naylor, the sum of $2,590.25, with interest from the 15th of Dec., 1793, and costs of suit "Aug. 24, 1799, I do hereby assign over unto John HOLLAND, Esq., all my rights, etc., to within judgment." s/ George NAYLOR.

1799, May 18
　　SHERIFF'S SALE - A. CRAWFORD, Esq., Sheriff, "At the suit of William RADFORD, against Richard P. WHITE, I do sell at public outcry, on the Columbia County Courthouse steps, to Capt. John SAVAGE, for $400., two negroes, Nancy, an old woman; Grace a girl."

1800, Jan 30
　　EMANCIPATION - Joshua GRINAGE, to servant Glouster (see sale of same), "I pronounce him to be perfectly free. He may have all the rights and privileges enjoyed by other citizens of this State, without fear of molestation, hindrance, or trouble."

1800, Jan 4
　　QUIT CLAIM - or RELINQUISHMENT - Joseph COOPER, and wife, Martha, to James HAMILTON, in consideration of the sum of $60., relinquish all title to the 1/3rd part of a 200 acre tract of land on East side of Kiokee Creek, known as Allison's Old Place, which 1/3rd, Martha COOPER claims as her dower as relict, or widow, of Henry ALLISON, dec'd. She has since married with Joseph COOPER.

1801, Mar 11
　　RELEASE - Robert HATCHER, to Ignatius FEW: "Many years ago I did sell to Ignatius Few, Esq., a tract of land containing 380 acres, then in St. Paul's Parish, now in Columbia County, granted to me Apr. 4, 1775. I do hereby assign and release all right and title to said land."

1801, Mar 10
　　CERTIFICATE OF RELEASE - "In or about 1786, I, Ignatius FEW, did sell and convey to James BELCHER, of Savannah, a 380 acre tract of land I purchased from Robert HATCHER. I do hereby release my title to said land to said James Belcher."

1801, July 6
　　MORTGAGE - John GREENE mortgages to William DUNN; Abraham FRANKLIN; and Alexander GARDNER, a waggon, and geer; 1 sorrel horse; 2 bay "mairs"; 1 sorrell ditto, for $350.

1801, July 8
　　MORTGAGE - Joshua GRINAGE, Planter, to George WOODRUFF, of

Savannah, for final sum of $3,000., mortgages 500 acre tract granted to Sir Patrick HOUSTOUN, Oct 4, 1774, bounded by lands of Absolom BEDELL; John SIDWELL; Jonothan SELL; and Robert MC CLUNG. Also one other tract granted to Sir Patrick, adj., Alexander SCOTT, and lands vacant.

1804, Jan 20
HEIRS' AGREEMENT - Zadock, George, John, Archibald, and Ellender MC GRUDER, and John OLIVE, and Sally (MC GRUDER) OLIVE, his wife, do relinquish to Elizabeth MC GRUDER, relict of Basil MC GRUDER, a tract of 150 acres, whereon said Basil did live.

1804, May 18
DEPOSITION - John MARCUS, of Hancock Co., for John HAYNIE, did swear that in 1796, in Columbia Co., he did see Robert MIDDLETON bargain and sell unto said Haynie, a negro slave named Gilbert, of yellow complexion, and rather a cripple in one hand.

1804, May 18
RECEIPT - Received of John BRISCOE, a certain mulatto girl, Amy, to sell and dispose of for said Briscoe, Mar. 21, 1803
s/ John HAYNIE.

1804, May 18
DEPOSITION - John DORSETT, swears that above handwriting is that of John HAYNIE, dec'd.

1796, Oct 4 - Rec. May 10, 1804
ACCOUNT - George NAYLOR, to John HAYNIE: Oct 5, 1796, to cash: $148.67; bal. due yet, $364.60. Total: $513,27. By two negroes, Sarah and Harriot, $513.27. To bal. brought down, as per contract: $364.60. To be discounted out of said Haynie's account for building a grist and saw mill, as per agreement.

1804, Apr 23
DEPOSITION - Anderson CRAWFORD swears that he was acquainted with handwriting of George NAYLOR, and identifies the above.

1801, Mar 4 - Rec. July 19, 1804
MORTGAGE - William DUNN, to Edward TELFAIR, Esq., of Savannah, being indebted to said Telfair for $800., plus interest, payable in 2 annual payments, mortgages 300 acres in Columbia Co., purchased from said Telfair in January 1780.

1804, July 23
RECEIPT - Solomon VERNON, who sold 27 acres on Maddock's Creek to Isaac PATTON, for $82., "have been paid to my full satisfaction."

1804, July 23
HEIRS' AGREEMENT - Elizabeth CALDWELL (heir to 1/3rd of 200 acre tract from father, Peter CULBREATH, dec'd.), and Delpha CULBREATH, now married to David HUBERT, also an heir, have sold their portions to James CALDWELL. James has sold all property to Thomas CUMMING, of Augusta.

1804, July 24
HEIRS' SALE - Philip JOHNSTON, and Elizabeth, his wife, (late the relict of Jesse NOE, dec'd.); Louden NOE, and Judah NOE, the only surviving children, sell to Thomas JONES, 200 acre tract, for $500.

1804, July 25
QUIT CLAIM - Mary ROUSSEAU, daughter of John, dec'd., for a valuable consideration, relinquishes "all claim to my share of the legacy willed to me by my father, John ROUSSEAU, as follows: negro woman, Patience, and all her present and future issue." (NOTE: Mary, daughter of John Rousseau, married William ROUSSEAU, of Oglethorpe Co., Ga., and gave above property to her brother, William Rousseau).

1804, Nov __
HEIRS' SALE - Robert and William GERMANY, of Oglethorpe Co., sell to John and James GERMANY, 300 acres of land on Uchee Island, in the Savannah River, at the mouth of Little River, granted to Robert GERMANY and his wife, Mary, by Governor James WRIGHT, in the years 1761, and 1766. Robert now dec'd.

1805, Mar 12
MORTGAGE - Thomas NAPIER, and Robert RANDOLPH (son-in-law), to James MOSSMAN, of Savannah, indebted by a promissory note for $1,200., secure the note by mortgaging 700 acres of land in Columbia Co., on Germany's Creek.

1805, Mar 13
MORTGAGE - Joshua GRINAGE, to James MOSSMAN, being indebted for $6,000., mortgages 1,000 acres in Columbia County.

1805, Mar 18
EXECUTOR'S SALE - Lewis GARDNER, dec'd., did, on the first of January 1798, execute his bond to John BENNING, giving title to 200 acres of land. Executor, Lewis GARDNER; Verlinder GARDNER, and Stephen HOGE, in consideration of the sum of $700., grant and assign said land to John BENNING.

1803, Oct 20 - Rec. Apr 10, 1805
NOTE - "I, William FULLER, for and in consideration of sum of Eight and Twenty Dollars ($28.), I borrowed from Keziah DAVIS, have secured the debt by agreeing to deliver one bay horse, 14 1/2 hands high, a star on his forehead, which I bought from James GUEST. To be yours, if I do not pay you on or before the first of December."

1804, Dec 24
RECEIPT - The above listed property was forfeited unto Hezekiah DAVIS, and delivered by William FULLER.

1805, June 11
MORTGAGE - John DORSETT, to Peter CRAWFORD, Exr., of Last Will and Testament of William APPLING, Esq. Dorsett indebted to the estate for $200.94 1/2, by note of hand. For further security of

Peter Crawford, Dorsett mortgages, "100 acre tract on Big Kiokee Creek, whereon I now live."

1805, June 20
ARTICLES OF AGREEMENT - John RICHARDSON, and brothers, Daniel and Enoch, heirs and representatives of late Daniel RICHARDSON, who died intestate in St. Paul's Parish, no regular Adm., ever having been appointed, the brothers mutually agreed to pay all debts, and in, "peace and friendship, equally divide all and singular, the real and personal estate, to our entire satisfaction." (The father must have died before 1777, when St. Paul's Parish was changed to Richmond County.)

1805, Aug 8
LEASE - John MC COY, of Richmond Co., leases to Adam LEDLOW, a plantation on Kioka Creek, near Major John WALTON, in return for Ledlow acting as his attorney, prosecuting a trespass case.

1805(?), _____
MORTGAGE - William PEARRE, indebted to James and George CARY, under the name of CARY & CO., for the sum of $800., secures debt with the, "Smith Tract, whereon I do now live," 294 1/2 acres on Kiokee Creek.

1804, Apr 13
PARTITION - James GERMANY; Charles CLAYTON (husband of Mary Germany); Jesse SANDERS (husband of Jane Germany); and John GERMANY, heirs and representatives of William GERMANY, who died intestate, agree to divide the estate, including a 300 acre tract purchased from Robert and William GERMANY, of Oglethorpe Co., legal representatives of James GERMANY, dec'd. Land divided by lot: James Germany, Lot #1, on the island and the main, 332 1/2 acres; John Germany, Lot #2, on the island and the main, 384 acres; Charles Clayton, Lot #3, on the main, 305 1/2 acres; Jesse Sanders, Lot #4, 609 acres, and 300 acres in Elbert Co., originally granted to John HEARD, near mouth of Vann's Creek.

1805, Aug 6
MORTGAGE - Yancey SANDERS, Planter, to William BULLOCK, of Savannah, Atty., indebted for sum of $1,120., mortgages 400 acre tract in Columbia Co.

1804, Jan 28
HEIRS' AGREEMENT - Edmond BOWDRE makes bond for $20,000., and is appointed Exr., and Admr., of estate of Richard BOWDRE, dec'd. Heirs: Millie BOWDRE; Joseph DORSEY (husband of Mary BOWDRE); Robert BOWDRE; Benoni BOWDRE; Samuel BOWDRE, and Thomas BOWDRE. "Whereas, Richard Bowdre died intestate, and at the time of his death held jointly, with the above Edmond, a considerable estate in lands, negroes, stock, etc., which Edmond now claims as his own, as brother and survivor of said Richard, and Whereas, the above Milly; Joseph Darsey; Robert; Benoni; Samuel and Thomas, are the mother; brother-in-law, and brothers of Richard, dec'd., said heirs have chosen Samuel Bowdre; Thomas Bowdre; Levi Marshall; William BECKHAM; and James SIMMS, as arbitrators, to determine their Rights.

1804, Jan 28
    ARBITRATORS' DECISION - Land and estate awarded to Edmond Bowdre, and heirs ordered to sign a relinquishment.

1804, Feb 24
    RELINQUISHMENT - Milly; Robert; Benoni; Samuel and Thomas Bowdre, and Joseph Darsey, in right of his wife, Mary (Bowdre) Darsey, do sign over all right, title, etc., to above estate, to Edmond Bowdre.

1805, Oct 5
    Floyd JARVIS, indebted to William LOWE, for $150., mortgages one parcel of land on Savage's Creek, 56 1/4 acres.

1805, Dec 5
    MORTGAGE - Rhesa HOWARD, in debt to the Hon. Edward TELFAIR for £1,200, sterling, dated July 5, 1777, mortgages 1,500 acre tract on Greenbriar Creek.

1805, Dec 7
    TAX SALE - Dixon PERRYMAN, Tax Collector, for Columbia Co., sells to Hillary BOSTICK, of Burke Co., for $20., a 140 acre tract seized from Floyd JERVIS for taxes.

1806, Feb 4
    QUIT CLAIM - Hezekiah JONES, and Edward Jones, Tennants-in-common to 275 acres, divided by mutual consent.

1806, Feb 28
    RECEIPT - Richard DARBY gives John GRIFFIN a receipt for $15., in full payment for 15 acres of land.

1806, Jan 27
    EXCHANGE - John SHACKLEFORD, exchanges 8 acres of land with Marshall KEITH, for 8 acres.

1806, June 30
    Seaborn JONES, Att'y., and Winifred JENKINS, relict of Col. James JENKINS. Mrs. Jenkins claims dower rights on tract she lives on, at Rae's Creek. Said property mortgaged to Seaborn Jones, by late husband. Jones agrees to let her live on the property, rent free, for 7 years.

1792, Aug 10 - Rec. Jan 31, 1809
    RELINQUISHMENT OF DOWER - Mary Candler FEW -vs- Ignatius FEW
    On receiving the sum of £500, sterling, Mary Few relinquished all dower rights. "We are mutually agreed this day to make a final separation as man and wife, and it is my sincere wish that the General Assembly may divorce me from said Ignatius Few." s/ MARY FEW

1794, Dec 3 - Rec. Apr 4, 1806
    AFFIDAVIT - Thomas SANDRICK, for Ignatius Few. Swears that Mary

Few signed renunciation of dower. Swears that he never heard Capt. Few mention her name, or any circumstance relating to her, but on that day Capt Few called at his house to borrow his pistols, and Dr. DeYamport was with him.

Deponent lent the pistols, but expecting they were about to be used in a duel, offered his services in conciliating matters. On their way to Wrightsborough, Capt. Few stated that William SLATTER had made his escape from justice, after having, in concert with said Mary Few, procured poison from said Dr. deYamport, to administer him, Few. Hoped that deponent would help him.

Procured new warrant at Wrightsborough, on most positive deposition of deYamport as to the facts. On the following day went out to a relative of said Slatter, where they stated that Slatter and Mary Few had slept the night before. Slatter's brother reprobated the conduct of said William in living with Mary Few, promising he should leave the State in 14 days, Capt. Few giving him that long to settle his affairs.

Deponent then came to Mrs. Few's and found her very violent, and denying the fact of procuring the poison, until she found that Capt. Few had brought Dr. deYaomport with him. She then burst into tears, and said, "The doctor is just as bad as me - he told me to give it." On being asked how she and Slatter came to give a bond for £200 to said deYamport, she made no answer. She continued to cry and begged forgiveness. Said she would write to her sister over the mountains, and live virtuous in future. Capt. Few reminded her of several deviations from virtue which she confessed, also to having taken two bonds for £120, each. She had been given £50 as separate maintenance, and assurance of pecuniary relief if she returned to her sister, and left the connection with Slatter.

But on Monday morning she had the audacity to tell the deponent she had altered her mind, and was determined to live with Slatter, because she was not yet 30 years of age, and people would always say she lived with somebody. She declared she once had had a consent from Capt. Few, to marry the said Slatter. (At this point others came in --- Flournoy, Atty.,Weatherby, preacher, etc.) It was proposed that an instrument of divorce should be drawn up, and deponent positively saith no threats were made.

Capt. Few has since proposed that if she would name a trustee to prevent her squandering away her property in the shameful manner lately practised, he would make any purchases she chose. Further deponent saith not.

1806, July 19
ASSIGNMENT - William NELSON -vs- Isaac WILLINGHAM, Feb. Term 1805. Judgment returned for Nelson. "I hereby assign my right and title to $139., to Thomas CARR, my attorney."

1806, Sept __
DEED IN TRUST - Owen and Rachel BALDWIN, for $140., do sell to James ROSS, guardian of Taylor WILEY, a 2/3rd interest in a 27 acre tract.

1806, Oct 8
Elijah MENDENHALL appoints, in his place, as guardian of his

brothers, John; James and Marmaduke, minors, his trusty friend, David JONES, also granting him power of attorney.

1806, Dec 4
RELINQUISHMENT - Lewis POWELL, to Archibald and Mary POWELL, legatees of estate of James and Michael MC NEIL, do relinquish to my two children, Archibald and Mary, all my rights, titles, and claims to the estate, both real and personal.

1807, Jan 14
MARRIAGE CONTRACT - Whereas, a marriage contract has been arranged between me, Thomas SHIPP, and Jedediah MOON, we do agree upon the following: I do make over to said Jedediah the tract of land upon which she now lives; 3 notes of hand....1 on John Espey; 2 on Wiley Espey. Four beds and furniture, all rest of household goods in the dwelling house.

1803, Feb 27
MORTGAGE - George Dent, being indebted to Richard and Charles TUBMAN, for sum of $970., mortgages three slaves: Sam; Mentor; Notley.

1807, Mar 14
AUCTION - Francis FARRER, Sheriff, sells at publick outcry, negro girl, Dafney, property of James JENKINS. Seaborn JONES highest bidder, $324.

1807, Mar 14
TAX SALE - Daniel MARSHALL, Collector of Taxes, sold at auction to Ashell GARDNER, 100 acres for $13.

1807, Aug 17
QUIT CLAIM - Rebecca COCKE, to Clem READE, of Halifax Co., Va., for $1.00, all right and title to a 690 acre tract in said county, being part of tract where William THORNTON, the Elder, father of said Rebecca lived, and to which she had a claim, according to her father's will. Her brother, William THORNTON, JR., sold said tract to Clem Reade.

1806, May 1
RELINQUISHMENT - Robert TOOMBS, of Wilkes Co., for $550., has conveyed all right and title to a tract of land in Columbia Co., to Thomas COBBS. Said land was purchased from Charles ELLIS and wife, Elizabeth; Garah DAVIS, and his wife, Peggy, Jan 23, 1806.

1807, Sept 27
ADMINISTRATORS' SALE - Heirs of James and Michael MC NEIL: John CULBREATH; John RAMSEY; Polly POWELL; Archer POWELL; Archibald CLARKE; John MATTHEWS, in right of his wife; and Mary MC NEIL, Adms., of estate of James and Michael MC NEIL, authorized to sell, by order of Inferior Court, whole of real estate of above. Property bought by John Ramsey, as highest bidder, 300 acres for $3,150.

1807, Sept 28
Same heirs sell to John MATTHEWS, who purchased 100 acres on

Little Kiokee Creek, and Washington Road, for $581.

1807, Oct 22
SHERIFF'S SALE - William FLEMING, Sheriff, seized property of Stephen COLLINS, dec'd., now in possession of widow, Sarah, Admx., on suit of William COLLINS, et al; property sold at auction, bought in by Richard SHACKLEFORD, @ $300., for 90 2/3rds acres.

1786, Feb 16 - Rec. Nov 24, 1807
ADMINISTRATOR'S SALE - John CRITTENDON; THOMAS CRITTENDON; Jonathon CRITTENDON; Isaac SKINNER, and wife Elizabeth; Anderson; Edward WILLIAMS, and wife Margaret; and Frances CRITTENDON, to William CRITTENDON. Heirs having equal shares in a 100 acre tract. William pays them each £5.

1807, Dec 1
HEIRS' SALE
Mary Ann CRITTENDON, and others, to Felix MC KINNEY; John MC KINNEY, and Barna MC KINNEY. (dated Nov 17, 1806) Ann Margaret CRITTENDON, widow of William CRITTENDON; Charles COUSINS, and Frances Crittendon COUSINS, his wife, dau., of said William Crittenton, sell all interest in 300 acre tract, originally granted to William Crittendon, Sr., dec'd., father of above William, on Sept 6, 1774. Also 150 acre tract granted William, Jr., dec'd., Feb 2, 1786; Also 150 acre tract granted to William, Sr., Oct 2, 1784. Total price: $250.

1806, Nov 17 - Rec. Dec 1, 1807
Elizabeth (Crittendon) Downs, wife of Jacob DOWNS, sells to above McKinneys, her 1/8th share of 300 acre tract left by father, for $125.

1808, Apr 17
SHERIFF'S SALE - William FLEMING sold at auction, 300 acres, originally property of Thomas MOORE, SR., to John RAMSEY, for $1,505.

1808, June 16
AGREEMENT - John FREEL, SR., and Elizabeth FREEL, wid., of John Freel, Jr., final settlement of all controversy, relative to property of Freel, Sr., which he now settles on said Elizabeth: A negro fellow, Stewart; negro wench, Peg, and Peter, her child; Margaret, and her child Hanna; Love, a negro boy. Elizabeth agrees to pay $100., by next Christmas. On her part, she agrees that John Freel, Sr., shall have negroes, Austen; Tom; and Bob.

1808, July 27
SHERIFF'S SALE - Reuben LANGSTON, Sheriff, sells at auction, 100 acres, to James CARTLEDGE, for $356.

1808, July 28
HEIRS' SALE - Stephen COBBS, and Mary COBBS, of Pendleton Co., S. C., Rachel COBBS, and Nancy Cobbs, of Columbia Co., Ga., heirs to estate of James COBBS, dec'd., sell to Elisha PERRYMAN, and David STANFORD, Exrs., of estate of Dixon PERRYMAN, their equal shares in

105 acre tract originally granted to James COBBS, and by him left to them in his will, for $165. apiece.

1806, Dec 27
AGREEMENT - Between Nancy RAY, and William BARNETT. Mrs. Ray agrees to rent her storehouse, gin-house, and gins, for a year from the 1st of April'1807, for $600. If he should board elsewhere, amount of board shall be deducted. She also agrees not to sell any spirits, only by wholesale (quarts, casks, or hogsheads), nor to allow anyone else to sell spirits on the premises.

1808, June 8
PROMISSORY NOTE - Francis FARRER, to Ross, Brown & Co., for $1,037., on demand, with lawful interest. Assigns tract of land on Greenbriar Creek, 331 acres, originally granted to Peter PARIS (PARISH), Oct 1, 1769.

1808, Nov 14
AGREEMENT - Heirs and representatives of David WALKER, dec'd., viz: James THOMAS; Mary POUNDS; James WALKER; Archibald WALKER; Willoughby SLATON, and widow, Elizabeth WALKER, and Elisha and David WALKER, Adms., of estate. Elizabeth Walker to receive mansion house and lands contiguous, 300 acres, to be enjoyed by her during her natural life and no longer, also sum of $900. She to pay all taxes. At her death, to be divided between heirs, equally. (Note: Willoughby Slaton was representing his wife, Elizabeth (Walker) Lowe, widow of Isaac Lowe).

1808, Nov 16
ADMINESTRATORS' BOND - To make a division of slaves, at public auction, heirs had themselves put under bond. Mary Pounds and John Hall, bound to Elisha Walker, David Walker, and John Smith, Adms., of David Walker estate, for $4,000. James and Archibald Walker, bound to the above for $4,000.,James Thomas and Peter Crawford, bound to above, for $4,000; Willoughby Slaton and Robert Crawford, bound to above for $4,000. At sale, James Walker was highest bidder for negro man, Joe; woman, Beck and two children, Boston and Lever. James Thomas bought negro woman, Hettie.

1809, May 24
RECEIPT - John CURTIS (CARTER?), to William OFFUTT, "Received of William Offutt, Aug 5, 1807, a deed of conveyance of two lots of land in Harrisburgh, and the other, including the ferry landing, conveyed to Offutt, Jan 21, 1801," (Harrisburgh was in Augusta).

1809, June 13
MORTGAGE - Jesse WINFREY, to Adms., of estate of Andrew WARREN, Jane WARREN and Jeremiah DARLEY. Winfrey being indebted to estate for $600., by note of hand, mortgages 200 acre tract he now lives on, on Little Kiokee Creek.

1809, June 15 - date recorded
MARRIAGE SETTLEMENT _ Francis FARRER (FARRAR), to Anne JONES "Whereas, a marriage is shortly to be arranged between us, we are

hereunto moved to a mutual agreement. Since Francis FARRER and Anne JONES, widow, both have property in their own names, they shall retain same. Said Francis' property shall not be subject to debts owing by Anne Jones at present, and said Anne shall not be liable for his present debts. Anne to be allowed to dispose of her property as she wishes, or to her own children. At the present time she holds 388 acres on Greenbriar Creek, and following negroes: John; Will; Anthony; Horatio; Isaac; Jesse; Charles; Jacob; Jane; Mary; Grace; Celina; Ann; Elizabeth; Henny; Susannah; all of the stock of hogs; cattle; horses, and household and kitchen furniture, and plantation tools. Francis is to manage the above property for Anne Jones. (Note: Anne was the widow of Basil JONES, maiden name, SEWALL. Had 1 dau., Elizabeth Brook Jones. Francis and Anne m. March 18, 1807.)

1808, Oct 6
APPOINTMENT OF ARBITRATORS - Robert CRAWFORD, and William BARNETT, Adms., of estate of William and Hannah BARNETT, dec'd., and John MADDOX; Hezekiah BEALLE, and Allen LOVELACE, divisors of said estate, have mutually chosen Hugh BLAIR; Anderson CRAWFORD, and John FOSTER, as arbitrators to settle all matters of controversy. Recorded June 15, 1809

1809, June 15
AGREEMENT - John FOSTER; Hugh BLAIR, and Anderson CRAWFORD, appointed by Robert CRAWFORD and Ann BARNETT, Adms., of estate of Hannah and William BARNETT, dec'd., and John MADDOX, in right of his wife, one of the heirs of Hannah's estate; Hezekiah BEALLE, and Allen LOVELACE, representatives of late Jesse BARNETT, also an heir to said estate. "We do award distribution of real estate of William Barnett, the Elder, as follows: John Maddox, 250 acres on Uchee Creek, 184 acres on Ogeechee, in Wilkes Co., 287 1/2 acres in Franklin Co. James SMITH, guardian to heirs of Jesse Barnett, dec'd., 500 acres on Broad River in Wilkes Co., 300 acres on Uchee Creek. Adms., to pay to John Maddox, $350.10 in full of his proportion of the estate. Also sum to Allen Lovelace of $573., as his full share. Hezekiah Bealle shall pay to Robert Crawford and Anderson Crawford, $102.84, with lawful interest from Nov 1, 1806, it being money overpaid to said Bealle.
(William Barnett m. Anna (or "Hannah") Crawford, in Richmond Co., Dec 23, 1789.)

1809, June 15
HEIRS' SETTLEMENT - Heirs and representatives of estate of William WILBORN, sell whole estate, as follows: 2 dishes, 75¢; 8 plates, 93¢; candlestick, 25¢; 1 tumbler, 18 3/4¢; one chest, 25¢; trunk and books, 25¢; negro boy, $159., negro man, 456., total: $615. 93 3/4. $1.68, brought forward, total: $617.61 3/4. Robert HENDERSON, purchased: 2 dishes, $1., pewter, 12¢; tinware, 62¢; 1 lot tinware, 37¢; 1 mortar, 62¢; Earthenware, 12¢; table, 87¢; Butterpot, 62¢; Butterpot, 62¢; jugg, 25¢; 6 chairs, $2.75; Featherbed and furniture, $18.00; Featherbed and furniture, $13.00; negro woman, and child, $299.00; 3 cowhides, $1.62; total: $339.58. Martha WILBORN, wid., purchased: 1 case, 50¢; pair flatirons 37¢; chest, 50¢; wheel and cards 18 3/4¢; two stays, 50¢; bed and furniture, $8.62; mare $62.12, total: $72.79 3/4. Martha Wilborn, (or WELBOURNE), relict of William; Reuben Welbourne, son of dec'd., and Robert HENDERSON, in right of his wife,

Jane (WELBOURNE) HENDERSON, do agree with each other that the foregoing sale represents the whole estate of said William, dec'd., and that we each renounce all title to articles in above sale, the purchasers thereof to enjoy them forever.

1809, June 15
ADMINISTRATOR'S BOND - Humphrey EVANS, Adm. of estate of Boswell SMITH, is bonded for sum of $5,000., unto Caty JENNINGS, guardian of property of Caty SMITH. Due to disagreements, Anderson and Peter CRAWFORD appointed arbitrators. On June 16, 1809, arbitrators demand that all controversy cease. Each party shall pay his own costs. Evans ordered to pay Caty Jennings $2,429.76 1/4, within a month, this being her share of estate, agreeable to a statement here. Caty shall give Evans a full release: STATEMENT:

1802	1/7th of $177.00	Overseer's share of crops sold		$25.03
1803	" " $370.93	" " " "		52.99
1803	3/10ths " $317.94	for negroes of H. EVANS		92.37
1804	1/7th " $558.49	Overseer's share of crop		79.78
1804	3/10th " $478.71	for 3 negroes of H. Evans		143.61
1805		Overseer's standing wages		130.00
1805	2/8th " two negroes of H. Evans ($17.48)			4.36
	Tax on land and negroes, for four years			18.16 1/2
	Blacksmith's work for four years			76.00
	Clothing for negroes for four years			90.00
	Rent of land and iron(?)			56.00
	Rent, 2 mares, 2 horses, 18.00 pd. R. TINDELL			19.25
	One mare a season(?)			11.00
	Bal. due Mrs. Evans by estate			111.23 1/2
	H. Evans comm. on $3,961.79 1/4 @ 5%			198.09
	H. Evans comm. on $1,358 3/4 @ 10%			135.08
	Cash paid Caty JENNINGS			2,429.76 1/4
				$3,672.72

1802	Crop sold for	177.00
1803	Crop sold for	370.93
1804	Crop sold for	558.49
1805	Crop sold for	147.48
	10 negroes val. @	3,325.00
	65 bbl. of corn	330.00
	Mare sold	65.00
	Stock, Plantation tools, household and kitchen furniture	1,128.57 1/2
		$6,102.47 1/2
	H. Evan's share	3,672.72
		$2,429.75 1/2

1809, Aug 19
MORTGAGE - Moses WHEAT, indebted to Phelps and Howard, of Augusta, for $600., mortgages negro man, Tab, 24 years old; negro child, Tun, 3 years old; negro child, Matilda, dau. of Tab; negro woman, Lu. Same day mortgages 230 acres of land for $700.

1810, Mar 7
Reuben LANGSTON, Sheriff, sells at auction to John LAMAR,

1/5th of a 307 acre tract, originally property of Anderson ROZIER, for $21.00.

1810, Mar 5
Richard JELKS, for his wife, Hannah, late GERMANY, Adm., of estate of James GERMANY, dec'd., sells to John FURY, of Richmond Co., at auction, 100 acres, originally property of James Germany; Jelks bid it in for $90., then gave up his bid to Fury, who bought it for $190.

1810, Mar 13
PUBLIC APOLOGY - John CRUMP, and others, to Dr. George BROWN, "The subscribers had the misfortune to be swindled out of a quantity of Cotton at a factor's store in Charleston, and the matter was advertised in Georgia and South Carolina papers. They have had the misfortune, in their anxiety and zeal to discover the swindler, unjustly and rashly to form a suspicion that Dr. George Brown, of Wrightsborough, was the person who had committed the fraud, and a religious congregation of citizens at the house of William HALBERT, in Pendleton Dist., S. C., publicly charged him with the act. Dr. Brown, like a man of integrity and honor, fully convinced us of our great mistake and error, and in consequence of us being poor men, actuated by mistake, has forgiven us. While Dr. Brown has it in his power to ruin every one of us, and to distress our families, we swear in Open Court at Pendleton Court House, to all the world, our mistaken and erroneous conduct. We certify his innocence, and declare our regret and sorrow for the injuries his feelings may have sustained. (They go on for half a page, about Dr. Brown's nobility of character.) s/ John CRUMP; William MITCHELL; George MITCHELL; William DODSON; Wit: William BROWN; John B. DEMPSEY; Wm. HARRIS.

1810, Aug 20
BOND - Joshua GRINAGE; Joseph CAMPBELL, and George MOORE, bonded for $4,000., as Adms., of estate of James CARTLEDGE.

1810, Aug 22
Henry MAULDEN swears that, "I know no harm of Matthew BOLTON, in whose behalf an action of slander is now pending against me, and I do not know of anything injurious I said against Bolton's character, and I am sorry for anything I may have said harmful to his reputation. I know him to be an honest man."

1810, Oct 5
DEED OF TRUST - James SIMMS appoints Robert SIMMS, and Jared POUNDS, Trustees for Obedience LEDLOW; Lewis LEDLOW; Adam LEDLOW, JR., and Temperance LEDLOW, children of Obedience LEDLOW, my daughter, to take charge of slaves, Jack and Lever.

1810, Dec 5
ARTICLES OF AGREEMENT - Mary WHEAT, widow of Basil WHEAT; Edward O'NEAL, in right of his wife, Rebecca; Moses; Harvey; Westley, and Ila WHEAT; concerning gifts given by Basil in life to his son, Eli, also in last Will and Testament, also will signed by my son, Eli. By the will, considerable advantage is given to some of the

legatees, more than others. Of right, an equal division should take place. We mutually agree to the above statement. Mary WHEAT, widow, is to set at nought the deeds of gift and the will of Eli WHEAT, is to be no longer in force, and we do consider ourselves as legatees of a person dying intestate. We agree to name three trustees to appraise estate, and make equal division. The heirs put themselves under $2,000., bond.

1811, Jan 23
   William WILKINS, Sheriff, on suit of Dr. Nathan CRAWFORD -vs- Michael SMALLEY, sells enough of Smalley's goods and chattels to make sum of $19.75, with interest from May 28, 1808, plus $1.50 costs.

1811, Feb 12
   AUCTION - Elisha PERRYMAN, Exr., of estate of David PERRYMAN, sells at auction, 275 acres of land. Hezekiah DEAKINS, highest bidder, for $915.

1811, Mar 2
   DISPOSITION OF ESTATE - John and Samuel RAMSEY, and John CULBREATH, (Isaac Ramsey not qualified), Exr., of estate of late John RAMSEY, in accordance with last Will and Testament, divided estate, as follows: Samuel Ramsey, 350 acres on Little Kiokee Creek, originally granted to Randol RAMSEY, sold to Thomas MOORE, then to John RAMSEY, dec'd., (Seized by him in accord with an execution against said Thomas Moore); also negroes Abram and wife, Sal, and their children, Hannah; Hagar, and Austin; Lewis and Nancy; 1 sorrel horse named, Tarleton; 1 rifle gun and apparatus.

1810, Dec 17 - Rec. Feb 15, 1811
   AUCTION - Robert L. LAZENBY, and Timothy Pittman LAZENBY, Adms., of estate of John LAZENBY, to Henry HANNON, by virtue of an order of the Inferior Court: Sell at auction 500 acres of land originally granted to Thomas AYRES, and sold to John Lazenby, May 8, 1792, by Thomas Ayres, and wife; William Wright and wife,; Francis Danielly and wife; William Ayers and wife, and Joshua Ayers, heirs of Thomas Ayers, Sr., dec'd. Henry HANNON highest bidder at $2,000.

1811, Jan 22 - Rec. Feb 14, 1811
   EXECUTOR'S SALE - Executors of estate of John RAMSEY sell to Archibald HAGA (HEGGIE), 300 acre tract on Little Kiokee Creek, known as the Race Path Trace. (No price quoted.)

1811, Mar 1
   MORTGAGE - John LUCKEY to Thomas EDMONDSON. Indebted for $500., on 25 separate notes of $25., each, mortgages 95 acres on Augusta-Washington Road.

1810, May 21 - Rec. Mar 12, 1811
   RECEIPT - George WHITTON and Robert WHITTON, acknowledge receipt of $200., from John GRIFFIN, for 100 acres on Whitton's Spring Branch.

1811, Mar 12
   John ROBERTS acknowledges receipt of $15., from John GRIFFIN, for 20 acres of land adjoining Whitton's Place.

1811, Mar 21
   AUCTION - Archer AVARY and Walter MADDOX, Exrs., of Amos SESSOMS, to Richard King. Whereas, Amos Sessoms desired that all his property should be sold, they auctioned off to Richard KING, for $614., a tract purchased by said Sessoms from Jeremiah LAMKIN, 60 acres, and one other purchased from John DOGGETT, 6 acres, including his house.

1811, Mar 22
   EXCHANGE - Cornelius SULLIVAN to Obadiah and Samuel SULLIVAN, exchanges 202 1/2 acre tract in Baldwin Co., Lot #236, for the legacies of Obadiah and Samuel from estate of father.

1811, Mar 26
   MORTGAGE - Warren Lewis KENNON, in debt to Thomas HOWARD, for $900., gives mortgage for 210 acre tract on Cane Creek.

1811, Apr 4
   RELINQUISHMENT - William, Archibald, and Nathan MAGAHEE, by last Will & Testament, heirs to all land where David MAGAHEE, Testator, lived, make following arrangements: Archibald and Nathan relinquish to William, 150 acres; William and Nathan relinquish to Archibald, 111 1/2 acres; William and Archibald relinquish to Nathan, 129 3/4 acres.

1811, June 20
   ADMINISTRATOR'S SALE - William UNDERWOOD, Adm., of estate of Isaac UNDERWOOD, sells 95 acres on Uchee Creek, at auction, to Peter CRAWFORD, for $60.

1811, June 22
   ADMINISTRATOR'S SALE - Archibald PRIOR, Adm., of estate of Hadden PRIOR, sells at auction a house and lot, "at the Courthouse," located on Courthouse Square, 1/2 acre, Lot #58, bounded by Baptist Society land, and William APPLING'S land, for $650.

1811, Aug 13
   GUARDIAN'S SALE - John FOSTER, Guardian to heirs and minors of Ephraim SANDERS, sells to Thomas COBBS, Esq., 133 1/3rd acres of land. Sale ordered by Inferior Court, and auction held. Thomas Cobbs highest bidder, @ $1,156.

1811, Aug 18
   William WILKINS, Sheriff, sells at public outcry, on Courthouse steps, 217 2/3rds acres on Little Kioka Creek, property of Richard SHACKLEFORD. Isham BAYLISS high bidder, @ $200.

1800, July 13 - Rec. Sept 3, 1811
   HEIRS' AGREEMENT - John SCHICK, and Winifred, his wife; George SCHICK, and Catherine, wife; Mary LEAVER; Isaac FELL, and Elizabeth (Schick) Fell, wife; Benjamin ANSLEY, and wife, Mary; and Peter Sch-

ick, all of Savannah, legal heirs of John SCHICK, the Elder, dec'd., who died intestate, agree to sell to Thomas GARDNER, 500 acres on Kiokee Creek, granted to John Schick, Nov. 1, 1774, for $1,600.

1811, Sept 10
MORTGAGE - Holt CLANTON -vs- David MIMS, Exr., of estate of Samuel SCOTT. In debt to Mims for $1,351., mortgages 250 acres of land on Red's or Savidge's Creek, also one other 200 acre tract.

1811, Oct 22
DEED OF TRUST - William CRAWFORD, appoints as trustees, Anderson CRAWFORD; John W. SMITH, and Peter CRAWFORD, to hold the following in trust for his wife, Alice (STROTHER) CRAWFORD, and children: 150 acres conveyed by father, Charles CRAWFORD; 165 acres conveyed by George DENT, where he now lives. All negro slaves: Jerry; Godfrey; Ben; Daphne; Clara; Luckey; and Sally. 1 wagon and gear; 1 gunn; 5 head of horses; all stock of cattle and hogs, and sheep; household and kitchen furniture; plantation tools; and every other specie of property I possess.

1811, Oct 30
MORTGAGE - Jonathon CITRAN, owing William STARKE, $300., mortgages the following:_____

1812, Jan 3
MORTGAGE - Thomas FEW, indebted to John HOWARD, for the sum of $757.52, mortgages negro man, Arch, his wife, Patience, and boy Jess, 3 years old.

1811, Apr 19 - Rec. Jan 21, 1812
HEIRS' AGREEMENT - William JONES; Edward JONES; James FLINT; John GARTRELL; Shadrack GIBSON; Samuel JONES; and Reuben WALKER, for $100., 250 acres on Kiokee Creek, representing seven out of eleven parts of a 405 acre tract, the same being 2/3rds of a 406 1/2 acre tract, after deducting Widow JONES' dower. s/ Edward Jones, and Arabella, wife; Samuel Jones, and Hesky, wife; Elizabeth Gartrell, wife of John; S. W. Gibson, and Jannet Gibson; Reuben Wilburn, and wife, Susannah; William and Lucy Jones.

1812, Feb 12
HEIRS' AGREEMENT - Thomas; John; William; Joseph; Jonathon; Nancy; and Esther STANFORD, and Thomas RICHARDS, in right of his wife, Sarah, to David STANFORD. Heirs of William, dec'd., sell 100 acre tract on Kiokee Creek, for $400.

1812, Mar 12
RELINQUISHMENT - Peter CRAWFORD, attorney for Obedience LOWE, widow of Beverly LOWE, relinquishes dower unto Obediah LOWE; James CULBREATH, and John FOSTER, Exr., of estate, of Beverly Lowe.

1812, Aug 30
John COLLIER, Trustee for Esther MC EACHIN, formerly STALLINGS; Martha STALLINGS, now STANTON; and James STALLINGS, for $800., sells to Notley WHITCOMB, 574 acres, part of a 1000 acre

tract formerly granted to James STALLINGS, SR., Esq., dec'd. Seized and sold as property of said Stallings, and purchased by Richard WAYNE, of Savannah, and put in trust by him for above heirs.

1812, Sept 2
   BOND - Marshall MIMS; Thomas M. WHITE; and Pleasant BENNING, bound to Thomas MERIWETHER, Exr., of estate of Nicholas MERIWETHER, Whereas, Nicholas did give and bequeath to Matilda MERIWETHER, who since intermarried with Marshall Mims, slaves Sucky; Charles; Fancy; and Esther, appraised at $975., and duly delivered by said Thomas.

1812, Sept 12
   WRIT OF PARTITION - Heirs of Lewis GARDNER; Sarah; Lewis, Jr; Jesse; Stephen HOGE, in right of wife, Ann GARDNER; Polly; Nancy Verlinder HARRIS, and Gray BYNUM, represented by their guardian, Lewis GARDNER, and Rachel ALLISON; represented by her guardian, Verlinda GARDNER, widow of Lewis Gardner, Sr., dec'd. They possess, as co-heirs, 610 acres on Kiokee Creek, 116 1/2 acres on Savannah River, being upper end of Germany's Island; one other tract of 14 acres on Savannah River. A petition that such lands be laid off, by Writ of Partition, agreed to by Act of Assembly, each heir to have 1/9th. Therefore, the Commissioners, Anderson CRAWFORD; Solomon MARSHALL; Hugh BLAIR, SR; William WILKINS; John CULBREATH; Levi MARSHALL; John WALTON; William LOWE; Thomas COBBS; Joseph BLUNT; and Ambrose JONES, or a majority of your proper persons, are to go to said tracts, and in presence of interested parties, cause to be assigned 1/9th of said lands to each heir, to be held severally by themselves.

1812, Oct 12
   RECEIPT - William SAMUEL to George TANKERSLEY, Rec'd., of G. Tankersley, Exr., of estate of William JACKSON, the legacy in full, both real and personal, devised to my wife, Maria (late JACKSON), by her dec'd father. (Wm. Samuel & Maria Jackson m. Aug 1, 1800) Receipt from Wm. Jackson to same, for legacy from father.

1812, Oct 21
   RELINQUISHMENT - Archibald MC EACHIN, to John COLLIER, Trustee, for $100., do sign over and relinquish all right and title I have, through my wife, Esther (STALLINGS) MC EACHIN, to estate of her father, dec'd.

1813, Mar 19
   HEIRS' AGREEMENT - Sarah and Rebecca LESLIE, to Notley WHITCOMB; since Joseph LESLIE died and left five heirs, and 113 acres of land, the following arrangement took place: Notley Whitcomb purchased the interest of John MORRIS, who intermarried with Nancy LESLIE. Sarah LESLIE has purchased the interest of Betty LESLIE, who has married Morriss KELLY. Robert LESLIE, having died, his share, by will, left to said Sarah and Rebecca, have petitioned commissioners to lay off the land so that Sarah is to have 3/5ths, and Notley and Rebecca 1/5th each. All parties put under $500., bond to abide by decision. (Name also given as "Lashley.") Notley Whitcomb m. Rebecca, Oct 4, 1813.

1813, Mar 24
  MORTGAGE - John HATTAWAY mortgages negro boy, Dublin, to Thomas COBBS, for $60.

1813, Apr 7
  DEED OF TRUST - George RAY, has entrusted to friend John STITH, 100 acres of land on Whiteoak Creek, for use and benefit of beloved dau., Sarah HILL, and husband, John HILL.

1813, May 17
  NULLIFICATION OF CONTRACT - George MURPHY to S. SULLIVAN, "I have this day taken back all the said land Sullivan holds by virtue of a deed from me, on Little River." (Land had been included in a contract, and Murphy declares that he no longer considers himself bound by it.)

1813, Dec 20
  RELEASE - Thomas W. COBBS, to heirs of William COBBS: Thomas; Lewis; and William Beckham COBBS, dec'd., by will, did devise the tract of land whereon he lived, 300 acres, to wife, Catherine, and at her death to go to Thomas Cobbs grandsons, Thomas and Lewis, and great grandson, William Beckham Cobbs, on compliance of said Thomas to his will; for $2.00, doth release said tract unto them as above named.

1813, Dec 24
  RELINQUISHMENT - Byrd FERRELL, of Hancock Co., to Abraham MARSHALL; William MC GRUDER; Eliza FERRELL (formerly McGruder-Graves), for $5.00, relinquishes all right in tracts of land, as follows: To William McGruder, 1/6th tract in Wilkes Co., at mouth of Long Creek, on Broad River, left to Elizabeth GRAVES, now Ferrell, by will of Humphrey GRAVES, dec'd. 1/6th of a 600 acre tract in Jackson Co., left as aforesaid; one other tract in Elbert Co., on Savannah River; 1/6th of 500 acre tract left as aforesaid. One other tract in Columbia Co., whereon Basil McGruder, dec'd., lived. Three negro women, Dinah; Caty; and Rachel; one bed and furnishings; mahogany bureau, with all and singular the rights I have in aforementioned land.

1813, Dec 31
  MORTGAGE - Thomas JONES, indebted for $118., to Thomas SHORT, and Joseph MILLER, agents for John MOTE, and a second note of $21.05, mortgages 200 acres on Germany Creek, sold to him by Robt. ROZAR.

1814, Feb 8
  BOND - Eleanor STURGIS, is bound to John STURGIS, for $3,000., to be paid to John by Exrs., of estate of Reverend David STURGIS, David left wife, Eleanor, whole of estate, during her natural life, and to go to John at her death. "Whereas, Eleanor Sturgis has contemplated moving out of the county," she agrees to relinquish all right and title, if John will let her take Bob and Milly, negroes, and one bed and furniture with her.

1814, June 22
    MORTGAGE - Lewis POWELL, in debt to Thomas CARR, attorney at law, for sum of $500., mortgages 100 acres of land on Little Kiokee Creek.

1814, Aug 14
    APPRENTICESHIP INDENTURE - Sally Scott, a woman of color, to Berry OLIVE: "For and in consideration of natural love I have for Berry Olive and his family, as well as his being owner of my husband, the father of my children,"'indentures and binds herself for a term of 99 years,' and "do oblige myself to serve the said Berry Olive and/or his legal representatives as a faithful servant. I also bind my two female children, being also persons of color: Dice, about 8 years old, and Rebekah, about 6, to faithfully serve him and at all times obey, until they reach the age of 21." Berry Olive, on his part, agrees to provide Sally and her two children with sufficient meat, drink, clothing and lodging, suited to the different seasons, and at all times treat them with humanity.

1815, Jan 23
    MORTGAGE - Dreadzil PACE, in debt to William JACKSON, for sum of $2,000., mortgages 230 acre tract on Savannah River.

1815, Jan 23
    MORTGAGE - Joseph DAVIS to Robert JOHNSON, and John MC HAMZIE, of Augusta, mortgages land on Big Sweetwater Creek, 559 acres, part of three tracts originally granted to Matthew BURNSIDES, of 100 acres; 350 acres; and 600 acres, respectively.

1815, Jan 23
    DEED OF TRUST - Sarah ROSS, widow, appoints John MC KINNE, of the City of Augusta, trustee for all land where Sarah now lives, on waters of Michael's Creek, 357 acres, to hold said land in trust for Caesar McCredie, a man of color, who said McKinne has purchased from Mrs. Ross, for $2,770.

1815, Jan 25
    DEED OF TRUST - Frances YOUNGBLOOD has appointed Littleton YARBOROUGH, trustee for, "my beloved daughter, Scinthia, a minor," and is to hold in trust for her, negroes: Ally and five children; Harry; Cary; Mary; Isaac and Sam; 5 head of cattle; 10 hogs; 2 featherbeds and furnishings; all household and kitchen furniture.

1815, Jan 25
    RELINQUISHMENT - Richard MERIWETHER; Mary WHITE; Thomas M. WHITE; Thomas MERIWETHER; William MERIWETHER; and Frances MERIWETHER, forever Quit Claim to following property, as heirs and representatives of Nicholas MERIWETHER, dec'd: Plantation containing 300 acres where said Nicholas lived; one square in Baldwin Co., 202 1/2 acres, drawn by Thomas Meriwether; household and kitchen furniture; 2 stills; wagon; plantation utensils; also stock of every kind; negroes, Stephen; Lucy, his wife; Jane; Ned; Frank; Jacob; Mercer; Isaac; Rache; Robert; Cass; Polly; Betsey; Sucky; and Frank. We relinquish all said property to Micah Evans, woman of color, according to the will of dec'd Nicholas Meriwether.

1815, Jan 30
AUCTION - Obediah and William JONES, Adms., of Hezekiah JONES, sell 130 acres on both sides of the Washington Road. John FURY high bidder, @ $1,400.

1815, Feb 2
PARTITION - A petition addressed to Commissioners Marshall KEITH; Samuel BLACKWELL; James BURROUGHS; Notley WHITCOMB; John COLLIER; William COLLIER; Thomas DENT; George DENT; Asaph WATERMAN; John SKINNER; and Littleberry CLANTON, by Henry STANTON, in right of his wife, Martha, late Martha STALLINGS, and Peter CRAWFORD, guardian of James STALLINGS, minor, which Martha and James have survived Esther MC EACHIN, late STALLINGS, heirs of estate they hold as tenants in fee simple, a tract of 712 acres on Savannah River, conveyed by Richard WAYNE to John COLLIER, in trust for above heirs. Petition for land to be partitioned granted. Partitioners appointed: Thomas Dent; John Skinner; William Collier; Asaph Waterman; Notley Whitcomb; and John Collier. They declare that 370 1/2 acres be alloted to Henry STANTON, in right of his wife, and 331 1/2 acres to Peter Crawford, for James Stallings, minor. (Something wrong with their addition - only adds to 702 acres.)

1816, Feb 6
PARTITION - Commissioners John B. BARNES; William UNDERWOOD; William THOMAS; Jonathon WOOD; Thomas DAVIS; Harwood ROBERTS; James WALTON; Peter James BURROUGHS; and John BEALLE, are petitioned for Writ of Partition by Eleanor DAVIS, widow of Blanford DAVIS; Arthur FOSTER, in right of wife, Polly; Thomas HOWARD, in right of wife, Henrietta; Nancy and Verlinda DAVIS (represented by their guardian, Eleanor Davis, relict. They wish the property divided into equal shares, also a Writ of Dower granted to widow.

1815, Mar 6
RELINQUISHMENT - Alexander MC DONALD, to Thomas COLEMAN, of Wilkes Co., for $750., all right, title and interest, "I have in estate of my Grandfather, James MC FARLAND, and do hereby empower said Coleman to request a partition of said estate."

1815, Mar 16
MORTGAGE - Vincent PERRYMAN to Joseph MARSHALL, for $438., mortgages negro man, Abraham, and all the blacksmith's tools.

1815, May 4
AUCTION OF SLAVE - Adms., of estate of Daniel MARSHALL, auction girl, Betty, to Joseph MARSHALL, for $414.

1815, June 19
QUIT CLAIM - John NOLAND, of Wilkes Co., renounces all right, title or demand on 467 acre tract in Columbia Co., to Willoughby BARTON, for $6,000.

1815, July 12
John NEILSON, to Thomas NEILSON, of Petersburg, Va., indebted by a certain obligation for $7,000., gives title to 865 acre tract

in Columbia Co., also negro woman, Caroline, aged 23, and her three
children, Diana, 7; Ossian, 5; John, 6 mos; also Joe, 10 years, and
Davy, husband of said Caroline, about 26.

1815, July 12
RELINQUISHMENT - William BALDWIN, to Owen BALDWIN, for $100.,
all right and title to, "my share of estate of my father, David
BALDWIN, dec'd." Also Aron PARKES, to Owen Baldwin, any claim to
estate of David Baldwin, dec'd., in right of first wife, Ann Parkes.
Parkes & Anne Baldwin m., Richmond Co., Aug 27, 1787. He m. Elizabeth Ryan, July 30, 1810.

1815, Oct 19
RECEIPT - Micah Evans, woman of color, to Thomas MERIWETHER,
gives receipt for estate left to her by Nicholas MERIWETHER, "But
not to be understood as excusing Thomas Meriwether from payment of
$2,000., left to me in last will and testament of Thomas Meriwether,
dec'd."

1815, Oct 12
SHERIFF'S SALE - William FLEMING, to Robert RANDOLPH, on writ
of Exrs., of James MOSSMAN, against Robert Randolph, Exr., of estate
of Thomas NAPIER. Sheriff seized a 700 acre tract of land, and
sold it to Robert Randolph, as high bidder.

1810, _____ Rec. Mar 29, 1816
INDENTURE - Sally Scott, woman of color, to Mary JONES, of
Wake Co., N. C., binds her female child, Rebecca, now about 4 years
old, to Mary Jones, until said child reaches age of 21. Mary is to
give the child sufficient meat, drink, lodging and clothing. Also
binds child, Dicy. (Evidently this indenture did not hold good,
as on August 14, 1814, she bound the same children to Berry OLIVE.)

1816, May 10
RELINQUISHMENT - John MC COY, and wife, Mary, relinquish all
claim and title to an 89 1/2 acre tract, to Peter FOUNTAIN, for $150.

1810, May 2 - Rec. May 8, 1816
Willoughby SLATON, and wife, Elizabeth (LOWE) SLATON, to heirs
of Isaac LOWE, dec'd., viz: Curtis; Isaac; Sarah; Elizabeth; David;
George; Hester; Martha; Rebecca; and Matilda LOWE, and Mary (Lowe)
Slaton, children of said Elizabeth by her former husband, Isaac
Lowe, dec'd. All right and title to property left by Elizabeth's
father, David WALKER, dec'd.

1816, June 6
APPRENTICESHIP - Sarah ROBERTS, mother and guardian of infant
son, Thomas, aged 2 years and 3 months, doth bind him as apprentice
until he reaches the age of 21, to learn the art of practical farming, under the care of John MILTON. He shall conduct himself in
orderly fashion, nor frequent taverns or gaming houses, not to play
at unlawful games, and is to obey the commands of his master.

_____ Rec. July 3, 1815
DEED GRANTED - Abraham HOWARD, Sec'y. of State, to the Commissioners of Wilkes Academy: Whereas, Nicholas LONG; Philip CLAYTON; and Josiah TATTNALL, Commissioners of Confiscated Lands, did expose to public sale, 1,000 acres then in St. Paul's Parish (No date given, but had to be before 1777), it was purchased by Micajah WILLIAMSON for Wilkes Academy. No deed of conveyance was ever given, and upon petition by said Commissioners, deed granted by Abner HAMMOND, to 1,000 acres originally granted to John GRAHAM, Oct 4, 1774.

1816, Oct 22
MORTGAGE - Mary Ann D. BARNES, indebted to Richard TUBMAN, of Richmond Co., for $7,824.78 1/4, by note of hand, for securing said debt, mortgages 808 acres on Uchee Creek; one negro man, Stephen, 25 years old, of dark complexion.

1817, Nov 13
EXECUTORS' SALE - John LYON, and Samuel CRUMP, Exrs., of estate of James EUBANKS, sell at auction, by order of Court, 150 acres on Keg Creek, to William EUBANKS, high bidder, @ $521.

1816, Nov 27
WRIT OF PARTITION - To Commissioners, William JONES; John LYON; William FLEMING; Jeremiah BLANCHARD; and Thomas AYERS, Greetings! Whereas, John CARTLEDGE; James ROBERTSON (in right of his wife, Polly Cartledge Robertson); James ALEXANDER, represented by his Agent, James BLANCHARD; and James B. BLANCHARD, guardian of Elizabeth and Sarah CARTLEDGE, minors, the heirs and distributors of the estate of John and Jane CARTLEDGE, dec'd. Desire partition of 200 acres on Keg Creek. Therefore, a majority of you are requested to go to the above tract, and in presence of the heirs or their agents, cause to be divided into 5 equal shares, the said lands: Commissioners' Return: To James Alexander, Lot #1 - 40 acres; to John Cartledge, Lot #2 - 73 1/2 acres; to James Robertson, Lot #3 - 73 1/2 acres; to Elizabeth Cartledge, Lot #4 - 62 1/2 acres; to Sarah Cartledge, Lot #5 - 100 acres. (If it appears that some of the heirs got more land than others, it only means that some of the land was not valued as highly as the rest, and an effort to equalize the shares was made, by making some of the lots larger)

1816, Nov 28
WRIT OF DOWER & PARTITION OF ESTATE - On estate of John O. PEARRE, same procedure followed as above. Elizabeth PEARRE, wid., of John Pearre, in right of self and as guardian of Alexander Pearre, minor; and James TOOLE, in right of his wife, Lucy (Pearre) Toole, desire a 430 acre tract divided by Commissioners: Return: 1/3rd, or 173 acres to Elizabeth, as dower; 100 acres to Elizabeth as guardian of Alexander; 117 acres to J. T. ALLEN, as guardian of James; 130 acres to James Toole, for wife Lucy.

1816, Dec 3
WRIT OF PARTITION- Usual procedure, for partition of 474 acres, estate of James GERMANY, dec'd. William COLLIER, and wife, Sarah

(Germany) COLLIER; William COLLIER, as guardian of Maria GERMANY; Richard JELKS, and wife, Hannah, widow of James GERMANY, heirs and representatives of James Germany, dec'd. Returns: 1/4 (no acerage given), to William Collier, and wife; 1/4 to William Collier, as guardian for Maria Germany (150 acres); 1/4 to Richard Jelks (no acerage given), and wife; 95 acres to John Collier, as guardian of Sarah.

1818, Jan __
Marshall MIMS to Thomas MERIWETHER; "Dear Sir: I rec'd your letter by Robert MERIWETHER, and learn that you are anxious to settle the $2,000., suit, for part. I do not wish to be contrary, and as they have all agreed to the compromise, you may proceed as quickly as possible to settle it, but it has turned out just as I always predicted. I must confess, it does not agree so well with me, but has been managed so imprudently, you must do the best you can." s/ Marshall Mims. (This has reference to a suit brought by Micah Evans, colored woman, and legatee of Thomas and Nicholas Meriwether).

1817, Feb 13
MORTGAGE - William THOMAS, for further securing a note for $4,000., mortgages to Andrew WATKINS, 200 acres (formerly granted to C. SMITH); 150 acres (formerly granted to William SIMS); 70 acres (formerly granted to D. TINSLEY); 30 acres (formerly granted to S. DARK); all tracts contiguous, on Savage's Creek, also 400 acres on Savage's Mill Creek, one mile from Saratoga, known as Tinsley's tract.

1817, Feb 13
RELINQUISHMENT - Daniel COLEMAN, to Andrew SHEPHERD, both of Wilkes Co., for $530., relinquishes all right and title to John MCDONALD'S estate, both real and personal, which was the estate of his grandfather, James MC FARLAND, negroes excepted. "Property was purchased by my father, conveyed by him to John McDonald, and by him to me."

1817, July 22
MORTGAGE - John AYERS, indebted to Peter and Nathaniel CRAWFORD, for sum of $150., gives a mortgage on 120 acres of land on Hart's Creek, originally granted to Henry JONES, by him to Richard JOWELL, by him to William WARE, and by him to me.

1817, Aug 9
WRIT OF PARTITION - Mary FLEMING, relict of James FLEMING, dec'd., Samuel; Robert; John; William; David BUSSEY, in right of wife, Eleanor, late Fleming; John FLEMING, in right of wife, Mary, formerly FLEMING, and Mary, relict, as guardian of Agnes; Laird Fleming, and Joel; petition to have division made of 204 acres. Return: 204 acres divided into 10 equal parts: Mary #8, 49 acres; Samuel #5, 35 1/2 acres; Robert, #4, 35 1/2 acres; John #3, 35 1/2 acres; William #6, 49 acres; David Bussey, #1, 33 acres; John, for wife, Mary, #7, 49 acres; Agnes, minor, #9, 49 acres; James, minor, #10, 35 acres; Laird, minor, #2, 35 acres; Joel, minor, residue.

1817, Aug 31
WRIT OF PARTITION - John COCHRAN, in right of wife, Mary for-

merly Stuart; Margaret WILLSON, formerly Stuart; John COLLINS, in right of wife, Nancy (Stuart); also as guardian of Elizabeth and Isabella STUART; Anderson CRAWFORD, guardian of Jane and James STUART; John MC CORD, next friend to William McCord, heirs and representatives of estate of James STUART, dec'd., partition to have 925 acre tract equally divided. Tract consists of 500 acres conveyed by Thomas YOUNG, May 12, 1795; 300 acres conveyed by Cornelius DYSART, Nov 27, 1789; 125 acres conveyed by Jason GARDNER, Oct 12, 1800. Returns: 1/4th share, including mansion house, delivered to John McCord, parent and next friend to William McCord. Balance divided into shares: #3, John Cochran, 101 acres; #2, Margaret Willson, 101 acres; #1, John Collins, 80 shares; #4, Elizabeth Stuart, 160 acres; #5, Isabella, 120 acres; #7, Jane Stuart, 135 acres; #6, James, bal.

1817, Aug 27
    PARTITION - William; Joseph; Samuel; Elizabeth; Artimissy; Henry; and Robert, heirs to Robert JAMERSON, dec'd., petition a division of land: #1, William, 47 1/2 acres, valued @ $248., #5, Joseph, 47 1/2 acres, valued @ $192., #6, Samuel; 47 1/2 acres, valued @ $180., #7, Elizabeth, 47 1/2 acres, valued @ $120., #4, Henry, 47 1/2 acres, on Keg Creek, valued @ $48., #3, Artimissa, 47 1/2 acres, on Bird's Branch, valued @ $72., #2, Robert, balance, valued @ $48. In order to make all shares equal 1/7th, or $129.71 3/7ths, some heirs had to pay certain sums, so it would all balance.

1817, Sept 3
    ARBITRATION - William MURRAY, and John SEAY, having disputed over ownership of certain piece of land on Mountain Branch, case turned over to panel of arbitrators: Billington SANDERS; and William WALTON. Decided in favor of Murray, Seay to pay all Court costs. Each put under $1,000.

1817, Oct 20
    GUARDIAN'S SALE - William BARNETT, guardian of minors of Joseph RAY, dec'd., received permission of Court to sell land from estate, for benefit of minors. Sells to William MURRAY, for $630., 70 acres at confluence of Little River and Upton's Creek, contiguous to Murray's holdings, part of a 750 acre tract sold to Ray, by Commissioners For Confiscated Lands, Josiah TATTNALL; Philip CLAYTON, and Nicholas LONG, in 1794.

1817, Oct 23
    MORTGAGE - Leonard THOMPSON, indebted to Thomas COBBS, of Oglethorpe Co., for $1,000., secures said debt by mortgaging land on North fork of Greenbriar Creek, adj., Thomas Cobb's land, 403 acres, and next, for $1,000., mortgages negroes: Philip; Aggy, and Pinkey.

1817, Oct 27
    MORTGAGE - Littleberry CLANTON, indebted to Thomas PARHAM, for $1,592., mortgages 324 acres on Euchee Creek, including plantation where Parham now lives.

1818, Jan 14
    MORTGAGE - Hundley BOSWELL, indebted to John HOWARD, for $800.,

mortgages a man, Edmond, and woman, Juno.

1818, Jan 14
    TRUSTEE'S PURCHASE - Walter DRANE, to James ROSS, trustee for Susan Ann Green WALL, minor daughter of Benjamin WALL, of Savannah. Drane being attorney for Abraham GINDRAT, of Bryan Co., sells 100 acres to Ross, for $300. Land located in Wrightsborough, and was granted originally to James MC CAY.

1818, Feb 23
    RELINQUISHMENT - Elias WELBOURNE, to John PITTMAN, JR., for $10., a 2 acre tract on road from Augusta to Washington, by Raysville.

1818, Feb 25
    DEED OF TRUST - "Know all men, by these presents, that I, Henry Willis COBBS, conscious of the uncertainty of life, and the frailty of human nature, do constitute my friends, Edmond BUGG; Capt. John WATSON; R. Y. LANGSTON, of this county, and my brother, John COBBS, and Mr. H. JACKSON, of Jefferson county, the lawfull trustees for my heirs, with control over my property, real and personal. 301 acres whereon I now dwell, and another tract of 340 acres, known as Fruit Hill, adj., above mentioned land. The following negroes: Will, and wife, Molly, their children, George; Ned; Sally; Nelly; Betsy; Danil; Jenny; Renny; Charity; Maryann; Adeline; William, and Edy. Nelly's children, Martha and Tubby. Sally's child, John. David and wife, Nanney. Reuben and wife, Rose, and their children, Louisa; Charlotte; Reuben, and Aggy. Isabel and her children, Eliza; Alfred and Nancy. The girl Betsy, the fellows, Old Bacchus and Young Bacchus, Neptune; Glasgow; Dick and Joseph. Likewise, the fellow, Joab, which I had at Sheriff's sale, property of John HATTAWAY. If heirs will pay $317., they can have him back. Likewise, Phillis and Jim, now in possession of brother, John Cobb. I own jointly with Roger HARKIN, negroes: Adam; Billy; David; Len; Howell; Jacob; Judith; Jack; Lucy, and her child Betsy, purchased from Augustus NAPIER. If Napier or his heirs pay $700., plus interest, my share of said negroes shall be returned to said Augustus Napier.

1818, Jan 25
    TRUST - Richard MERIWETHER, to Peter CRAWFORD, for $95., has conveyed a tract of 21 acres on Lloyd's Creek, in trust for Jack BARNES (or BURNES?).

1818, Mar 19
    TAX SALE - John LAMAR, Tax Collector, sells to William WALTON, for $10., 100 acres seized from Richard RYAN, who is in default.

1818, Apr 14
    TRUST - Bennett CRAFTON, of Richmond Co., appoints John MC-KINNE, of Augusta, trustee for Caesar McCradie, a man of color. For sum of $4,164., paid by McKinne, does sell tract of land whereon Sarah POPE lived, 400 acres on Michael's Creek, held in trust for Caesar McCredie.

1818, July 10
QUIT CLAIM - Robert GILMER, and William PATTERSON, of Baltimore Md., to Henry Willis COBBS, for $1,000., sign a Quit Claim, relinquishing all right and title to estate known as Fruit Hill, which the above purchased from Charles CROOKSHANKS, May 4, 1792.

1818, July 19
AGREEMENT - Between, Sarah TELFAIR; Thomas; Alexander; Mary; Margaret TELFAIR, and Sarah HAIG, and Thomas and Alexander TELFAIR, trusteed under a marriage settlement between George HAIG, and said Sarah, of first part, and Jared POUNDS, for $1,000., 200 acre tract on Greenbriar Creek, part of tracts granted to Benjamin FEW; John HOWARD, and John UPTON.

1818, July 15
GUARDIAN'S SALE - William BARNETT, guardian of minors of Joseph RAY, dec'd., sells, by order of Court, to Jeremiah GRIFFIN, 470 acres on Little River, for $3,525.

1811, Mar 26 - Rec. July 21, 1818
RELINQUISHMENT OF DOWER - Eliza LAMAR, formerly WINFREY, of S. C., wid., of Thomas LAMAR, dec'd., relinquishes all right and title to a 300 acre tract in Columbia Co., conveyed by Thomas LAMAR, to William JONES. (She did not renounce her dower rights at the time the land was conveyed, but realizing that Jones had paid a valuable consideration for land, now renounced all rights of dower.)

1818, Nov 6
EXECUTORS' SALE - Nathan and Peter CRAWFORD, Exrs., of estate of Charles CRAWFORD, dec'd., are authorized by Inferior Court to sell land. Auction held, and Edward BOWDRE was high bidder for 2,400 acres on Dyas' Creek. The tract included 5 different surveys. Price $12,000. Same day, Bowdre resold land to Peter Crawford, $12,000.

1818, Nov 12
AGREEMENT - Between John T. ALLEN, Esq. and Frances A. WINFREY, relict of Jesse WINFREY, dec'd., and Benjamin, their son, by will of of said Jesse, wife is entitled to a considerable part of personal estate and mansion house on plantation. Agreed, that Frances shall live on land until she remarries, or until minors reach 21, when it shall revert to them. Whereas, a treaty of marriage hath been "agitated?" and concluded between said Allen and Mrs. Winfrey, it is understood that after they are married, she shall be at full liberty, without let nor hindrance from said Allen, to hold, use, and enjoy any of said property she now possesses, as if she were unmarried, any law, usage or custom to the contrary, not withstanding. If said Frances shall outlive John Allen, he shall leave her in as comfortable, eligible, advantageous, and ample a situation as regarding a mansion or residence as she now enjoys, on the property of Jesse Winfrey, which upon the solemnization she will relinquish. Any property which shall be legally hers is to be under her own separate control.

1818, Dec 12
DEED OF TRUST - William PEARRE, to Jesse OFFUTT, for $1.00., property in trust for wife, Agnes Pearre, and heirs of her body: All

my estate, both real and personal, including 1/3rd of tract on
Satilla. All negroes: Lucy, 27; Jude, 20; Rachel, 7; Sal, 5; Hannah, 2; Sidney, 6 mos. All household and kitchen furniture.

1819, Jan 4
MORTGAGE - Farley ADAMS, indebted to David LANGSTON, of Oglethorpe Co., for sum of $2,566.66 2/3, for better securing said debt, mortgages 730 acre tract on Germany Creek.

1819, Jan 13
AGREEMENT - Between Garah DAVIS, Peggy, his wife, and William MC GRUDER. Whereas, serious, dispassionate, consultation and understanding has taken place between Garah and Peggy, by reason of justice, propriety and prudence of providing and securing to said Peggy a competent maintainance suitable to the abilities of said Garah, and commensurate with the industry, thrift and exertion which said Peggy put into the accumulation of estate, to prevent all interruptions, expenses and delays, they have agreed to division of estate: Garah gives to Peggy, negro women: Sylvia and Margaret, and girl, Frances; 1/4th of money arising from whole residue of estate, when sold and converted, will pay off all Peggy's debts as long as they shall mutually cohabit. After death of Peggy, property to go to Richard Davis and Erasmus P. H. Davis. (Seems couple contemplated divorce).

1819, Feb 15
TRUST - John LARKIN appoints James and Elizabeth trustees for a negro girl, given in trust, "for kindness and affection I have for Mary TOOLE, daughter of Dr. James TOOLE, and his wife, Lucy."

1819, Apr 27
MORTGAGE - George and James CARY, indebted to Barrett AMES, and Richard ALLEN, of Augusta, for the sum of $2,469.95, "mortgage a store, house and lot, in Fredricktown, Md."

1819, Aug 2
DEED OF TRUST - Triplett SHUMATE, to Arthur FOSTER, and John W. BEALLE, as trustees for beloved wife, Rebecca SHUMATE, property as follows; negro woman, Chloe, and child Solomon; $1,000., in cash; gray mare and gig; 4 head of cattle; 20 hogs; 3 bedsteads and furnishings; 1 mahogany dining table; 1 pine sideboard; all balance of household and kitchen furniture, all present growing crops, and all claim I may have in undivided estate of Timothy BARHAM, real and personal.

1819, Aug 20
RELINQUISHMENT - Samuel and Frances COBB, former wife of William WARE, possessing a tract of land on Headstall Creek, by will of William Ware (Will entered in books as "Wheer"), relinquishes all right and title to said land to John MC CORMICK.

1819, Aug 30
RELINQUISHMENT - James WALTON, and wife, Elizabeth, to William YARBOROUGH, for $450., paid, renounce all claim to estate of Littleton YARBOROUGH. (Elizabeth was wid., of Littleton, m. in Richmond

County, 1788.)

1819, Nov 2
   Whereas, Triplett SHUMATE left certain property in trust with Arthur FOSTER, and John BEALLE, said trustees hereby relinquish trusteeship, and return property to control of Rebecca SHUMATE.

1820, Jan 11
   MORTGAGE - Patrick ROBINSON, of Wrightsborough, to Gregory MC KENZIE, and Hardin BANNOCK & Co., to secure notes for $1,520., and $760., mortgages negroes: Ralph, a black boy, about 16; Daniel, a black boy, about 9; Cynthia, a yellow girl, about 12; and Luanda, a black girl, about 7.

1820, Mar 15
   LEASE - Joel WILLIS to Frances YOUNGBLOOD, spinster, 1 acre of land on East corner of Willis' land, adj., Union Meeting House land, including house, etc., with privilege to cut wood for her own fire, only, on remaining Willis land. No price mentioned.

1820, Apr 25
   DEED OF TRUST - Henry COBBS, to brother John A. COBBS, of Jefferson Co., Edmond BUGG, and John WATSON, of Columbia Co., for $10., property in trust for wife, Obedience, and children. 300 acres conveyed by E. Bugg to Henry Cobbs; 310 acres conveyed by Thomas DUNAWAY, as agent for William PATTERSON and Robert GILMER, of Baltimore, Md., known as, "Fruit Hill." 400 acres conveyed by Leonard THOMPSON, whereon Cobbs now lives. Also negro slaves: Will; Molly; George; Ned; Sally; Nelly; Betsey; Davy; Jenny; Rang(?); Charity; Maryann; Adeline; Willis; Eady; Nelly; Martha; Tabby; John; David; Nancy; Reuben; Rose; Louisa; Charlotte; Little Reuben; Aggy; Isabelle; Eliza; Alfred; Nancy; Betty; Old Baccus; Young Baccus; Neptune; Glasgow; Dick; Joe; Ann; Phillip; and Sally, with the little children. All stock of horses; cattle; hogs; and sheep. Carriages, gears; plantation tools; implements of husbandry; household and kitchen furniture; and every species of personal property, which I now possess, without specific detail.

1820, Apr 27
   TRUSTEES' SALE - Trustees of William CRAWFORD (Anderson CRAWFORD; John SMITH; and Peter CRAWFORD), sell to John HOWARD, of Augusta, for $2,500., all property on Savage's Creek, which was left by William in trust for his family. By order of the Court.

1820, May 11
   AUCTION - William WILKINS, Sheriff, to Obedience OFFUTT, wid., of Jesse OFFUTT, property sold at auction, at order of Court, on suit of Jesse CAWTHORN, for $40., paid by Obedience Offutt, highest bidder. Sheriff sells 425 acres on Main Road, and Sweetwater Creek, now occupied by William PEARRE.

1820, Nov 20
   DEED OF TRUST - Nathan PEARRE to Lindsey COLEMAN, for $5., negroes: Amy; Sylvy; Mariah; Joe; Jim; Henry; Moll; Darkas; Tiller; Charley; and Jincey. The sorrel mare; 13 head of cattle; 60 hogs;

5 beds and furniture; and all other property, in trust for my wife, Rebecca PEARRE, and our children.

1820, Nov 22
    HEIRS' SALE - Elijah WILLINGHAM; Thomas WILLINGHAM, and Thomas, as agent for Jesse ROBERTS; Elizabeth WILLINGHAM; George WILLINGHAM; for self and as agent for Beverly WILLINGHAM; John WILLINGHAM; Nancy WILLINGHAM; and Reuben WILLINGHAM; Edward GAITHER; Isaac WILLINGHAM, for self, and as agent for Caleb WILLINGHAM; sell to William WILLINGHAM, 180 acres on Keg Creek, for $550.

1821, Jan 3
    AWARD - Thomas HEMPHILL, Exr., of last Will and Testament of Joseph RAY, dec'd., heirs of same: By order of the Superior Court: William BARNETT, in right of wife, Nancy (or Ann), formerly RAY; William BARNETT, as guardian of William and Henry RAY, minors; Jeremiah GRIFFIN, as Exr., of John RAY; Andrew WEST, as Exr., of Henry WEST, and James Ray, legatees. Thomas Hemphill is ordered to pay to said heirs all monies he holds as Exr., of estate of Joseph Ray, dec'd. All bonds; notes; accounts and books of accounts.

1821, Jan 3
    RECEIPT - Heirs of Joseph RAY to Thomas HEMPHILL, "Rec'd. all monies, notes, accounts and bonds, and do absolutely and forever acquit, release, and discharge said Thomas as Executor."

1821, Jan 3
    AGREEMENT - Joseph TANKERSLEY, of Columbia Co; Elizabeth CRAFTON; Lucy SAMUEL; and Mary WARE, of Edgefield Dist., S. C., William B. TANKERSLEY; Joseph TANKERSLEY, JR; George TANKERSLEY; Robert TANKERSLEY; Dread PACE, JR, in right of wife, Elcy (or Alice); Elizabeth TANKERSLEY, by her guardian, Dreadzil PACE, SR., -vs- Elizabeth TANKERSLEY, relict of George TANKERSLEY, dec'd., they having no children, and a considerable estate, both real and personal, the heirs and representatives bind themselves to a division of property. Administrators hereafter to be appointed shall deliver to Elizabeth, wid., all bonds; notes, etc., of estate of Williams JACKSON, dec'd. On payment of $10,000., will relinquish all claim to estate of Tankersley to said Elizabeth. (Elizabeth, former widow of Williams JACKSON, m. Tankersley on July 8, 1798.)

1821, Jan 4
    LETTERS OF ADMINISTRATION - Heirs of George TANKERSLEY grant Letters of Administration to Dreadzil PACE, SR., William B. TANKERSLEY; John WILLIAMS; and Bennett CRAFTON. If John Williams declines, George Tankersley shall serve in his place.

1821, Jan 18
    AGREEMENT - Heirs of George TANKERSLEY, in consequence of sum of $6,050., being paid by Elizabeth TANKERSLEY, relict, have relinquished all title to tract of land on Savannah River, 335 acres, between Big and Little Kiokee Creeks, granted to Thomas HAYNES, Dec. 5, 1796; part of a tract of 200 acres granted to Ralph KILGORE, Dec. 15, 1796, on Savannah River, and Big Kiokee Creek, purchased by Williams JACK-

ON, dec'd. Left by will, to his three children, Richard; Mariah; nd Williams F. JACKSON. Sold by them to G. TANKERSLY, dec'd.

1821, Mar 20
BOND - William MURRAY and John LYNN are bound to each other for $1,000., if either shall dissent from decision of Joel LOCKHART, whom we agreed upon to run a dividing line," bond will be forfeited.

1821, Mar 23
HEIRS' SALE - Sarah and Shadrack W. GIBSON, Adms., of estate of Dexter GIBSON, do, by permission of Court, sell to H. BIRON, Lot # 27, in Wilkinson Co., 202 1/2 acres, for $75.

1821, Sept 4
TAX SALE - Ayers CARTLEDGE, Tax Collector, sells to Obedience OFFUTT, for $5.50., 200 acres on Kiokee Creek, the property of Jesse OFFUTT, dec'd., estate, defaulted. (Obedience was Jesse's widow).

1822, Jan 14
MORTGAGE - Nicholas WARE, indebted to Elizabeth TANKERSLEY, for $6,030., by three notes of hand, further secures said debt with a mortgage on three tracts of land on Savannah River, totalling 335 a.

1822, Jan 20
LETTERS OF ADMINISTRATION - John DORSETT granted Letters of Administration on estate of Richard JONES, who died intestate, rec. Jan 11, 1822. Jones left nuncupative will, in Wilkinson Co., Miss.

1822, Mar 5
MORTGAGE - Thomas BATTLE, indebted to John GIBSON, for $4,880., in promissory notes, secured debt with mortgage on 198 acres, bounded on East by Town of Wrightsborough, North by REES.

1822, Feb 9
HEIRS' SALE - Heirs of George TANKERSLEY, viz: Elizabeth CRAFTON; Lucy SAMUEL; Margaret WARE; Joseph TANKERSLEY, of Edgefield, S. C., Joseph TANKERSLEY, SR., Robert; William and George TANKERSLEY, of Columbia Co., Ga., and Dreadzil PACE, in right of his wife, Alice, sell to Elizabeth TANKERSLEY, widow of George Tankersley, dec'd., 269 1/2 acres on Uchee Creek, for $3,500.25.

1822, Mar 11
QUIT CLAIM - George WOODRUFF to William JONES, for $5.00., relinquished all claim to a 500 acre tract originally granted to Thomas MOORE, in Columbia Co.

1822, Mar 25
MORTGAGE - Thomas BAYLISS, to Isham BAYLISS, indebted for sum of $1,000., gives mortgage on 100 acres on Greenbriar Creek. Further indebted for $1,000., mortgages negroes: Monday, a man of 40; Louisa, and her two children, May and Allen; negro man, Bill, 21. All stock of hogs; cattle and sheep, and household and kitchen furniture.

1822, Apr 17
   William WILKINS, Sheriff, seizes and auctions off 700 acres on Little River, the property of William STARKE, whereon he lived, and owned a mill. Originally granted to Isaac DENNIS, in 1770. James HARVEY, high bidder, @ $1,000.

1822, May 2
   MORTGAGE - James STALLINGS, to John HOWARD, of Augusta, having signed promissory note for $3,144.96, secures note with a mortgage on 329 1/2 acres on Savannah River, formerly the property of his father, Joseph STALLINGS.

1822, May 7
   Angus FLINT, to James WRIGHT, for $300., negro boy, Floyed.

1822, May 9
   DEED OF TRUST - Elias WELBORNE, for love and affection for daughter, Mary FLEMING, and her children, gives, in trust with Elias A. WELBOURNE, and Marshall H. WELBOURNE, negroes, Fanny, 18; Rhoda, 11; Fanny's infant child, Eliza.

1822, June 9
   AUCTION - Triplett SHUMATE, Exr., of Benjamin BARHAM, sells at auction, by order of the Court, "16 acres where the house stands," formerly property of Timothy BARHAM. Zachariah GARNETT, high bidder for $50.

1822, June 9
   ADMINISTRATOR'S SALE - Perry GRAVES, Adm. of estate of Joshua GRAVES, upon petition of Bird FERRELL; Perry GRAVES; James PEARRE; Chloe GRAVES; and George GRAVES; for leave to sell, auctions off 143 3/4 acres in Jackson Co., granted to Thomas Perry. Michael DOUGHERTY, high bidder ...no price shown.

1822, June 11
   MARRIAGE CONTRACT - Whereas, Treacy MC GRUDER, widow of Zadack, and Samuel PAUL, have entered into an agreement to be married, George MC GRUDER, for the sum of $100., paid by said Samuel, as marriage portion, and for a competent provision for said Treacy, confirms all stock of horses; sheep; cows; hogs; plantation tools; carriage; household and kitchen furniture, together with 1/7th part of real estate.

1822, June 21
   HEIRS' AGREEMENT - "From the peculiar situation of personal property of John BEALLE, dec'd., the heirs agree that all, except negroes, should be sold at auction."

1822, Aug ___
   MORTGAGE - John FOSTER, by virtue of a note for $52., is bound unto Jonathan WOOD, for safe delivery of a bay horse, abour 9 years old; 1 roan mare, 4 years old; 2 bedsteads, beds and furnishings; 1 red cow; 1 red calf; and 1 white cow.

1821, _____ - Rec. Sept 17, 1822
Stephen TODD, agent for Robert HODGENS, both of Ohio, for $45., paid by Adam IVEY, relinquishes all claim to a tract of land in Columbey Co., and partly in Warren, it being Robert's share of estate of father, John HODGENS, on waters of Maddock's Creek.

1822, Sept 5
ASSIGNMENT - Jeremiah REES, to Adam SCOTT - "Whereas, I am indebted to Richard JONES, and Thomas DOOLY, Adms., of estate of Alan JONES, dec'd., for sum of $483., towards payment of said debt, I assign 2 negro boys, Ellick, 25, and Jack, 12."

1822, Oct 7
TAX SALE - Ayers CARTLEDGE, Tax Collector, sells to Thomas BEALLE, for $2.64 1/2 (back taxes for 1821), 350 acres on Greenbriar Creek, formerly the property of H. W. COBBS, in default.

1823, Jan 5
MORTGAGE - Charles BEALLE, indebted to Andrew JENNINGS, by a promissory note, for $1,087.68, secures note with mortgage on 115 acres on Kiokee Creek; also negroes: John, 18; Christian, 18; Nathan, 26; Nancy, 25; Esther, 30; Bill, 14; and Elizabeth, 9.

1823, Mar 28
Sheriff G. TANKERSLEY, sells at auction, 130 acres on Uchee Creek, to John MORRIS, high bidder, @ 80. Sheriff also auctions property of James WATSON, as result of suit brought by John OLIVE. Isaac WATSON purchases as high bidder, 1/6th of a 200 acre tract on Sweetwater Creek, adj., widow Watson, for $41.

1823, Mar 28
RELINQUISHMENT - William and James CARROLL relinquish to Mitchell CARROLL, 150 acres on Boggy Gut Creek, whereon he now lives, part of estate of William CARROLL, dec'd.

1823, May 26
MORTGAGE - Jubal Orion MARSHALL, to secure debt of $808.93 3/4, to Andrew JENNINGS; mortgages negroes: Sam; David; and Polydore.

1823, May 26
MORTGAGE - Ignatius A. FEW, in debt to John HOWARD, of Augusta, for the sum of $5,286., secures said note with a mortgage on 350 acres on Green Briar Creek, and three other tracts adj., 200 a., 53 a., 40 acres, respectively.

1823, Feb 4
AUCTION - George TANKERSLEY, Sheriff, seizes property of Allen LOVELACE, and sells it at auction. Waters BRISCOE, high bidder, @ $201., on tract on Germany Creek; also all estate and property of Allen Lovelace, in fee simple.

1823, June 1
MORTGAGE - Thomas D. CARR, bound with Nicholas WARE, on a note to Thomas CUMMING, of Augusta, $3,320., secures his share of note

with mortgage on negroes: Brittain; Big Daniel; Little Daniel; Sam;
John; Joe; Sue and Harry, also 1/2 share in lands in Columbia Co.,
"Whereon I now live, lately the residence of Col. Thomas CARR, dec'd.,
called, Alexandria."

1823, June 2
    AUCTION - George TANKERSLEY, Sheriff, on suit of Durger & Elliot,
agents of M. G. DAVIS, and Jeremiah REES, sells property of Jeremiah
at auction, consisting of Lots 64; 65; 66; and 67, in Town of Wrightsborough. Talbot REES, (son of Jeremiah), high bidder @ $596.

1823, June 26
    DIVISION - William THOMAS; Peter CRAWFORD; and Edmond ROBERTS,
divide a piece of land between John and Charles BEALLE. (No amt gvn.)

1823, Mar 23
    AGREEMENT - Whereas, Col. Thomas CARR, dec'd., did, by Will,
leave all lands on Germany Creek to son, William CARR (2,250 A.),
and, whereas, said Colonel Carr did by deed give son, Thomas CARR,
half of said property, we, William and Thomas Carr, agree to partition said land between ourselves, and relinquish to each other,
one-half of said land.

1823, Sept 24
    AUCTION - George TANKERSLEY, Sheriff, seized land of Harrison
KINNEBREW, on Keg Creek, 219 acres. Auction held, Edmond CARTLEDGE
high bidder, @ $500.

1823, Sept 29
    ADMINISTRATORS' SALE - Administrators of Sarah MARSHALL; Nath-
an CRAWFORD; and Thomas BAYLISS, apply to Court to sell all real estate on Greenbriar Creek, 28 acres adj., lands of Levi MARSHALL, and
Jabez MARSHELL. 3 acres were willed to Mrs. Marshall by Levi M.
dec'd., including mill and its seat, and 25 acres by Rev. Abraham
MARSHALL, dec'd. Sold at auction, bought by Jabez Marshall for $400.

1823, Sept 2
    AUCTION - Sheriff G. TANKERSLEY, sells at auction; lands of
John DUNN, 100 acres on Little Kiokee Creek, adj., HEGGIE land.
William JONES, high bidder, @ $350.

1823, Nov 2
    LETTERS OF GUARDIANSHIP - Robert W. ROBERTS, of Limestone Co.,
Ala., is appointed guardian of Emily BOWDRE, a minor under 14 years,
"in right of my wife, Harriet Roberts," Bonded for $5,000.

1823, Nov 27
    MORTGAGE - Edmond BLUNT, of Putnam Co., indebted to Jacob
HORN, of Richmond Co., for $325., secures debt with mortgage on
300 acres on Kegg Creek, purchased from Joshua GRINAGE.

1823, Dec 15
    HEIRS' SALE - Elizabeth; Rebecca; James Benjamin; Eleanor;
and Thomas YOUNG, sell to John F. YOUNG, 100 acres on Upton's Creek,
for $200.

1823, Dec 17
   MORTGAGE OF PERSONALTY - Eugene FINNEL, mortgages to Guilford ALFORD, for $50., 1 road-waggon; 4 horses; 1 bay horse; 1 gray horse; 1 brown mare; 1 bay horse, blind.

1823, Dec 22
   QUIT CLAIM - Lucinda BRADBURY, widow of Henry, signs over all title to parcel of land containing 43 1/2 acres; 3 head cattle; all household and kitchen furniture; 1 bed, and two trunks, to George MOY, and wife.

1814, Jan 6 - Rec. Jan 6, 1824
   RELINQUISHMENT - Eleanor BUSSEY; Robert FLEMING; John FLEMING; of Putnam Co., to William FLEMING, in consequence of $300., relinquish four tracts of land drawn by them in division of land from father's estate, in all 155 1/2 acres.

1824, Jan 29
   HEIRS' SALE - Hillary PHELPS, and his wife, of Jasper Co., Marcus FLOURNOY, and his wife, of Jefferson Co., Tabitha BEALLE, of Richmond Co., and William FULLER, Exr., estate of Clementius DAVIS, dec'd., to Benjamin A. WARREN, Exr., of Walker LEIGH, said heirs, for $3,000., sell to Benjamin Warren, 200 acres in Columbia Co., where Davis, dec'd., lived at the time of his death, formerly the property of Thomas DAVIS, dec'd.

1824, Feb 6
   MORTGAGE - William GERMANY, of Richmond Co., to Peter LESQUIEUX, and Maria COTTON, of Richmond Co., by promissory note, indebted, for $733.75. For further securing said debt, mortgages 150 acres on South side of Savannah River, which I inherited from my father, James GERMANY.

1824, Feb 28
   MORTGAGE - Sheriff, sells at auction, property of David COOPER, 9 Lots in Wrightsborough, of 1 acre each. Henry WILSON, high bidder @ $120.

1824, Feb 27
   AUCTION - Sheriff TANKERSLEY, sells land of Dreadzil PACE, at auction, 180 acres. He is high bidder, @ $100.

1824, Apr 20
   MORTGAGE - Farley ADAMS, in debt to David LANGSTON, for sum of $906., secures said debt with mortgage on negro men: Cyrus and Jesse, and yellow woman, Clarissy.

1824, May 4
   AUCTION - Sheriff sells land of George JOHNSTON, 12 acres on Hart's Creek, to Isaac BRYAN, high bidder at $29.

1824, May 17
   DEED OF TRUST - Jeremiah BUGG sells to Benjamin HURST, of S. C., for $3,000., negroes: Cyrus; Peter; Molly, and her child; all

horses; cattle; household and kitchen furniture; and plantation tools now in my possession, in trust for Martha Sarah BUGG (relationship not given).

1824, June 11
RECEIPT - Frances MERIWETHER, relict of Nicholas MERIWETHER, to Thomas MERIWETHER, Exr., of estate. "I have received full satisfaction for all demands I have made upon him as Exr., of estate of my husband, Nicholas MERIWETHER, dec'd. Also in his services as Exr., of Thomas MERIWETHER, SR., dec'd. s/ Frances Meriwether; Robert Meriwether; Pleasant BENNING; Thomas WHITE; and William Meriwether, heirs.

1824, June 21
MORTGAGE - William HUTCHINSON, indebted to Dr. David BUSH, of Habersham Co., for note of $540., secured debt with a mortgage on 500 acres on Little River.

1820, June 12 - Rec. _____1824
ARBITRATION - "We, the undersigned, being called upon to establish a line between the properties of Harwood ROBERTS, and Dreadzil PACE, and to divide the two tracts whereon they now live, after viewing the premises, do run a line." (They gave marks). "Each shall peacably cultivate and take off the crops now growing, and shall have the privilege of removing all rails and fenceposts." s/ Peter CRAWFORD; John FOSTER; James BURROUGHS; John GERMANY; Jeremiah DARBY; William THOMAS; Amos ALBRITTON.

1824, Aug 12
MARRIAGE CONTRACT - Edmond CARTLEDGE, of State of S. C., and Sarah WALKER, of Columbia Co., Ga., do send greetings: "Whereas, we have entered into a contract of marriage,".. for sum of $6,000., paid by Dr. John CUMMINGS, and John FORSYTH, they have sold property held in trust for Sarah WALKER, and her heirs forever, the plantation whereon she now lives; slaves Tom; Chloe; Nancy; Cyrus; Milly; Sally; Martha; Henry; Violet; Maria; and Esther; household and kitchen furniture, all stock of cattle, and hogs; 4 wheel carriage and harness; 1 horse; 1 cart; and all and every species of property she is now in possession of.

1824, Aug 20
AUCTION - William WILKINS, Sheriff, seized property of Thomas BAYLISS, 100 acres where house stands, on Greenbriar Creek. Elizabeth BAYLISS, widow, high bidder @ $350.

1815, Mar 11 - Rec. Sept 14, 1824
William SHEFFIELD, of Hancock Co., to William SATTERWHITE, relinquishes all title, and claim to his share of negroes in hands of Milly SATTERWHITE; Sarah WALKER, and Robert POE, Exr., of estate of Elisha WALKER, dec'd., and under bond to his brother, David WALKER, for $150. Sarah did claim certain objects, and disputed sale of them to Dr. CUMMINGS, viz: 1 doz. silver teaspoons; 1 doz. silver tablespoons, a 2-branch candlestick; 2 small candlesticks; 1 soup ladle; 4 castors; 2 tumblers; 1 tea pot; 1 milk pot; and sugar dish;

1 pair brass firedogs; shovel and tongs; 1 large looking-glass; 3 large pictures; 2 knife boxes. "We agree to appear at Superior Court the second Monday in March, to establish ownership of above."

1824, Oct 14
   TAX SALE - Ayres CARTLEDGE, Tax Collector, sells to William SCOTT, JR., for $101., a 290 acre tract on Germany Creek, property of Beverly SPIVEY, in default of tax for 1822.

1824, Nov 10
   PARTITION - Petition for partition of real estate of John CRAWFORD, dec'd., granted. Return of Commissioners: Property divided in two parts, 94 acres on Watery Branch, valued @ $824., to William L. CRAWFORD. Residue, 150 acres, valued @ $1,080., granted to Peter CRAWFORD, in his own right, and as guardian of Ann L. CRAWFORD.

1824, Dec 2
   LETTER - Mr. Newman ALLEN, Exr., of estate of Elizabeth C. ALLEN, late of Culpepper Co., Va., dec'd. "Dear Sir: Please to pay to Col. Stanton SLAUGHTER, for use of Mrs. Elizabeth WHITE, of Columbia Co., Ga., all my right and title of the estate of my brother, James ALLEN, dec'd. Your ob'd't. servant. s/ Frances T. Allen.

1825, Jan 5
   LETTERS OF GUARDIANSHIP - Owen WEST, SR., appointed guardian of person and estate of John WEST, his son, aged 15 years, makes bond to amount of $120.

1825, Feb 12
   MORTGAGE - William Beckham COBB, in debt to Thomas Edgehill BURNSIDE, for a promissory note of $500., mortgages 325 acre tract on Greenbriar Creek.

1825, Mar 11
   MORTGAGE - Elizabeth STARKE, Admx., of estate of William STARKE, SR., dec'd., to Bowling STARKE, under a promissory note for $1,543. 16 1/4¢, secures note with mortgage for 8 head of cattle; 1 yoke steers, and cart; 4 horses (1 bay mare; 1 sorrell mare; 1 sorrell colt, and 1 sorrell horse); 40 hogs; 18 sheep; 3 beds, and furniture; 1 gin and gear, and all interest I have in my husband's estate.

1825, Mar 14
   DEED OF PERSONALTY - William STARKE to Bowling STARKE, all right and title I have to father's estate.

1825, May 31
   RELINQUISHMENT - Jubal Orion MARSHALL, to Isaac BRYAN, mortgages negroes for $1,001.18, Phillis 29, her children Frances, 14; Abram, 8; Adeline, 6; Dave, 2; and William, a sucking child.

1825, May 31
   RELINQUISHMENT - John A. COBB, of Clarke Co., to heirs of Henry Willis COBB; Obedience COBB, widow; Mary (Cobb) MESSINGER; Susan Amanda

COBB; Edmond Bugg COBB; Lydia Eliza COBB; and Martha Margaret Cobb; (John COBB; Edmond BUGG; and John WATSON were appointed trustees of H. W. COBB'S estate, Apr 25, 1820. Edmond Bugg and John Watson having died, John Cobb releases all property to Obedience COBB, and relinquishes trusteeship).

1820, Apr 13
RELINQUISHMENT - John and William KINNON, to Nicholas WARE, all right and title to property on bank of Little River, from a ford known as Downing's, up to the mills which we have this day sold to said Ware.

1822, May 9
MORTGAGE - Warner KENNON to William SCARBOROUGH, of Chatham Co., to secure a note for $1,755.83, mortgages 210 acres on Cane Creek.

1825, June 14
MORTGAGE - Thomas BOWDRE, in debt by means of a promissory note for $264.37 1/2 to John SMITH, mortgages one negro boy, Harry.

1825, Nov 8
TRUST - Hannah LEITH leaves in trust, with her brother, Charles LEITH, negro Jacob, for brother James LEITH, 'now absent," until he shall return.

1825, Nov 23
RELINQUISHMENT - Elizabeth BOOTHE, of Monroe Co., for $150., paid by Bradley CATLIN, of Litchfield Co., Conn., does sell all right and title which, "I do claim, as widow of Andrew BOOTHE, dec'd., in a tract of land of 193 acres, whereon William SMITH now lives."

1826, Jan 10
AGREEMENT - Hester; James; Ann; and Sarah NEWSOME, have sold interest in estate of Claiborne NEWSOME, to William NEWSOME.

1826, Mar 7
MORTGAGE - Jeremiah GRIFFIN, indebted to Walter APPLING, for $3,000., gives mortgage on 3 tracts of land on Little River, all adj., 200 acres in all.

1826, Apr 12
AGREEMENT - Between Jabez Pleiades MARSHALL, and Jubal Orion MARSHALL, as follows: Jabez P., is to let Jubal O., have negroes, Polydore; Delphia; Leonidas; Milly; Goldy; Nancy; and Cornelius, also $1,000., in consequence of Jubal O., letting Jabez P. have 425 acre tract of land.

1826, July 7
AGREEMENT - Nancy and Deborah LAZENBY agree that, Whereas, in the course of nature, all persons are subject to death, "so we do this day agree that in consequence of the death of either, the survivor shall inherit property owned jointly."

1826, Sept 5
MORTGAGE - Thomas CARR mortgages negroes to Benjamin LEIGH, for $3,200., Buster; Scias; Sue; and Hannah; also 1,500 acres of land on Greenbriar Creek and Germany Creek, comprising what has been called the Alexandria establishment, the residence of my late father, Col. Thomas CARR, dec'd.

1826, Nov 2
RELINQUISHMENT - Whereas, Benjamin JONES, son and heir of William JONES, dec'd., near Raysville, having received what he thought was to be his distributive share of father's estate, having intermarried with Nancy JONES, and died intestate, Dec. 30, 1824, without issue, but leaving a widow, who by law is to receive only 1/2 the estate, the next of kin to get the other half, Robert JONES, Admr. Elizabeth JONES (widow of William, mother of Benjamin); Mary RAY, widow of Joseph RAY, and sister of Benjamin; John REED, in right of wife, Elizabeth (sister to Benjamin); Burton CRABB, in right of wife, Sally (sister to Benjamin); and William JONES, brother of Benjamin, for the great love, maternal, brotherly and sisterly, for dec'd. brother and son, and to our dearly beloved daughter and sister, Nancy, widow of dec'd., Benjamin, do absolutely relinquish all claim to estate.

1827, Jan 31
TRUSTEE'S SALE - Jabez P. MARSHALL; Cornelius COLLINS; David STANFORD; William UPTON; and John EUBANKS, trustees of Kiokee Baptist Church, for $50., sell to Isaac BOWEN, 1/4th of an acre in village of Appling.

1827, Feb 12
MORTGAGE - Edmond CRAWFORD, to William L. CRAWFORD, to secure promissory note for $95.04 3/4, mortgages negro girl, Henrietta.

1827, Feb 17
INDEMNITY BOND- Benjamin and James REYNOLDS, under $1,696.96 bond to Turner CLANTON and James BURROUGHS, Exrs., of estate of Hannah CLANTON: Whereas, it is provided in Last Will and Testament of Hannah Clanton that money due her at time of death is to be collected and laid out in slaves, and equally divided among heirs, and that if any child shall die without issue, the property reverts to remaining children: Larkin REYNOLDS, intermarried with Eliza G. CLANTON, received of Exrs., a negro boy, Charles, valued at $430; and there being a balance of estate that could not be divided in slaves, he secured an order of the Court to divide remaining money. Demands $377.68, as his share, in right of his wife.

1827
RELINQUISHMENT - Sterling JONES, SR., with love and affection for dau-in-law, Martha JONES, wid., of Sterling Jones, Jr., dec'd., (she formerly WINFREY), relinquishes all right and title to estate.

1827, Mar 23
DIVISION OF LAND - William WRIGHT, and Alexander TELFAIR, Exrs., of Thomas TELFAIR, of Chatham Co., agree that the line between

land granted to Williams JACKSON, now the property of William WRIGHT, and the HOWARD-FEW tract, now property of Thomas TELFAIR, dec'd.,

1827, Mar 24
MORTGAGE - Edward CRAWFORD, to Peter CRAWFORD, to secure a $1,000., note, mortgages 1/2 tract of land on Uchee Creek, containing 1,280 acres, being tract whereon Robert CRAWFORD lived in his lifetime, and where Elizabeth, widow of Robert, now lives. Also 1/2 share of 250 acre tract drawn in land Lottery by said Robert, in 1st District, Early Co., Lot #328.

1827, Apr 10
MORTGAGE - Henry DOZIER to Thomas WHITE, guardian of Constancia Louisa Catherine ROBERTS, mortgages negro, Jim, for $255.

1827, Apr 11
SHERIFF'S SALE - George TANKERSLEY sells at auction all right and title of David COOPER in estate of Jesse WINFREY, dec'd. William C. CLIFTON, of Richland Dist., S. C., high bidder @ $1,000.

1827, May 25
RELINQUISHMENT - Jeremiah REES to Sarah WALTON, Warren Co. Whereas, Robert and Sarah WALTON, wid., of Benjamin REES, did sign a Deed of Gift, June 6, 1811, giving Jeremiah; Talbot; Taliaferro; and Albert, sons of said Sarah and Benjamin, dec'd., all estate of Benjamin REES, and Sarah, now not satisfied with the manner and form of the instrument, and wishing that an equal division be made, after her death, to ALL her children: Martha BULL; Jeremiah REES; Ephatha BOWDRE; Sarah AMOS; Taliaferro; Talbot; and Albert REES, we, the signers do relinquish all right and title to property mentioned in said deed of gift, as if there had never been no such writing.

1827, June 6
MORTGAGE - Edward CRAWFORD to William CRAWFORD, to secure note for $307.50., mortgages negro boy, Daniel.

1827, June 6
MORTGAGE - Samuel PAUL to Polly JENKINS, to secure two notes of $750., each, mortgages 850 acres of land on Greenbriar Creek, originally granted to Richard SHACKLEFORD.

1827, June 26
MORTGAGE - James STALLINGS, indebted to Thomas HAMILTON for $5,367.66, in promissory notes, assigns and mortgages 582 acres on Savannah River, being the land that Stallings now cultivates and where he permanently resides. Also negroes: Wally, 35; George, 30; Tom, 14; May, 10; Isaac, 7; John, 2; Austin, 2; Daphna, 21; Harriot, 25; Tamar, 20; Belinda, 18; Lucinda, 14; Phillis, 10; Lucy, 5; Isabella, 2; Charles, 1; Robert, 1; and Tenah, 3.

1827, July 11
TRUSTEE'S SALE - Jabez MARSHALL; David STANFORD; Cornelius COLLINS; William UPTON; trustees of Kiokee Baptist Church, sell to Simmons CRAWFORD, 1/5th of an acre in village of Appling, for $40.

1827, July 11
    TRUSTEES' SALE - Trustees of Kiokee Baptist Church (above named), sell to Thomas BURNSIDE, for $50., 3/10th of an acre in the village of Appling.

1827, Aug 9 (date rec.)
    TAX SALE - Ayres CARTLEDGE, Tax Collector for year 1821, to Thomas COBB, sells 1/4 of a 200 acre tract on Greenbriar Creek, returned by Gatewood DUNN, for tax of 1821, and being in default. Sold at public outcry, Sept 3, 1822, bringing $9.95

1827, Nov 28
    DEED OF TRUST - John B. TINDALL to Allen GREEN, for $200., hath sold, in trust for Alitha YOUNG, during life, (at her death the trust is to be dissolved, and property given to her children), negro girl, Mariah, 10.

1827, Dec 1
    RELINQUISHMENT - James CLANTON, of Natchitoches Province, La., to Catherine E. CLANTON, all right and claim to estate of dec'd., brother, Littleberry CLANTON.

1827, Dec 1
    DEED OF TRUST - Mary BEALLE, to Anderson MADDOX, of Taliaferro Co., for $10,000., in trust for, "my children, 1/4th part of total estate of Thomas BEALLE, dec'd."

1828, Jan 5
    MORTGAGE - James ROGERS, to Morris ANSLEY, for 7 promissory notes, totaling $143.37 1/2, mortgages tract whereon he now lives, 130 acres on Germany's Creek.

1827, Sept 10
    MARRIAGE RECORDED - Cassius STODDARD, of Tuscaloosa Co., Ala., to Emily POUNDS, "Pursuant to a license issued from Clerk's office in Tuscaloosa Co., Ala., dated Sept 10, 1827, I celebrated the rites of marriage between the above, and joined them in Holy Matrimony." s/ Robert MARTIN - "I certify that Robert MARTIN was acting Justice of the Peace at the time specified." s/ John HODGES, Clerk 10/5/1827.

1828, Jan 14
    TRUST DEED - Alexander PEARRE, to James PEARRE, for love and affection, "to my sister, Lucy TOOLE, wife of Dr. James TOOLE, in trust, 1 negro girl, Ann, between 12 and 15."

1828, Jan 21
    MORTGAGE - Thomas BURNSIDE, to Isaac BRYAN, to secure a promissory note for $663., mortgages 38 1/2 acres whereon Burnside now lives, and following negroes, Aggy and Martha.

1828, Jan 24
    MORTGAGE - Samuel HICKS, to Daniel DUBOSE, to secure four promissory notes: 1. payable Jan 1, 1829, for $812.50, with interest from Jan 1, 1828. 2. payable Jan 1, 1830, for $812.50, with interest from

Jan 1, 1828. 3. payable Jan 1, 1831, for $812.50, with interest from Jan 1, 1828. 4. payable Jan 1, 1832, for $812.50, with interest from Jan 1, 1828, mortgages 1 tract, formerly granted to John BOYD, whereon Sarah POPE lived, on Germany Creek, 347 acres. 1 tract adj., of 53 acres, where DuBose now lives. One other tract of 110 1/2 acres on Savannah River, originally granted to William GERMANY, and another adj., of 150 acres.

1828, Jan 29
   TAX SALE - James CARTLEDGE, Tax Collector, Esq., for unpaid taxes for year 1826 due on 202 1/2 acres in Dooly Co., Lot #68, Dist. 1, returned by William BASTON, now in default, of $3.39, sells said property to Thomas WILKINSON.

1828, Jan 30
   MORTGAGE - James WALTON, indebted by seven promissory notes, totaling $186.36, secures this debt to Archibald HEGGIE, by mortgaging 10 chairs; 4 pine tables; 1 slab, or sideboard; 1 bed; 2 bedsteads; 2 sets of ploughs; 1 waggon and gear; 1 bay mare; 1 gray horse; 10 head of hogs; 1 white and red cow; also 1/2 of 837 acre tract lying in Richmond Co., on Spirit Creek.

1828, Jan 30
   MORTGAGE - Elizabeth HOWARD secures a promissory note to Mark Price DAVIS for $1,620., by mortgaging negroes John, 30; Harriot, 26; Nathan, 8; Sawney, 6; Jesse, 4; Elizabeth, short of a year; and Judy, 15 years.

1828, Feb 13
   DEED OF TRUST - William MC GRUDER, JR., to William MC GRUDER, SR., and John POWERS, of S. C., negroes Rachel; Jim; Anderson; Darius; Rhoda; Emeline; Melinda, children of wench, Rachel; Rosetta; Amanda; and Louisa, children of wench, Rhoda. In trust for, "my wife, Mary Ann, late POWERS."

1828, Feb 15
   WRIT OF PARTITION & DOWER - Superior Court, Jan 26, 1826, Frances BLACKSTONE, widow of James BLACKSTONE, dec'd., petitions to lay off 1/3 of the real estate of her late husband. Commissioners, Archibald HEGGIE; William ZACHRY, and T. TUDOR, on Feb 6, 1828, delivered 66 acres of Blackstone land to widow.

1828, May 17
   Mary GRAVES, in trust with William MC GRUDER, for benefit of Cassandra PEARRE, 1 negro girl, Rebecca, about 4 years old.

1828, Apr 1
   EXECUTOR'S SALE - James CULBREATH, Exr., of Beverly LOWE, to Edward WOODING, for $40., a 20 acre tract originally the property of said Beverly LOWE, in compliance with the law.

1828, May 8
   QUIT CLAIM - Mark P. DAVIS, for divers good reasons, to William STEED, relinquishes all right, title and claim to a 350 acre tract on Germany Creek, originally granted to David ROBERSON.

1828, May 6
>MORTGAGE - Jacob BUGG, to secure three promissory notes, one for $3,852., payable 12 months after date, and one for $2,137.22, payable two years after date; also one other for $4,422.60, payable three years after date, to John P. KING, mortgages 212 acres in Richmond Co., purchased from Anderson WATKINS, with a grist mill. The 85 acre Handley tract; 100 acres purchased from Basil LAMAR; 124 acres purchased from Basil LAMAR; slaves: Joe; Jack; Sam; Akey; Ned; Prissy, and her child; Tidy, and her three children; Eady, and her three children; Lucy; Sally; Harriette, and her child; Betty, and her youngest; David, a carpenter; Malinda, and her child; and Billy Walker. Also a 150 acre tract in Columbia Co., also negroes held in Columbia Co: Charles, 35; Sappho, same; Peggy, and her six children, to-wit: Webster; Dinah; Tom; Rachel; Jerry; and Lucy; Jack, 20; and Violett, and her child.

1828, July 12
>MORTGAGE - Henry MEALING, of Richmond Co., to Lewis VANSANT, to secure a $1,000., promissory note, mortgages 759 acres in Columbia Co.

1828, July 12
>RELINQUISHMENT - Nathaniel Holt CLANTON, and Turner CLANTON, of Columbia Co., Larkin REYNOLDS, of Baldwin Co., to John CAMPBELL, for $75., relinquish all claim to 2 tracts of land; one of 100 acres, originally granted to David BOYD, June 7, 1774, being the tract whereon Isaac SKINNER lived and died. The other of 16 1/2 acres granted to **Isaac** SKINNER, on Michael and Germany Creeks. The two tracts being included in a deed from John BEALLE to said Campbell, the same bequeathed from Isaac Skinner to his widow, Jane, and at her death to children, Henry; John; Elizabeth; Howard Richard, and **Thomas** Hiram SKINNER, which was then conveyed to Howard and Henry Skinner, and by them to Charles CLAYTON, who died intestate. In the division, it became the property of aforementioned Nathaniel and Turner Clanton. The aforementioned Nathaniel and Turner Clanton, and Larkin Reynolds being intermarried with the three daughters, only children of said Charles Clayton, they thereby became entitled to a third share, each, which they hereby relinquish to John Campbell.

1828, July 26
>MORTGAGE - Thomas SHIVERS, indebted for three $2,000., notes, mortgages three tracts of land in Columbia and Warren Counties, on Sweetwater Creek, including the Sweetwater Mill tract, consisting of 400 acres. Each of the other tracts contains 111 1/2 acres, adj., to each other. Originally the property of German TUCKER, and Jonathon STANFORD.

1828, Nov 4
>DEED OF LEASE - James COLLINS, guardian of Hartwell COLLINS, to John HARRIS, leases 125 acres, until Hartwell shall come of age, for $50.

1828, Nov 5
DEED OF TRUST - Edward WELCH, to Edward BARBAREE, in trust for "my wife, Cassandra WELCH, 3 head of cattle; 6 hogs; 1 cupboard; 2 chests; 1 spinning wheel; 2 bedsteads; 1 bed and furniture; 2 pots; 1 oven and skillet; 1/2 doz. chairs; 3 tables; crockery; knives and forks.

1828, Nov 11
ADMINISTRATORS' SALE - Administrators of estate of Nathaniel BENTON, (Nelson BENTON and James CARTLEDGE), sell to Archibald HEGGIE, 202 9/10th acres, originally granted to Rosborough and George SMITH, for $300.

1828, Nov 11
ADMINISTRATRIX' SALE - Elizabeth GARNETT, Admx., of John GARNETT, to Peter CRAWFORD. Elizabeth petitions to sell 240 acres of estate. Petition granted, and land sold at auction. Crawford was high bidder, @ $800. This is to comprise of parts of several tracts. 1. Part of a 200 acre tract granted to John CRITTENDON, Mar. 1772. 2. Part of a 200 acre tract granted to John Crittendon, Nov. 1, 1774. John died intestate, leaving nine heirs, and distributees. Aforementioned John Garnett married Elizabeth, one of the heirs, and received 1/9th of the estate. Other shares, to make up 247 acres bought by Garnett.

1829, Jan 8
HEIRS' AGREEMENT & SALE - Rebecca GRIFFIN, SR., Michael; Rebecca, Jr; John KNOX, of Lincoln Co; John GRIFFIN, of Walton Co., Joseph BAKER, of Abbeville Dist., S. C., John SCOTT, Edgefield, S. C., Troy GRIFFIN, Tuscaloosa, Ala., Isaac WILLINGHAM, Fayette Co., Ala., all heirs and legatees of estate of John Griffin, dec'd., of Columbia Co., sell to Charles GILL, for $1,631., the 551 acre tract whereon J. Griffin lived and died, on Little River.

1829, Jan 9 (Date rec.)
tax sale - Daniel MARSHALL, Tax Collector for 1794, sells to Nimrod JONES, 300 acres originally granted to John TINDELL, and William SULLIVAN, who are in default. Jones high bidder at public sale, $11.00. (Jones sold above tract to Burwell BULLOCH, Jan 9, 1828, for $10.00.

1829, Feb 25
TAX SALE - James CARTLEDGE, Tax Collector for 1826, sells to Washington Jefferson SANDERS, for $3.36, a 109 acre tract in Lincoln Co., turned in by Daniel TRAMWELL, and who defaulted.

1829, Feb 25
ARBITRATION - Rebecca RUSSELL, under $1,000., bond -vs- William YARBOROUGH, guardian for Elizabeth YARBOROUGH. Whereas, doubt has arisen and does exist with said Rebecca, and she denies that the said Elizabeth is one of the heirs and residuary legatees of estate of Littleton YARBOROUGH, dec'd., said Elizabeth being the only surviving child of Beall YARBOROUGH, dec'd., who was an heir of Littleton. Rebecca and William Yarborough agree to settle the

dispute by arbitration, and select as arbitrators: Archer AVERY; Juriah HARRISS; Isaac RAMSEY; and William WRIGHT. Decision: Elizabeth is entitled to her father's distributive share of estate of Littleton Yarborough, left to him in will of said deceased.

1829, Mar 5
AGREEMENT - "Taking into consideration of my age and infirmity, and being wholly unable to attend to my pecuniary affairs and temporal concerns, I have released to Edward JONES, in consequence of his paying all my just debts, all the real estate left me by will of my late husband, Aquilla HOWARD. Mr. Jones has agreed to find me a comfortable home, and clothes and maintenance, and treat me in a kind and humane manner. I also relinquish unto him all the horses; hogs; and cattle, left by my late husband. Also all my interest in the negroes bequeathed to me, except 1 negro girl I lately bought from Thomas BOLTON."

1829, Mar 16
DEED OF TRUST - John REYNOLDS to Reuben and Walker REYNOLDS, for sum of 12 1/2¢, and fraternal love and affection I bear to my brothers: All parcel of land on East side of Little Germany Creek, 635 acres; negroes: Anthony; Linny; boy Patum; Spencer; Sam; Peter; and Vinny, together with articles of every description I purchased at recent sale of property of late Father, Reuben REYNOLDS, in trust for use of me, John Reynolds, and heirs of my body.

1829, Apr 1
RELINQUISHMENT - Amzey PARKES, relict and widow of John PARKES, to heirs, William; Lewis; Richard; Gabriel; John; Cornelius; Hardy; Elizabeth KINDRICK, and Richard GRIFFIN, legatees of said Parkes, named in his will. For and in consequence of their relinquishing all claim and title to the sum of $1,000., 2 beds and furniture, and 2/5ths of the household furniture, which was left me during my lifetime, and then to be divided among my children at death, in return for which I relinquish all claim and title to 5 tracts of land, three of them in Columbia Co. 1. 350 acres on Little River, whereon said Parkes did live. 2. 21 acres adjoining above. 3. 395 acres adj., Reuben SANDERS, and others. 4. 1 tract in Wilkerson Co., Lot 85, 14th Dist., 202 acres. 5. 1 tract in Wilkerson Co., Lot No. 95, 12th Dist., 202 acres.

1829, Aug 6
MORTGAGE - Benjamin BUGG, to secure debt of $413.50, mortgages negroes, Cleo, 31, and her 5 children, Ann, 13; Flora, 11; Littleton. 9; Juliet, 6; and a sucking child.

1814, Sept 12 - Rec. Sept 10, 1829
John LOVELACE received of General TWIGGS, $100., consideration money for 5 acre lot, including the Mineral Springs. On Sept. 10, 1829, George TWIGGS sells above to J. J. CARTLEDGE, "I, George Twiggs, Exr., of estate of late Gen. John TWIGGS, have sold unto Mr. J. J. Cartledge, the 5 acre lot, known as Rousseau Springs, for $100."

1829, Nov 19
   DEED OF TRUST - Hester COLE, to the issue of my body, after
my death, negro man, Frank, 35; 1 parcel of land in Pike Co., formerly Monroe Co., drawn by orphan Mark COLE, in 2nd Dist., Lot 21, 202 1/2
acres. Also a Chickasaw mare and colt; 2 featherbeds and furniture;
all to be equally divided. In trust with friend, Rese HAMILTON. If
I die without issue, to be property of said Hamilton.

1829, Dec __
   DEED OF TRUST - Rese HAMILTON (his name in marriage book
spelled "Rhesa"), in trust with Isaac RAMSEY. "Whereas, a marriage
has taken place between Rese HAMILTON and Hester COLE, and the following property was in the possession of said Hester, said Rese is desirous of securing it to her." Describes above property, in addition, "4 head of cattle; milk and neat cattle; one mare and colt;
1 Gig. To be held in trust by Isaac RAMSEY, for use of said Hester."

1830, Mar 15
   TAX SALE - John COLLINS, Tax Collector, for 1828, sells 250
acres in Early Co., of Ephraim WHITTINGTON, defaulter, to Archibald
HEGGIE, for $10.06 1/4.

1830, Apr 14
   DEED OF TRUST - William WILKINS, upon his marriage to Polly
AVARY, dau. of Archer AVARY, received from her father, negroes:
Rachel; Pinky; Milly, and child; Alfred; Tishy; and Dick, as dower,
for said Polly. It is Wilkins intention to secure said property to
Polly, and leaves it in trust with her father, Archer Avary, Sr.

1830, Apr 29
   MORTGAGE - Th. NAPIER, to secure Jared POUNDS, cosigner with
NAPIER, on 14 promissory notes to John SMITH, totaling $417.60, mort-
gages 230 acres in Columbia Co., 2 negroes, girls, Harriet, 8 years
old, yellow Complexion; Dilcey, 8, dark complexion.

1830, May 4
   MORTGAGE - Green SANDERS, to secure a debt of $500., to Reuben
SANDERS, mortgages negroes, Betty and 3 children; Jerry, 13; Vice, 10;
Keziah, 8; Sorrel mare, and a small black mare.

1816, May 27
   WRIT OF PARTITION - Estate of James MC FARLAND, heirs John
DOZIER; John LEE; Curtis LOWE; Nathan BEALLE; Jeremiah SANDERS; John
WEST; Jeremiah GRIFFIN; Robert JOHNS; John PARKES; and Collin FINNEY,
-vs- Thomas COLEMAN. Whereas, said Coleman, in right of his wife,
Elizabeth, Dau. of James MC FARLAND, dec'd., and guardian of Betsy
MC DONALD, minor dau. of Jane McDonald (formerly McFarland), also
claiming under Alexander McDonald, by conveyance, Andrew Shepherd,
who claims under Ann McFarland; John McFarland, and John McDonald,
by conveyance; Russell BRANHAM, father and natural guardian of his
two children by wife, Jane Branham, late McDonald, late McFarland,
claimants to the estate of James McFarland, dec'd., are in controversy over 6 tracts of land on Little River, containing 1,000 acres.
300 acres granted to James McFarland; 150 acres to Jacob DENNIS; 100

acres granted to Jacob DENNIS; 200 Acres granted to Illy; 150 acres granted to James MC FARLAND. Heirs petition for a partition of said land. Commissioners' return: Thompson COLEMAN, for wife, 443 acres; Andres SHEPHERD, 480 acres (other grants very complicated, such as "2/5ths of a 1/4th of tract, etc." Russell BRANHAM, 224 acres.

1830, May 20
    WRIT OF DOWER - Decision of Hon. William SCHLEY, for Mrs. Elvira WRIGHT, widow and relict of James WRIGHT, entitled to dower - 1/3 of all that tract, 160 acres on Hart's Creek and Carson's Creek, whereon said James resided at time of death; also four lots in Town of Wrightsborough, formerly owned by Benjamin PERRY, value to be decided by Thomas BOWDRE; Bushrod PETTIT; and Charles PORTER.

1830, June 24
    MORTGAGE - Jesse MOORE to secure $344., in promissory notes, to Isaac RAMSEY, mortgages 170 acre tract on Kiokee Creek, on the road from the Columbia Co., Courthouse to Wrightsborough. Also, Jesse mortgages slaves Jacob, 24; and Beckey, 24., to John SMITH, on a $580., debt.

1830, July 19
    RELINQUISHMENT - Thomas REYNOLDS; Walker REYNOLDS; Reuben REYNOLDS; and John REYNOLDS, legal heirs of Reuben REYNOLDS, dec'd., -vs- Charles EVANS. Charles in right of his wife, Margaret Ann (formerly Reynolds - m. June 21, 1817), for $8,000., relinquishes all right and title to estate of Reuben Reynolds: 291 acres on Carson's Creek; negroes: Logan; Isaac; George; Sarah, and her 4 children, Solomon; Robert; David; and Daniel; also all property left to Margaret Ann EVANS.

1830, Oct 30
    MARRIAGE CONTRACT - Robert Raymond REID and Elizabeth D. N. V. RANDOLPH, in trust with James STALLINGS: Whereas, it is the intention of Robert Reid to secure such property as Elizabeth Randolph may possess unto her, so that the same shall be in no way liable for the debts of said Reid: 250 acres, near Few's Old Place, known as "The Cluster," also negroes Dinah; Venus; Sidney; Easter; Nancy Louisa and George, to be held in trust by James Stallings, for said Elizabeth.

1830, Dec 2
    MORTGAGE - Isaac BOWEN, to Archibald HEGGIE, co-signer on a $2,000, note in Central Bank of Georgia, secures Heggie from loss by mortgage on 1 1/4 acre lot, including the dwelling house, on public road between Appling and Augusta, in Appling.

1831, May 7
    DEED OF TRUST - Jesse MORRIS, with love and affection for his wife, Martha, places in trust with friend, James BURNSIDE, tract of land on Kiokee Creek, 160 acres. Lot #101, Dist. 1, Coweta Co; Lot #101, Dist. 3, Troup Co. Also 4 negroes, Rebecca, 22; Ben, 25; Jacob, 24; and Edmond, about the same age; also household and kitchen furniture.

1831, May 11
    ADMINISTRATOR'S SALE - Lewis PARKES, Adm. estate of John PARKES, sells at auction, 395 acres on Little River. Richard GRIFFIN high bidder, @ $450. (This in gold mine district, brought good price).

1831, Nov 10
    SALE - Samuel ARNETT, from John Q. WEST, and John COLEMAN, joint purchasers of a certain tract of land on Little River, sell to said Arnett the J. MC FARLAND tract called the "Fish Dam." Two other tracts formerly said McFarland's, one called "Horse Shoe Bend," and one of fifty acres on Little River, below Quirn's(?). William MARTIN'S share of Ganaway MARTIN'S Old Survey; 1 tract in Columbia Co., called, "Water's Bend," originally granted to Holland MIDDLETON, all for $1,538.08, totaling 524 1/2 acres.

1831, Dec 1
    MARRIAGE CONTRACT - Between William SEAY and Mary Ann HOWARD: Whereas, Mary Ann is entitled to a 1/4 share of a tract on Upton's Creek, under will of Mark Price Davis, and to 1/3rd share in a 202 1/2 acre tract in Muscogee Co., drawn in Lottery by Orphans of Dorsey HOWARD; hogs; and household and kitchen furniture, William relinquishes all claim on said property forever, and confirms it to the use of Mary Ann and the heirs of her body, only.

1831, Dec 24
    MARRIAGE CONTRACT - John BURCH, of Wilkes Co., and Obedience (Bugg) COBB, widow of Henry Willis COBB: Whereas, said Obedience is possessed of Lot #214, Troup Co., 202 1/2 acres; 200 acres pine land in Columbia Co., also as one of heirs of estate of H. W. COBB, dec'd., possesses negroes: Sally and 5 children, John; Clarence; James; Dave and William; Tyro, and 3 children: Andrew; David and John; Wonder; Will; Bacchus; Reuben, and Charlotte, also stock of cattle; horses; hogs; household and kitchen furniture, and plantation tools. John agrees to have no claim on said property, and "For making it official in law," it is placed in trust with Obedience's brother, Charles BUGG.

1831, Dec 30
    MARRIAGE AGREEMENT - Between Charles WILSON; Sarah Ann HARRISON; and Edward JONES, Trustee: Whereas, a marriage is intended between the above, it is agreed the property she now possesses, as one of heirs of Father, (Terrell) Cook HARRISON,(son of Richard and Elizabeth HARRISON), be placed in trust with Edward Jones, for the sole use of Sarah and her heirs.

1832, Mar 13
    ORDER OF CONSENT - Treacy PAUL, to George MAGRUDER (Treacy Magruder Paul was sister of George, and he was her trustee): Sir: You will please dispose of, and sell Lot #1, in disposition of estate of Zadock Magruder, which was conveyed by Marriage Settlement dated June 11, 1822.

1832, Nov 21
    ADMINISTRATOR'S SALE - Property of Jared POUNDS sold at auction

by Thomas BEALLE, Adm. Leonard STEED high bidder @ $2,010. 995 acres on Greenbriar and Germany's Creeks, comprising what was originally the Alexandria Establishment, belonging to Thomas CARR, Sr., and left by him to his sons, Thomas and William.

1832, Dec 2
SALE - James BULLOCK, to the Trustees of the Methodist Camp Ground at Whiteoak, viz: James BURROUGHS; Edward WOODING; Harmong LAMAR; William ADAMS; George GUNBY; Thomas BOWDRE; Thomas DAWSON; and William HARRIS, for $237., sells 158 acres on Germany Creek.

1833, Jan 9
APPOINTMENT - Washington STONE; Harvy WHEAT; John BARNES; James DARSEY; in behalf of self, and James DARSEY, as guardian of Mary DARSEY, heirs of Joseph DARSEY, dec'd., appoint Stone; Wheat and Darsey commissioners to make prompt and speedy distribution.

1833, Apr 8
James GERMANY to Turner CLANTON, to secure 2 promissory notes totaling $562.50, land on Island in Savannah River, commonly called Germany's Island, containing 67 1/2 acres, and also for $500., negro woman, Polly, 26.

1833, May 2
MORTGAGE - Edward WOODING, indebted to Thomas HAMILTON, for $1,896.73, in promissory notes, mortgages a 240 acre tract, including 200 acres originally granted to Beverly LOWE, and following negroes: Betty, 24; Amey, 21; Anny, 24, and her child, Mary, 8, her child, Eliza, 3, her child, Milly, 2, and her child, Jane, 1.

1833, May 7
MORTGAGE - James CARTLEDGE; Uriah BLANCHARD; James BLANCHARD; and Edmond CARTLEDGE, for $5,700., mortgage to Thomas HAMILTON, 648 acres on Little River, whereon James Cartledge now lives. Also the following negroes: Tom, 47; Page, 16; Mariah, 18; Sally, 29; Jane, 14; Tolbey, 4; Harriet, 12; Julia, 7; Isaac, 10; Sally, 40; Elcy, 12; Hannah, 40; Baldwin, 22; Sandy, 18; Kit, 22; Osbourne, 22; Matilda, 20; Willis, 3; Polly, 7 mos; Lucy, 35; Kissy, 15; Margaret, 15.

1833, May 20
Shadrack GIBSON mortgages to Isaac BRYAN, for $400., negroes, Sam, 40; and Jim, 28, both dark complected.

1833, June 28
MORTGAGE - Edward JONES, to secure promissory note for $375., mortgages to William DRIVER, Lots 111; 112; 113; 18 and 22, in Wrightsborough, purchased from Thomas BOWDRE, cont. 5 acres in all.

1833, July 2
REVOCATION - Jemima BLAIR, having made deeds of gift to Robert BROWN and William BENNETT, and whereas, Mrs. Blair hath quit her former residence in Columbia Co., to live in Lincoln Co., doth hereby annull and renounce said deeds of gift, and desires property returned.

1833, July 9
    TAX SALE - Ayres CARTLEDGE, Tax Collector, for 1820, sells at auction 55 acres on Uchee Creek, formerly property of Duncan MC NEIL, in default. Stephen HOGE high bidder @ $11.25.

1833, Nov 18
    MORTGAGE - Jubal O. MARSHALL mortgages to Isaac BRYAN, for $1,428., slaves: Davy; Phillis, and their seven children, Adeline; Duncan; Will; Anderson; Golding; Mary Ann, and John Evans. (Mortgage paid in full Jan 15, 1838).

1833, Nov 23
    MORTGAGE - Ansel HUDGINS mortgages to Jeremiah GRIFFIN, for $216., 200 acres, formerly the property of Stanton PORTER, sold by Sheriff, known as the Tanyard Tract, in Wrightsborough, and originally owned by Henry JONES, Quaker.

1833, Dec 4
    ADMINISTRATORS' SALE - Peter SHORT and William SCOTT, Adms., of estate of Terrill HARRISON, dec'd., sell at auction to Guilford ALFORD, 320 acres on Germany Creek for high bid of $1,310.

1834, Jan 7
CORONER'S DEED - John HARRIS, Coroner, to Isaac RAMSEY, Sheriff: Whereas, said Harris did lately seize upon a tract of land on the Milledgeville Road, 200 acres belonging to Samuel PAUL, and sold it at auction. Ramsey high bidder @ $35.

1834, Jan 8
    LEGATEE'S RECEIPT - Milton GARTRELL, to Thomas and Nancy CULBREATH, Exrs., of John CULBREATH, a receipt for his share of estate of said Culbreath in right of wife, Lucy. (m. May 20, 1817)

1834, Feb 5
    DEED OF TRUST - Abner ROBERTSON to Thomas SKINNER, in trust for use and benefit of Frances Ann COOK, infant daughter of James COOK, 315 acres in Columbia Co. (140 acres formerly granted to Jonathon WARD. Part of tract has been conveyed to the Baptists, and is where Aberleen (Abilene) Meeting House now stands. The same not included in this conveyance.

1824, Mar 29
    RECEIPT & ACQUITTANCE - "I, James HILL, in right of my wife, Rebecca, late WHITCOMB, and formerly LESLIE, one of heirs and distributees of Sarah LESLIE, have received of James STALLINGS, Adm. of said estate, $57.90, in full share, and hereby exonerate and acquit James Stallings of all liability on my account, in right of my wife."

1834, Apr 28
    DEED OF TRUST - Between Jesse CLARK and Elizabeth OLIVE, who appoint Thomas W. OLIVE, as trustee, "to secure to said Elizabeth such property as she is entitled to from estate of her late husband, Berry OLIVE, to her sole and separate use." (Elizabeth Wilkins m. Berry OLIVE, May 17, 1813).

1834, May 2
TRUST DEED - MARRIAGE CONTRACT - "Whereas, a marriage, by God's permission, is intended between Wesley HOBBY, and Martha Rowena MARTIN, it is the said Wesley's intention to secure all property she possesses, to said Martha, and it is hereby put in trust with Thomas DAWSON, for her sole use and benefit, to-wit: Slaves, Bob; Tom; Peter; Jacob; George, a boy; Bob, a boy; Tom; Evalina, and her two children, Fanny and Martha; Ursula, and her child, William; Lydia, and her child, Alvin; Bird; Frances, and her children, Henry and Eugene. If Martha dies intestate, trust will be in force for her children. If she dies without issue, property to go to Wesley."

1834, May 12
TRUST DEED & MARRIAGE CONTRACT - Whereas, a marriage is intended between Edward BALLARD and Elizabeth PEARRE, and Whereas, said Elizabeth is a legatee of late husband, John PEARRE, to 1/4th part of total estate, it is agreed that said property shall be placed in trust with Benjamin BUGG and Isaac GIBSON. If couple have no children said Edward to inherit.

1834, May 12
MORTGAGE - Joseph GRANT mortgages to Thomas HAMILTON, for $2,160., a tract of land whereon said Grant now lives, on Savannah River, opposite Germany's Island, containing 1,018 1/2 acres.

1834, May 23
James STALLINGS mortgages to Thomas HAMILTON for $4,152.19, 582 acres on Savannah River, whereon said Stallings now lives, also negroes: August, 40; Will, 25; Sandy, 24; Polydore, 23; Cuff, 21; Jim, 19; May, 17; Isaac, 16; and Sam, 22.

1834, May 27
MORTGAGE - James, Eleanor and William GERMANY mortgage to James BURROUGHS, for $927., all of an improved lot in village of Appling, known as Franklin Hotel, containing 1/2 acre.

1834, July 22
TRUST DEED - Joel FLAKE, for love and affection towards wife, Mary, leaves in trust with John DENSON, 4 slaves, Claiborne; Ben; Andrew and Ephraim, the first three being mulattoes and the last black.

1834, Oct 2
AUCTION - Isaac RAMSEY, Sheriff, sells at auction, some of property of Jeremiah REES; Alfred HALL, high bidder @ $55., buys "a one acre lot in Wrightsborough, on Broad St., on which is a two-storied building formerly occupied as a tavern and store."

1834, Oct 2
Albert HOLLIMAN sells to Pliny WHEELER, one-half acre lot in Wrightsborough, containing a red house, formerly occupied as a grocery by Theodosius MASSENGALE, also one other house, un-occupied, and much dilapidated.

1834, Oct 9
   ADMINISTRATOR'S SALE - Benjamin WARREN, Adm. of Lindsay COLEMAN, estate, sells to James LYNES, 303 acres, by order of Court, at auction. Property known as Quaker Springs, for $3,320.

1835, Jan 7
   MORTGAGE - Thomas HARDEN mortgages 530 acres on N. W. side of Keg Creek to George TANKERSLEY, for $666. 2/3¢,

1835, Jan 7
   RELINQUISHMENT - Frederick JACKSON, of Union Dist., S. C., to George MAGRUDER. Whereas, Davis VINSON, dec'd., of Richmond Co., did devise, by last will and testament to Charlotte (Vinson) JACKSON, certain property, Frederick and Charlotte have sold, and relinquished their interest to George MAGRUDER for $2,300. Jackson gives Magruder power of attorney to attend to legal matters in Columbia Co. Charlotte Jackson signs relinquishment and power of attorney.

1835, Mar 19
   INDENTURE - Between Marshall KEITH, and William JONES, a cotton-gin maker of Augusta, Ga. Marshall Keith, guardian of person and property of Tarleton KEITH, hath this day bound and put to apprentice said Tarleton, to learn the art, trade and mystery of a cotton-gin maker in all its various branches and improvements, for the full term of five years, all of which time his master he shall faithfully obey; he shall do no damage to his master, nor see it done by others without giving notice thereof. He shall not contract matrimony during this time. He shall not absent himself day or night, but shall behave himself as a faithful apprentice should. William Jones does promise to teach the art of a cotton-gin maker, provide said Tarleton with decent Sunday clothes, and a moderate amount of pocket money, also sufficient meat, drink and lodging, and all other things. Marshall Keith also apprentices a negro boy, Frank, property of Tarleton Keith, to learn the art of blacksmith (makes same provisions). Jones covenants to pay, at expiration of apprenticeship, $200., for use of Tarleton Keith.

1835, Apr 27
   ADMINISTRATOR's SALE - William L. CRAWFORD, Adm. of estate of David VINSON, Richmond Co., dec'd., sells, by order of Court, at auction, to Benjamin WARREN, and James L. COLEMAN, 380 acres on Uchee Creek, as advertised in the Augusta States Rights Sentinel. High bid @ $626.

1835, May 6
   RECEIPT - Daniel MARSHALL, Adm., estate of Thomas POLLARD, to Martha POLLARD, Admx., estate of Robert POLLARD, dec'd., "Received of Martha Pollard $234.06, it being the lawful share of Thomas Pollard, dec'd., in estate of Robert Pollard, dec'd."

1835, May 23
   Certified Copy of Will of Ozias MORGAN, Sept 16, 1829, S. C., leaves property to: Son, Archibald, 275 acres land, negroes, Stephen and Jim. Son, Elbert, 275 acres of land, and negroes, Tom and Peter.

Daughter, Martha, negro boy, Reuben, negro girl, Mourning. Dau., Eliza, negroes Harriette, Ned and Solomon. Beloved wife, Elizabeth, all balance of estate during natural life, with use of house and plantation whereon I now live. At her death, land to go to son, Elbert, but personal property to be divided between daughters. All property left to daughters to be managed and controlled by sons, Archibald and Elbert. $25., to be paid to Daniel and William PRESCOATT. Exrs., sons, Archibald and Elbert.

1835, June 21
   MORTGAGE - Wesley HOBBY, mortgages to Simmons CRAWFORD, for $125., 1 fine mahogany table, consisting of one large table and two ends; 4 beds; 3 matrasses; 4 bedsteads; 6 fine chairs.

1835, July 30
   RATIFICATION - Whereas, by a marriage settlement made and executed in 1827, by John BURCH and Obedience COBB, I, Charles Burch, was named trustee, and, whereas, said John hath departed this life, and Obedience hath made a deed of conveyance of certain tract of land to one William WRIGHT, I, as trustee, do hereby ratify said sale.

1784, Jan 24 - Rec. Sept 17, 1835
   Commissioners of Confiscated Estates, viz: Hugh LAWSON; Abraham RAVOT; and Hepworth CARTER, to George HANDLEY, and Christian HILLARY, of Savannah, lease for £35, 400 acres in Richmond Co., (later Columbia Co), in Wrightsborough Township. (The original deed is so badly tattered it is impossible to tell from whom the land was confiscated. From the location, it could have been that of Governor WRIGHT.)

1835, Sept 22
   QUIT CLAIM - Allen GREEN, in consideration of $100., relinquishes all and any share or claim in estate of James TINSLEY, dec'd., in right of his mother, to William Tinsley. (Mother was Mary Tinsley m. Philip Green, Dec 8, 1804)

1835, Sept 25
   MORTGAGE - Middleton HILL, mortgages for $4,900., a tract of land on Little River and Upton's Creek (gold mine area), to the mouth of Jones Spring Branch, then up said branch to a road, and a cliff of rocks, to Jeremiah GRIFFIN.

1835, Sept 25
   MORTGAGE - Daniel JONES to Jeremiah GRIFFIN, for $3,255., mortgages tract on waters of Little River, a branch called Jones Spring Branch, and another branch called West Spring Branch, containing in all, 465 acres.

1835, Dec 2
   TRUSTEE'S SALE - Fergus LINN, trustee for Reese and Amanda LINN, to Turner CLANTON and William COOK. Whereas, said Reese did make a promissory note for $787.50., and secured debt with a mortgage on negroes Nathan, 21; Cherry, 24; Grace, 18. Trustee ratifies mortgage.

1835, Dec 16
   SETTLEMENT - Richard BRANHAM, for self and children, William Thomas; Mary Priscilla; Sophronsiba E. M. Branham; Joseph Perrin, and Susan, his wife -vs- Axton WHITECOTTON, of S. C., a settlement of a claim against Branham for slaves mentioned in a marriage contract between the late Edward WINGATE, and wife, now Mrs. Branham. The arbitrators order a division made of following slaves: Old Hannah; Sam; Dinah; Sambo; Cornelius; Young Hannah; Mariah; Duke; Doll; Quash; Mahala; Young Hester; Dick and Judy. Both Branham and Perrin place their wives' shares in trust with Whitecotton.

1836, Jan 21
   RELINQUISHMENT - Nathan CRAWFORD, for $300., paid by Benjamin COXE, renounces all right and title to interest in estate of Robert CRAWFORD, dec'd. Joel CRAWFORD makes same arrangement.

1836, Feb 17
   TRANSFER - Nathan CRAWFORD, to Emily M; Caroline M; Charles T; and Elizabeth F. BAYLISS - 175/200th of a share in negro girl, Latisky.

1836, May 2
   MARRIAGE CONTRACT - Between John CARTLEDGE and Elcy JONES. Whereas, Elcy Jones is in possession of certain lands in Columbia Co., consisting of 1,050 acres; also 13 negroes: Rendor, 65; Lidia, 55; Nancy, 28; Marthy, 8; Livy, 5; Ugina, 2; John, 45; Jonathon, 45; Jim, 28; William, 25; Jabez, 18; Allen, 23; Lewis, 70. She is further possessed of 4 mules; 4 horses; a waggon and carriage; furniture; loose stock and provisions. And, whereas, a marriage is shortly to take place between parties, they have agreed to appoint John REID, trustee, for said property, and it is to be held for the only and separate use of said Elcy JONES, reserving to herself, family, and such other family as may be added to hers, including Rebecca CARTLEDGE, and Jane, when not boarded out; and their clothing while in a single state, and a competent and decent support. At Elcy's death the property is to be divided between James PACE, her son; Susan AVARY, her daughter; and Levina PACE, her daughter, and the heirs of their bodies. Cartledge relinquishes all right and title to any of above, in event of wife's death.

1836, May 27
   MORTGAGE - John CARTLEDGE acts as security, (co-signs) a note for $3,294.30, which his brother, James, borrowed from Juriah HARRIS. In order to protect his brother, John, from any possible loss, James mortgages negroes: Osbourne; Matilda; Willis; Polly; Susan, and her child Osbourne; Balaam; Sandy; Page; Kit; Maria; Tom; Mary; Elcy; Lucy; Kissy; and Isaac.

1836, July 19
   QUIT CLAIM - Elizabeth STAPLER to Booker SUTTON, for $87., gives up all claim to a portion of land in Columbia Co., her distributive share of estate of Samuel CRABB, dec'd., known as share #3., 39 1/2 acres. (Samuel Crabb was Elizabeth's step-father).

1836, Sept 8
TRUST DEED - John REYNOLDS to Reuben and Walker REYNOLDS, for 12 1/2¢, 635 acres on Little Germany Creek, also negroes, Anthony; Linney; Patum; Spencer; Sam; Peter; Vincey; also a dark bay horse; and all articles bought by me in a recent sale of my late father's estate. (Father, Reuben REYNOLDS, SR.). The above to be held in trust for the above named John Reynolds. REVOCATION - Reuben and Walker Reynolds, with the consent of John Reynolds, revoke and make void the above trust.

1836, Nov 4
GUARDIAN'S BOND - Alexander DORTCH, guardian of minors of Stephen HATCHELL, of Mecklingburg Co., Va. At a meeting of Quarterly Sessions, on motion of Stephen Hatchell, A. Dortch was appointed guardian of Stephen Jones Hatchell; Peterson Hatchell; Angelina Hatchell, and William Hatchell, infant children of said Stephen. Alexander Dortch placed under $5,000. bond, and given power of attorney to recover all property due the Hatchells from estate of John Hatchell.

1836, Dec 10
ARTICLES OF SEPARATION - John EMERSON and Louisa EMERSON -vs- Henry MASSENGALE, trustee for Louisa EMERSON. Whereas, marriage under all due forms and ceremonies was solemnized on the evening of the 26th of July 1836, between John Emerson, of Morgan Co., and Louisa Matilda BARNES, widow of Joseph BARNES, dec'd., of Wrightsborough, Ga., "Since the marriage certain difficulties, inequietudes and bickerings have arose, destructive of matrimonial harmony and concert of action, which renders married life a blessing, and after duly reflecting, and considering the insuperable obstacles which lie between them and connubial happiness, have resolved, as a choice of evils, to separate." Emerson, wishing to leave Louisa in a "comfortable situation," returns all the property Louisa, as widow of Barnes, brought to the marriage, and relinquishes all claim to same. (Louisa Matilda REESE m. Joseph BARNES, Oct 4, 1830; Louisa Matilda Reese BARNES m. John EMERSON, July 27, 1836; Louisa Matilda Reese Barnes EMERSON m. A. L. HOLLIMAN, Nov 21, 1840).

1836, Dec 20
RECEIPT - "Received of John W. REID, my late guardian, 6 negroes; $700. in cash, in full of all property placed in his hands, and to which I am entitled," s/ James M. PACE

1837, Nov 17
GUARDIAN'S SALE - Nathan BEALLE, guardian for Richard DOZIER, minor son of John DOZIER. Alpheus FULLER, guardian for Cicero DOZIER, minor son of John DOZIER. James F. DOZIER, guardian for John A. DOZIER, minor son of John DOZIER. Above guardians applied to the Court to sell balance of real estate, cont. 300 acres, being the residence of late John Dozier, bequeathed in will to youngest child, Fidelia DOZIER, whose guardian is Green DOZIER. Permission granted, property sold at auction, on Courthouse steps, in Appling. Green Dozier high bidder @ $900.

1837, ____
WRIT OF PARTITION - Of lands held in common by Gazaway DAVIS, in his own right, and as trustee for Sarah WILLIAMS. Gazaway Davis, in own right, Zachariah WILLIAMS, in right of wife, Sarah, and the said Davis, as trustee for said Sarah, present petition of partition to Superior Court, being tenants-in-common of a tract of land conveyed by Isaac WILLIAMS in 1802, to D. and John ANDERSON (Book L, pp 262-269, S/C Minutes). They are desirous of having land partitioned. Stephen DRANE; Benjamin DRANE; Thomas BOWDRIE; John MEGAHEE; and George GUNBY, appointed arbitrators. Decision: To Gazaway Davis, on Big Kiokee Creek, 4 tracts: 545 acres; 760 1/2 acres; 273 1/2 acres; and 297 1/2 acres. To G. Davis, as trustee for Sarah Williams, 4 tracts: 502 acres; 560 1/2 acres; 273 1/2 acres; and 301 acres on the Old Furlough Road.

1837, Feb 23
RELINQUISHMENT - William DEARING for $300., relinquishes all title and claim to estate of Margaret SHAW, to Henry THOMPSON.

1837, Mar 27
MORTGAGE - Henry Bradford PORTER, indebted to Pinkney PERRY, by note for $40.06 1/4, mortgages, 1 sorrel mare, 7 yrs. old; one negro woman, Patty, 60 yrs. old; 10 head of stock; 1 featherbed and bedstead; 1 wooden clock; 1 pine sideboard; 1 Derben (Dearborn) Wagon and Harness. On note to Albert HOLLIMAN, and Pinkney PERRY for $60.31 1/4, he mortgages, "all my interest in a parcel of land known as the Porter Tract on Hart's Creek, 140 acres."

1837, Mar 27
MORTGAGE - James BURNSIDE mortgages to Daniel HAND, for $750.80, all stock of goods and wares of merchandize in Village of Appling, consisting of Dry Goods; Crockery; Hardware and Groceries.

1837, Mar 29
QUIT CLAIM - James BURRAGE to Joshua WHITAKER, "doth relinquish all rights in 126 acres, part of a 252 acre tract surveyed by Solomon FUDGE and Silas MONK."

1837, Apr 8
MORTGAGE - McCullen POLLACK, indebted to Daniel HITT, both of Richmond Co., for $1,700., mortgages 221 acres on Fury's Ferry Road.

1837, May 12
MORTGAGE - George THOMAS, indebted to James F. W. BURROUGHS, on two notes of $1,000., each, mortgages negroes: Easter, 21; Mima, 18; also a carriage more commonly called a buggy, and two horses, one a sorrel with a flax mane and tail, bought from Arthur GUEDRON, and the other a bay bought fron Benton; a one horse wagon, bought of Arthur SMITH, and household furniture, consisting of a mahogany sideboard, and dining table; tea table; secretary; candlestand; 2 large mirrors; mantle clock; 1 doz. parlour chairs; 4 curtained bedsteads, beds and furniture.

1837, May 26
   SHERIFF'S SALE - Isaac RAMSEY, Sheriff, to Mark Price DAVIS, plaintiff in suit against Elizabeth HOWARD. Sells, at auction, all interest Mrs. Howard has in following: John, light complected negro, 25 years old; Harriet, light complected negro, 27 years old. Her children, Nathan; Sawney; June; Elizabeth; and Cynthia, $1,650.

1837, May 27
   MORTGAGE - William BEALLE, in debt to Thomas HAMILTON, of Clarke Co., for $1,080, mortgages 481 acres in Columbia Co.

1837, May 29
   RECEIPT - Peter MARSHALL, to Nathan CRAWFORD, Exr., of Joseph MARSHALL, for distributive share of estate. "Land, negroes, stock, provisions, farm utensils, and all cash and accounts to which I am entitled."

1837, Sept 5
   RECEIPT - Joseph COTTON to Martha POLLARD, for, "my share of estate of Richard POLLARD, dec'd., to which my wife, Lucinda was entitled." $276.76. Lucinda POLLARD m. Joseph COTTON, Jan 1, 1836.

1837, Sept 25
   MORTGAGE - Micajah BOND mortgages negro woman, Mourning, of a yellow color, and her two children, Job and Eleanor, for $1,000., to Benjamin BUGG.

1837, Sept 26
   ARTICLES OF SEPARATION - Between Abraham HEARD, and Harriet (Magruder) HEARD. Whereas, it is found to be inconvenient and impractical for the two parties to live together as man and wife, for cause which need not be enumerated, they have agreed to live separate and apart from each other. Abraham states he is, "no longer responsible for debts contracted by wife. All the gains arising from the care and industry and good management of Harriet, and all money and property which were her dower, shall be hers to enjoy free from all claim of said Abraham." William MAGRUDER appointed guardian of his daughter's dower, and property. Both parties given right to visit their daughters, Antoinette and Cornelia. The girls to be placed in a school in Greensboro, Ga., one now, and the other when she is five years old, and are to be boarded in a home selected by Abraham. If either parent wishes to remove children from school and town of Greensborough, he or she must get permission of other parent.

1837, Oct 10
   RECEIPT - Receipt in full for distributive share of Rebecca and Martha, in estate of Robert CULPEPPER, dec'd. $539.71, for the two girls, signed by John MADDOCKS, guardian.

1837, Nov 14
   MARRIAGE CONTRACT - Between Lucy WELLBORN, George LEWIS, and Mary WELLBORN, who was appointed as trustee for her daughter's property: Negroes, Kit; Abby; Amanda; Malinda; Charlotte, and her

children, Henry; Sampson; Abraham; Daniel; Jane; Angela. (Lucy and George m. Oct 18, 1837).

1837, Nov 23
 DEED OF TRUST - Abraham HEARD places in trust with wife's father and brother, for separate maintenance of wife, Harriet, negroes: Sukey; Jackson; Felix; Allen; Violet; Addison. Trustees to pay Harriet income on labors of said slaves and their increase. If she dies, to go to her infant son, William Lloyd HEARD.

1837, Dec 8
 RECEIPT - Martha POLLARD, one of heirs of Susannah MARSHALL, dec'd., has received from Daniel MARSHALL, the sum of $200., whereof "I have conveyed to Daniel Marshall all my claim to the estate."

1837, Dec 28
 INDEMNIFYING BOND - John MONCRIEF; Wiley MONCRIEF; John H. LITTLE; John FLEMING; Delila MOORE; and James H. MAYES, heirs of David MONCRIEF; and Caleb MONCRIEF, are under bond of $20,000., to Josiah STOVALL, att'y., of Henry SPAULDING. Whereas, Henry became possessed of certain property from the estate, by intermarriage with late wife, Mary MONCRIEF, and since Henry is disposed to give up said property, it is the purpose of present bond to secure his attorney from any loss. s/ John Moncrief; Caleb Moncrief, by John Moncrief. Wiley Moncrief; Wiley, as attorney for William Moncrief; John B. Little; John Fleming; Delily Moore, for husband; James H. Mayes. They sign receipt for negroes: Dick; Betty; Pheriby, and child Marianne; Charity; Polly; Betty, and Dick, a small boy.

1838, Jan 4
 RECEIPT - James YARBOROUGH, Adm. de bonis non, from James BURROUGHS: A receipt in full for negroes, Charles, val. @ $260., negro man, Kit, and boy, Henry @ $930; Mary; Maria, and Bob @ 865., and Clarissa, @ $400.

1838, Jan 4
 RECEIPT - John WILEY, one of heirs of William WILEY, receives from Thomas WILEY, guardian, the following negroes: Charlotte; Epsey, and her son, Romaldus; Isaac and Charles. Also $187.50, in cash, in accordance with will of father, William Wiley. Releases Thomas Wiley from guardianship.

1838, Jan 27
 RECEIPT - John REID, guardian of Thomas H. YARBOROUGH, received from William YARBOROUGH, late guardian of said Thomas, 3 negroes, Jim; Alfred, young men, and Trim, an aged man. Also a note on Nancy YARBOROUGH for $35.46, the same being in full of property and money which came into the hands of William as guardian of Thomas. I hereby exonerate William Yarborough of responsibilities of guardianship.

1838, Jan 27
 RECEIPT - James YARBOROUGH, guardian of William O. P. YARBOROUGH, received from William Yarborough, late guardian of above, negroes: Jacob; Edmond, and Mary. Also $545.70, full share of money and property in hands of William Yarborough, after deducting annual expendi-

tures and advances. Exonerates W. YARBOROUGH from guardianship.

1838, Jan 27
    RECEIPT - James YARBOROUGH receives from William YARBOROUGH, Adm. of estate of John YARBOROUGH, 5 negroes: Frank; Eady; and their children, Charles; Fanny and Moses; notes in amount of $232.41, it being "my proportionate share of estate of John Yarborough, dec'd., my father, sold at advertised sale, Dec. 15, 1835."

1837, Jan 27
    RECEIPT - Nancy YARBOROUGH, and Anne CLARK, late Yarborough, relict and daughter of late James YARBOROUGH, acknowledge receipt of whole interest in personal property of James, dec'd., as follows: Negroes, Lucy; Thornton; David; Jeff; and Robin; also $464.82, our share as heirs in common.

1838, Jan 29
    LETTER - From John W(?) MADDOCK, agent for Isaac WATSON, to Gabriel JONES, Adm. of Robert CULPEPPER, dec'd. "Mr. Jones: If thar is any more coming from the estate of Culpepper to be divided among the heirs, as I come in for to shears, you will pay it over to Mr. J. W. Maddock, and he will receipt for same. Dec. 25, 1837." s/ Isaac Watson, by Mr. Maddock

1817, Mar 24 - Rec. Apr 25, 1838
    AGREEMENT - Between Sarah; Alexander; Mary; Margaret and Thomas TELFAIR, and trustee, Alexander TELFAIR, for $5,500., heirs sell all of Josiah TELFAIR'S plantation to Thomas TELFAIR. Property consists of 1,000, more or less, in three tracts. 150 acres granted formerly to Benjamin UPTON; 300 acres granted formerly to John COBB; balance granted to firm of Howard & Few.

1839, Apr 5
    AGREEMENT - On location of dividing line between Peter LAMAR, and Mary TELFAIR; Mary E. COBB; Margaret L. TELFAIR, by their atty., George JONES. Dispute settled, and each person agrees to release to other, land lying on his side of line.

1839, Apr 16
    MARRIAGE CONTRACT - Between Robert JONES and Nancy A. CRAWFORD, with Eli HOLLY as trustee for Nancy's property, to be used for benefit of Nancy and her two children, Joice and Enoch.

1839, June 11
    DEED OF TRUST - Cornelius COLLINS to Elbert and Archibald MORGAN, of Edgefield Dist., S. C., in trust for Eliza JONES, and children, in accordance with will of late Ozias MORGAN, 169 2/3 acres of land on road from Appling to Old Kiokee Church, adj. land of Joseph MARSHALL, and Martha MOORE, etc.

1839, Oct 11
    BOND FOR MAINTENANCE - Malachi GUY, under $3,000. bond, to John GUY, to furnish John and Mary GUY with the necessaries of life, namely, food and raiment, sufficient for comfort during their natural life.

1839, Oct 11
QUIT CLAIM - Mary REYNOLDS relinquishes all claim on 224 acre tract on Uchee Creek, to James KIRKPATRICK, for $40. Mary inherited part of said tract as wid. of Robert REYNOLDS.

1840, Jan 18
RECEIPT - Received of Thomas M. WATSON, "my former guardian, $250., in full of all demands against said Watson, being my share of estate of late father, Allen JONES."

1838, Jan 29
DEMAND - "Mr. Jones, you will send by John MADDOCK, my part of estate of Robert CULPEPPER, of which I am entitled to two shares, my own, and that of Nathaniel CULPEPPER." (Jane received $66.32).

1838, Feb 13
RECEIPT - Dickens REYNOLDS, who intermarried with Mahala P. A. GILPIN, heir of Green GILPIN, has received from Gabriel JONES, Adm., of Gilpin estate, $654.17, share of wife, in full; $67.50 having been previously paid for a horse, at sale of Gilpin personalty, and balance in cash.

1838, Feb 15
CLAIM - James CRISSMAN; Jacob PRINTUP; and Elisha CRISSMAN, master carpenters, claim an incumberance on house lately belonging to William G. BONNER, now the property of James KILPATRICK, and occupied by Sherwood ROBERTS, adj. lands of Loyless and Ga. Railroad, for repairing and putting addition on said house, at request of William BONNER, Nov., Dec., and Jan., last.

1838, Mar 26
INDEMNITY BOND - Eliza KINNEBREW and Alfred DUNN, to William DUNN, Exr. Alfred Dunn; Eliza Kinnebrew; and Mary Dunn, guardians to minor children of Waters DUNN: Gatewood S. Dunn; Waters M. Dunn; and William Dunn, and Waters for Eliza Kinnebrew, under $20,000., bond to William DUNN, Exr., of estate of Winifred Dunn, dec'd. Petition for partition. Alfred signs receipt for 9 negroes: Airy, val. @ $800., Ellen, @ $325., Mary @ $375., Abraham, @ $1,300., Violet @ $900., Sally @ $525., Julia @475., Jim @ $200., Winny @ $500., share in full. Elizabeth signs receipt for slaves: Catherine, and child, Susan @ $1,100., Matilda @ $500., Mahala @ $400., Jo @ $350., Jane @ $200., Bill @ 1,100., Louis @ $1,100., Lucretia @ $850., share in full.

1839, May 18
RECEIPT - In full, for legacy in right of wife, Samuel STANFORD, to George A. P. WHITEFIELD, guardian of E. P. SANDERLIN. "I acknowleged the receipt from said Whitefield, late guardian of my wife, Eleanor STANFORD, late Eleanor P. SANDERLIN, the following negro slaves: Tenah and her children, Adam and Frank; 1/2 interest in negro woman, Penny, owned jointly by my wife and her sister, Anne KESTERSON; also 1/2 interest of my wife in lot in Lee Co., drawn by her mother; also $821., paid in full at sale for negro woman, Hester, and her child Tom; $280 on hire of negroes. Releases Whitefield from guardianship.

1838, June 5
RECEIPT - John LANGSTON, guardian of Cassandra CULPEPPER, to Gabriel JONES, Adm. estate of Robert CULPEPPER, receipt for $294.81 1/4¢, share in full.

1838, July 10
DEED OF TRUST - Sarah TOMKINS, about to be married to Francis TOMKINS, places in trust with Dr. Charles M. HILL, negroes, Joe and Lucy, with their 5 children; also July; Jerry; Alfred; and Little Alfred; Amy; Hannah; Noe; Ralph; and Susan; also the 300 acre tract known as Quaker Springs.

1838, Oct 20
"AMENDE HONORABLE" - Jefferson TRAMMELL, and wife, Mary, to Mrs. Rebecca KEELING. "To all whom it may concern: Know that an unfortunate difficulty arose in consequence of a misunderstanding between myself, my wife, and Mrs Rebecca Keeling. Whereas, in anger, and without reflection, myself and wife, made use of very improper language, calculated to injure the character of Mrs. Keeling. We do now, after due reflection, feel it due to her to say that we are truly sorry we ever made use of such language, and further say we know nothing derogatory about Mrs. Keeling's character in relation to her virtue."

1839, Nov 7
MARRIAGE CONTRACT - John BYNAUM, of Baldwin Co., to James D. GREEN, in trust for Mary LANSDALE, a certain support and maintenance for herself, and her children now in being, Eliza Ann, and William, and for those who may hereafter be born of her body, all property Mary now possesses, or may expect from her parents, or any other person. John and Mary state their intentions of marrying.

1840, Jan 16
PURCHASE - Commissioners of Town of Wrightsborough, viz: Thomas DOOLY; Edward JONES; Charles WADE; and Thomas WHITE, also the trustees of Wrightsborough Academy, purchase from Sherwood ROBERTS (the Innkeeper), for $175., the house and ground attached thereto wherein Luke LANDSDELL kept a tailor's shop, and known as Bailey's Schoolhouse.

1840, Jan 19
MARRIAGE CONTRACT - As a marriage is to be solemnized between Josiah JONES, and Elizabeth PARHAM, Jones places in trust with Arthur FOSTER, for said Elizabeth and her present children: James; Joel; Edmond; Sarah; Julia; and Savannah, all property Elizabeth now possesses: Negro woman, Rhoda, one draw in the Gold Lottery; one draw in public land lottery.

1840, Feb 14
Holland MC TYRE to Phillips MANTZ, of Augusta, and Simmons CRAWFORD, of Columbia Co., places in trust for Mrs. Ann McTyre, wife of "my son, John, and children; 2 mahogany Tester bedsteads; 1 mahogany bureau; 6 flag-bottomed Windsor chairs; 2 mahogany end tables, alike in size, with fluted posts; 1 pr. Superior Brass andirons; 1

bay horse; 7 head of horned cattle. Most of this was the property of Ann, and sold as property of her husband at his death, and bought by me."

1840, Jan 20
RECEIPTS - John P. BACON; Nicholas C. BACON; John B. MOORE; and Edmond B: BACON, give receipts to Mary BACON, Excx., of Last Will and Testament of John P. Bacon, dec'd., for their shares in full. $1,382. each.

1840, Mar 6
DEED OF TRUST - Samuel GOODE, of Wilkes Co., James HAMILTON, and Thomas HAMILTON, of Columbia Co., and Joseph BYNUM of Hancock Co., place in trust, negroes: Jack and Jenny and their children, Henry; Young Jack; Pamela; Willis; Judy; Nat; Albert, and Felix; Moses and Critty Randall, and children, Peter; Lucy; Charlotte, and Young Moses; Vinny and Horace, and children, Jenny; Esther; Keziah; Billy; Jeff and his wife, Milly, and children, Milly and Seaborne; Lucinda and Wesley, and children, Joe; Wesley, Jr; Prissy; Nancy; Minton; Nancy Dixon and Beverly. Part of personal property of said Samuel Goode, in trust for use and benefit for wife, Frezon; Ann Eliza; Emily; Samuel Jr., and Hines Goode."

1840, Feb 15
DEED OF TRUST - Between Eldredge IVEY, of Columbia Co., Seaborn ARNETT, of Wilkes Co., Zebedee IVEY, of Warren Co., and Elias IVEY and James M. IVEY, of Columbia Co. Whereas, it is "my intention to secure to Martha ARNETT; Thomas ARNETT; Elizabeth ARNETT; and John L. ARNETT, certain property, they being the children of Seaborn Arnett and his wife, Elizabeth, formerly Ivey, daughter of Eldridge Ivey, the following negroes in trust with Zebedee, Elias, and James Ivey: Amy, and her six children, Jim; Bob; Ann; George; Will, and Ellick. For education and maintenance of above children of Arnett."

1834, MARCH TERM - GRAND JURY PRESENTMENTS
"We present Elias SCOTT, for the offense of keeping a tippling-house open on the Sabbath." (Two sets of informers). "We present Reuben WINFREY for keeping open a common, ill-governed and disorderly house, for the purpose of gaming and drinking, and disturbing the citizenry." "We present Abijah HOLLIMAN for keeping open a tippling-house on the Sabbath." "We present John _____, for living in an open state of adultery with a single woman. We present C_____, for living in an open state of adultery with a married man, John _____." "We present William BARDEN, residing in the village of Appling, keeping a disorderly house with open doors on the Sabbath, and a notorious place of resort for slaves." "We also present as a great grievance to the community, the fact that certain free negroes or persons of color, namely Betty and Charlotte, are keeping disorderly houses in and about the village of Appling, places of general resort on the Sabbath, for large numbers of slaves, drinking, rioting, blaspheming, and profaning the Lord's Day."

APPLICATIONS FOR PENSION - Revolutionary War Service

Declaration of HENRY SPAULDING, in order to obtain the benefit of an Act of Congress, passed June 7, 1832.

On this 19th day of September 1832, personally appeared in open court, before the Superior Court of Columbia County, State of Georgia, Henry Spaulding, a resident of said State and County, aged 85 years, and nine months, who declared he was born in Charles County, Maryland, and being duly sworn, doth on his oath make the following declaration: That he entered the service of the United States under the following named officers, and served as herein stated, and that he has a record of his age in a Bible at home.

At the time he was drafted, it was either in the month of June or July, (he cannot now recollect) in the year 1780. He lived in Granville County, N. C., where he was on the date mentioned drafted into the Militia Service, in the Regiment commanded by General Butler. That he was drafted for the period of three months, and entered the service sometime in the month of July, of the year 1780, and marched to the South, by way of Hillsborough, crossed the Yadkin River at the Island Ford, stayed encamped there for a short time, and then marched to Rocky River, where the body of the Troops to which he was attached was met by the American Army returning from Gate's defeat.

That William Moore was Colonel of the Regiment, and William Davidson was the General commanding the detachment, and Capt. Harrison (whose Christian name he believes was, Richard), was Captain of the Company into which he was drafted and with which he marched and served.

Upon meeting the Army as aforesaid, marching from Gate's retreat, the Militia detachment to which he belonged joined them, and marched back to Granville Co., N. C. After a short interval returned under the command of Col. William Moore, General William Davidson, and Capt. Richard Harrison to the South again, as far as Mayhaw Creek in S. C., and was there discharged under a written discharge dated Nov. 9, 1780, and signed by said Col. Moore, and Gen. Davidson, which the declarant has still in his possession, served out his tour of duty of three months, according to law. That he was not engaged in any actual battle, tho often in momentary expectation of being engaged.

That about a year previous to above tour of duty, (he cannot recollect the date), he was called out on another tour of three months, under Capt. Bennett, and was engaged a considerable length of time in hauling the Seine in the River Roanoke to supply the American Army, by catching and bringing up fish for their use, which was instead of a tour in the Army as a soldier.

That he believes his service in the draft, and upon the occasion of service in fishing for the Army exceeded in all, six months, but of the first service he has no documentary evidence, and that he knows of no person who can testify as to his service aforesaid.

That since shortly after the Revolutionary War he has lived in Ga.

The said Henry Spaulding hereby relinquishes any pension or claim, other than the present, and declares that his name is not on the pension rolls of any other Agency or State. He is known to Juriah Harris (preacher); Archer Avary, and James Boyd in his neighborhood.

Petition granted: s/ HENRY SPAULDING (Seal)

THOMAS MURRAY, in order to obtain the benefits of an Act of Congress, passed June 7, 1832, on the 12th day of September 1832, personally appeared before the Superior Court of Columbia County, in the State of Georgia. Thomas Murray, aged 74 years, and being duly sworn, doth on his oath make the following declaration:

That he volunteered his services in the year 1776, in Bedford Co., State of Virginia, under Capt. James Beauford; William Renfrow and Jacob Early being the two Lieutenants.

That the term of this volunteer service was 6 months. That he and his company marched to Williamsburg, State of Va., and was stationed there some time, and as well as he recollects, Patrick Henry was the commanding officer of this station.

From Williamsburg, he and the Company to which he belonged was ordered out against the Cherokee Indians, but as his term of service expired during the march, he volunteered again in the same company, under the same officers.

Col. Charles Lewis commanded the regiment that went against the Indians, and Col. William Christie was Commander in Chief of the expedition against the said Indians. That the Army burned a number of villages, so that peace was made there and then by the Indians with the Commanding Officer, and the Army returned to Virginia on the 24th of December 1776. That the whole length of the service was 9 months.

In 1779, the applicant volunteered in said State and County in the Light Horse Company, under Maj. John Calloway, (Charles Calloway and Barney Price being the two Lieutenants), and marched to Petersburg, Va., and was stationed there for some time, Baron Steuben being the Commanding Officer of that Station. After completing this tour of service, he and the Company returned to their respective homes.

In the Spring of 1780, the applicant volunteered in said State and County under Col. Charles Lynch, Alexander Cummings being Capt., of the Company. This service was to defeat the Tories who were rising and embodying themselves to join Lord Cornwallis, in the State of North Carolina.

This regiment marched over the mountains to the lead mines, and all through that country in pursuit of the Tories. That they defeated the Tories, and took many prisoners. This applicant served seven months, in this tour of duty. After this service was over, said applicant volunteered under Col. Lynch, (Bourne Price, Capt., and Nicholas Welch, Lieut).

In this service, he stayed at least three months, and was during this time, engaged in the Battle of Guilford Courthouse. During this hot battle the regiment to which this applicant belonged acted as Infantry to Col. Washington's Corps of Horse, and fought on the right wing of the Army commanded by Gen. Greene. After the Battle of Guilford, (March 15, 1781), the British retreated across Deep River, at Ramsaw's(?) Mills, to which place they were followed. The regiment to which this applicant belonged was ordered forward to give the British battle, but they had crossed the said Deep River before they could be overtaken, and the pursuit ended at that place. The Regiment was dismissed, and returned home.

About the 1st of August 1781, this applicant was appointed keeper of a depending station at New London Va., and acted as Quartermaster (Deputy), and issued provisions to the Continental Troops stationed there. Altho this station was discontinued about the first of the year, 1782, this applicant stayed there until the end of the year, in discharge of his duty, making out the public accounts, settling the same, taking care of the public stores there, and afterwards sending them to Petersburg. The wages which the applicant received as Deputy Quartermaster was 12 shillings a day, equal to $2.00 a day now.

That the whole time of his service was, as near as he can ascertain at this time, three years and six months.

He hereby relinquishes any claim to a pension or annuity except the present, and declares that his name is not on the pension rolls of any other Agency or State.

Petition granted: s/ THOMAS MURRAY (Seal)

WILLIAM YOUNG, in order to obtain the benefit of an Act of Congress, passed on June 7, 1832, personally appeared before the Honorable, the Superior Court of Columbia County, State of Georgia, Sept 11, 1832.

William Young, a resident of State and County aforesaid, and aged between 70 and 80 years, doth on his oath, make the following declaration: That he entered the service of the Army of the United States as a substitute in the year 1781, with Capt. Lavarsh, and served in the 4th Maryland Regiment of the Infantry, under the following officers: Major Roxburgh commanded the Regiment, Capt. Lavarsh commanded the Company, Bettes (or Bettis) was the Lieutenant I served for, during the term of six months.

I resided in Montgomery County, Maryland. I was in the Siege of York.

Deponent hereby relinquishes any pension or bounty other than the present, and declares that his name is not on the rolls of any other Agency or State.

Petition granted: s/ WILLIAM YOUNG (Seal)

Declaration to obtain a pension, State of Georgia, County of Columbia, under an Act of Congress, passed June 7, 1832.

Personally appeared before the Honorable, the Superior Court now sitting, JOHN LAMBERD (or LAMBERT), a resident of the State and County aforesaid, aged 79 years, who being duly sworn according to the law, doth on his oath, make the following declaration, in order to obtain the benefits of a provision made by an Act of Congress, passed June 7, 1832.

That he enlisted in the Army of the United States in the year 1776, and served in the First Regiment of the Virginia Line, commanded by Col. George Gibson, in the Company of Thomas Ewell.

That he was then a resident of the County of Prince William, in the State of Virginia, and enlisted for the term of three years. That he does not recollect the exact date at which he entered the service, but joined the Army under General Washington a few days after the

Battle of Brandywine, and remained through the winter at Valley Forge and until the British evacuated Philadelphia. That he then accompanied the Army under the Commander in Chief in pursuit of the enemy thru the Jersies, and was engaged in the Battle of Monmouth in a detachment commanded by General Scott.

That he accompanied the main Army to White Plains, and was present when Major Andre was hung. That at Middlebrooks encampment, having nearly served out his time or tour of three years, he enlisted for the duration of the War in the Continental Line; as well as now recollected, into Capt. Crump's Company, and the Regiment commanded by Col. Charles Dabney.

That he returned with the Army to Philadelphia, where he received a furlough of four months, and returned home. This interval of four months was the only time during which he was out of service from the time of his first enlistment until the close of the War. That at the expiration of his furlough, he again joined the regiment at Goochland Courthouse, State of Virginia. That he was present at the Siege of York, and the capture of Cornwallis, and was the second man who entered the gates on that occasion. That he went from York to Portsmouth, where he spent the winter, and returned to York in the Spring, where he remained until finally discharged in the Spring of 1783, by Col. Charles Dabney.

That he was in possession for a number of years of his discharge, but under the impression that it never would be of any service to him, had permitted it to be lost or mislaid, and cannot now find it.

He. doth further declare that on rejoining his regiment at Goochland Courthouse he received the appointment of Non-commissioned Officer, viz: Serjeant, in which capacity he continued to act, until the end of the War.

The above statement is true, as to all material facts, and if any unimportant errors should exist, he claims a charitable indulgence as he has been compelled to rely exclusively on his memory, being able neither to read nor write.

Claims that his name is not on the pension rolls of any Agency or State.

Petition granted: s/ JOHN x LAMBERT

1794, Mar 25

FRANCIS GRIFFIN, a soldier in the 3rd Reg., S. C. Troops, Col. TOMSON, Commanding, appoints JOSHUA GRINAGE.
JOSHUA GRINAGE, appoints ABRAHAM BALDWIN of Philadelphia. Grinage was, "late a soldier in a detachment commanded by Col. William HETH, at the siege of Charleston, belonging to the Va. Line.

Declaration in order to obtain a pension, under an act of Congress, June 7, 1832, State of Georgia, County of Columbia.
On this 15th day of March, in the year 1853, appeared in open court before me, WILLIAM HOLT, one of the Judges of the Superior Court of Law and Equity now sitting: JOHN LYNN, a resident of the State and County aforesaid, now in his 77th year of age. Who, being duly sworn, doth on his oath make the following declaration in order to obtain the benefit of an Act of Congress, passed June 7, 1832.
That he entered the service of the United States under the following officers, and served as herein stated, viz: He entered the service as a volunteer in the Militia of the State of North Carolina at the age of 16 years; and in the year 1780 (as well as this deponent can recollect at this distant period) under the command of Captain MORRIS (MORSE-MOORE --edge of page frayed, writing indistinct) in an expedition against the Cherokee Indians. This expedition was commanded by Gen. RUTHERFORD, the service continuing about three months. The Indian huts were burnt, and their cornfields destroyed. The regiment to which I belonged was under the command of Col. LOCKE. I was born and raised in the county of Rowan, State of N. C., and was a resident of the said County when I entered service as a volunteer in the expedition against the Indians.
I served another time, as will appear by reference to a certificate of discharge signed by Capt. MYRICK DAVIS, herewith exhibited, 28 days in guarding prisoners taken at Tarleton's defeat by Morgan, at the Cowpens, to the Virginia Line. This deponent further states that he served another tour of duty as Light Horseman in Capt. Daniel MC KISSICK'S Company, under the command of Brigadier General CASWELL, as will fully appear by reference to a certificate of discharge herewith exhibited, signed by JAMES BEARDEN, Lieut. Col. (--word missing) by DANIEL MC KISSICK in pursuit of the Tories who had assembled in considerable numbers at Ramsauer's(?) Mills, on the Catawba River. They were dispersed and some prisoners taken, and their plunder.
This deponent further states that he served as a volunteer in an expedition against the Tories upon the Yadkin River under the command of Captain Cole, in which they were defeated, and many prisoners taken.
This deponent further states that he was born in Rowan County, N. C., as informed by his parents, on the first day of January, in the year 1757. I have no record of my age, the record of my age and the rest of my parents' children was made in a family Bible, which was taken by some of the other children.
When I entered the service as a volunteer, I lived in Rowan Co., N. C. Since the close of the Revolutionary War, I have lived in the State of Ga., and for the last 35 years, a resident of Columbia

County, State aforesaid.

I entered the service as a volunteer, never having been drafted or substituted. During my service, I have no recollection of having served with any troops commanded by Regular Officers, the circumstances of my service having been detailed. I have no discharges, but such as have been exhibited. I am known in my neighborhood to the Reverend ROBERT MC CORKLE, WILLIAM BARNETT, JOHN LAMAR, JEREMIAH GRIFFIN, etc. They can testify as to my character and veracity, and their belief as to my service in the Revolutionary War.

This deponent further states that he has no documentary evidence other than the two certificates herewith exhibited, and that he knows of no person whose testimony he can procure, who can testify to his service.

He hereby relinquishes any claim whatsoever to a pension or annuity other than the present, and declares that his name is not on the rolls of any other Agency or State.

WITNESSES:
ROBERT MC CORKLE
WILLIAM BARNETT   (Petition granted)

s/ JOHN LYNN

WILLIAM HOLT, Judge

1801, May 12

Know all men, by these presents that I, DAVID HODGE, of the County of Columbia, and State of Georgia, for divers good causes and considerations, have made, authorized, nominated, and appointed Richard Bullock my true and lawfull attorney, for me, and in my name, for my own proper use and benefit, to ask, demand and receive of and from the Honorable Assembly or Land Office of the State of Virginia, or any other person or persons, for the Bounty of land due me for a tour of duty by me done and performed in the said State of Virginia, or otherwise in the service of the Country done by the said David Hodge in the year of 1755, under the command of General Braddock, in Captain Chumbler's Company, and for me to make, seal and deliver, and for me to do all lawfull acts and things whatsoever, concerning the promises, as fully and in every respect as I myself might or could do were I personally present at the doing thereof, ratifying and confirming by these presents, and allowing whatsoever my said attorney shall in my name legally do, act, or cause to be done, in and about the premises, by these presents.

IN WITNESS WHEREOF, I have hereunto set my hand and seal, this 9th day of May 1801.

his
DAVID X HODGE   Seal
mark

1801, May 12

Know all men by these presents that I, JOHN MC DONALD, SR., Lieutenant, and CALEB RUSSELL, of Columbia County, State of Georgia, for divers good causes and considerations have made, authorized, nominated and appointed RICHARD BULLOCK our true and lawfull attorney, for us, and in our names, for our own proper use and benefit, to ask for, demand and receive of and from the Honorable Assembly or Land Office of the State of Virginia, or any other person or persons, for the Bounty of Land due us for a tour of duty by us done and performed in the said State of Virginia, in the service of our Country. The said McDonald in the year 1758, under the command of GEORGE MUNROE, in the 67th Regiment commanded by ARCHIBALD MONTGOMERY; and the said CALEB RUSSELL in the year 1755, in Captain ARMSTRONG'S Company, commanded by Colonel HANTO HAMILTON.

IN WITNESS WHEREOF, we have hereunto set our hand and seal, this 10th day of April 1801.

s/ JOHN MC DONALD, SR.   Seal

his
CALEB X RUSSELL   Seal
mark

1818, May 1

POWER OF ATTORNEY - PHOEBE EDWARDS, appoints W. W. HALL, att'y., Know all men by these presents that I, PHOEBE EDWARDS, admx., of the estate of JOHN MARTIN, late of Capt. TATNALL'S Company, of the 43rd Regt., U. S. Infantry, have made, constituted and appointed W. W. Hall of the city of Augusta my true and lawful attorney, for me and in my name to ask for and receive from such officers or persons as may be authorized to settle and pay the same whatever may yet be due me, and owing from the United States for the service of said JOHN MARTIN, either for balance of bounty, monthly pay, or any other account, and a full receipt for the same for me and in my name to give, and ask other acts and things necessary for settlement of the accounts of said John Martin, dec'd., for me and in my name to do in every respect as fully as I could myself do were I personally present. Hereby ratifying and confirming whatever my said attorney may lawfully do by virtue of these premises.

IN WITNESS WHEREOF, I have hereunto set my hand and seal, April 24, 1818.

PHOEBE EDWARDS

Signed, and witnessed by:
JOSEPH WALKER
THOMAS WHITE, J. P.

1792, Nov 10

"ROBERT DIXON appoints BRITTAIN SANDERS, of Wake County, N. C., Attorney to receive all bounties and pensions due me from the United States Government and the State of North Carolina."

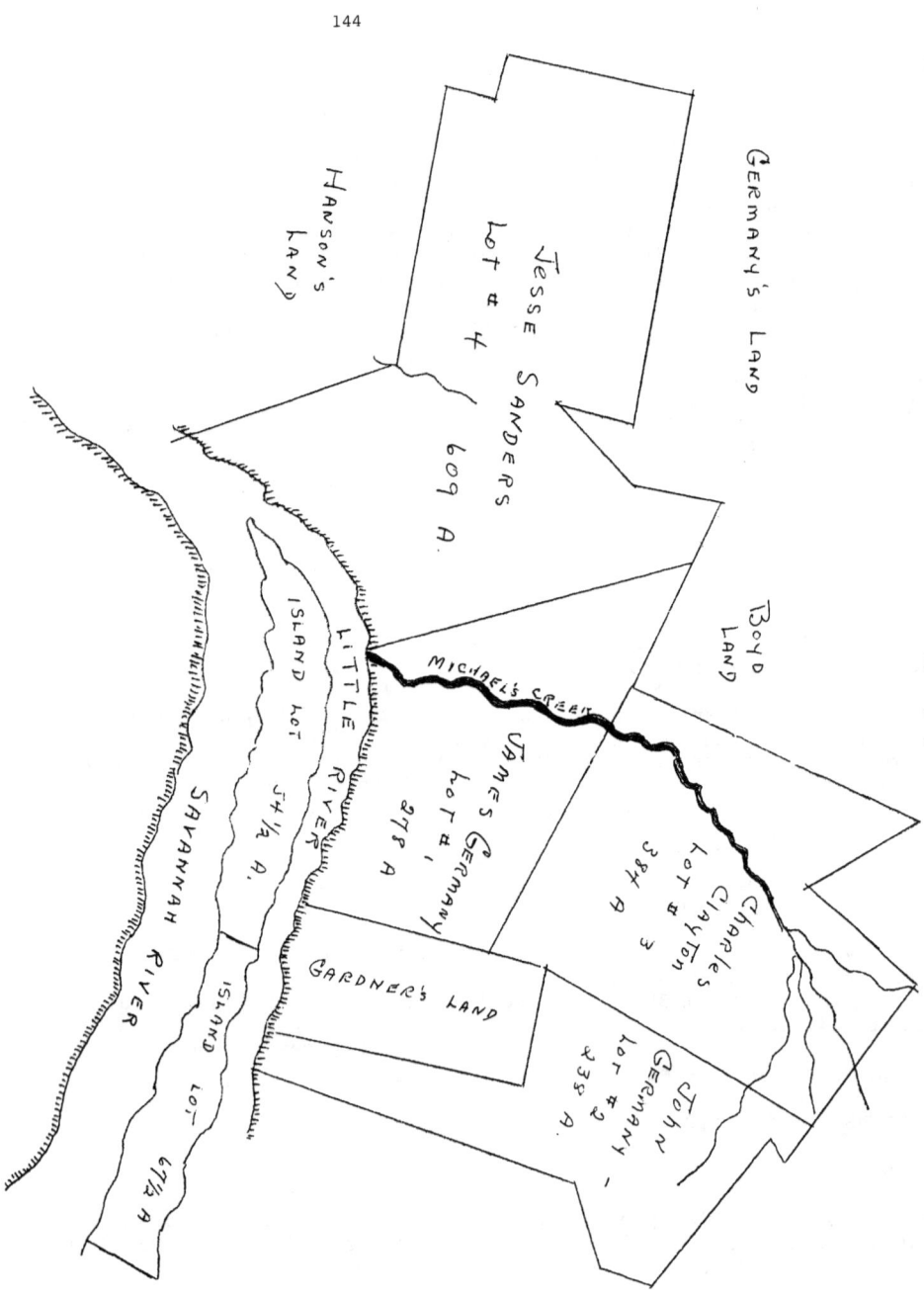

I N D E X

ADAMS 67 69 102 109 123
ADKINS 20
ALBRITTON 41 65 110
ALEXANDER 68 97
ALFORD 63 66 109 124
ALLEN 7 10 13 14 15 16 17 20 33 38 39 42 59 66 101 102 111
ALLISON 77 92
AMES 102
AMOS 114
ANDERSON 46 47 55 58 74 130
ANDRE 140
ANDREWS 11 12 32 75
ANSLEY 90 115
APPLING 51 53 79 90 112
ARMSTRONG 7 14 143
ARNETT 122 136
ATHEY 76
ATKINSON 55
AUSTIN 34
AVARY - AVERY 5 9 10 13 15 18 20 67 68 90 119 120 137
AYERS - AYRES 8 45 70 89 97 98

BACON 38 136
BAILEY 67
BAKER 118
BALDWIN 2 8 41 53 66 82 96 141
BALLARD 76 125
BANKS 49
BANNING 28
BANNOCK 103
BARBAREE 118
BARDEN 136
BARHAM 7 56 102 106
BARKER 21
BARLOW 8
BARNES 59 60 67 68 95 97 100 123 129
BARNETT 48 85 86 99 101 104 142

BARTON 95
BASTON 63 116
BATTEY 43
BATTLE 105
BAYARD 57
BAYLESS-BAYLISS 10 32 42 44 45 52 58 65 90 105 108 110 128
BEALLE 1 3 9 11 17 20 34 43 46 58 63 77 86 95 102 103 106 107 108 109 115 117 120 123 129 131
BEARDEN 141
BEASLEY 9
BEAUFORD 138
BECKHAM 12 32 33 80
BEDELL 78
BELCHER 77
BELL 11
BELLAMY 1
BENNETT 123
BENNING 10 14 35 79 92 110
BENNOCK 70
BENTON 21 32 35 118
BERRIEN 60
BERRY 16
BETTERTON 17
BETTS-BETTIS 41 139
BIBB 57
BINION 31
BIRCH 73
BIRON-BYRON 105
BLACKSTONE 62 116
BLACKWELL 7 45 56 95
BLAIR 45 74 77 86 92 123
BLANCHARD 11 97 123
BLEDSOE 2 51
BLUFORD 1
BLUNT 19 22 92 108
BOLTON 20 88 119
BOND 131
BONNER 28 39 74 134
BOOKER 44
BOOTHE 112

BOROUM-BORUM 9
BOSTICK 81
BOSWELL 13 33 55 99
BOWDRIE-BOWDRE 6 15 28 52 54 58 59 64 65 69 80 81 101 108 112 121 123 130
BOWEN 67 113 121
BOWERS 63
BOYD 23 32 37 74 116 137
BRADBERRY-BRADBURRY 2 109
BRADDOCK 6 142
BRAGG 50
BRANHAM 120 121 128
BRIGHTWELL 73 77
BRINSON 58
BRISCOE 7 25 45 46 47 55 78 107
BRISON 55
BROADUS 15
BROOKING 7
BROOKS 14
BROWN 8 36 42 47 49 55 85 88 123
BROWNSON 72
BRUNSON 54
BRYAN 109 111 115 123 124
BUGG 21 28 37 49 62 63 64 71 100 103 109 110 112 117 119 125
BULL 28 43 67 114
BULLOCH-BULLOCK 1 6 24 80 118 123 142 143
BURCH 72 122 127
BURGAMY 32
BURKE 74
BURNETT 6
BURNLEY 63
BURNSIDE-BURNSIDES 18 70 94 111 115 121 130
BURRAGE 130
BURRISS 66

BURROUGHS 2 18 58 61 63
    95 110 113 123 125
    130 132
BURTON 23
BUSH 110
BUSSEY 98 109
BUTLER 137
BUTT-BUTTS 6 36
BUYS 20
BYNAUM-BYNUM 4 18 42 92
    135 136
BYRD 39

CALDWELL 70 78
CALLOWAY 138
CAMPBELL 10 88 117
CAPEL 7
CAPERS 8
CARLETON 3
CARMICHAEL 4 24 75
CARNES 71
CARR 4 19 40 54 64 68
    82 94 107 108 113
    123
CARRELL-CARROLL 19 75
    107
CARRINGTON 16
CARTER 55 85 127
CARTHIEL 29
CARTLEDGE 19 20 21 26
    41 64 67 69 76 84
    88 97 105 107 108
    110 111 115 116
    118 119 123 124
    128
CARY 12 17 63 80 102
CASTLE 74 75
CASWELL 141
CATHELL 29
CATLIN 112
CAWTHORN 103
CHAMBERLAIN 72 75
CHENNAULT 10 34
CHRISTIE 138
CHUMBLER 142
CITRAN 91
CLAIBORNE 39
CLANTON 17 18 20 21 22
    43 91 95 99 113 115
    117 123 127
CLARK-CLARKE 4 8 9 15
    50 83 124 133
CLARKSON 4

CLAYTON 9 80 97 99 116
CLEVELAND 47
CLIETT 36 65
CLIFTON 18 114
CLOUD 6
COBB-COBBS 5 12 33 41
    42 61 67 83 84 85
    90 92 93 99 100
    101 102 103 107
    111 112 115 122
    127 133
COCHRAN 45 98 99
COCKE 37 58 59 60 83
COLE 76 120
COLEMAN 3 39 49 58 76
    95 98 103 120 121
    122 126
COLLIER 11 91 92 95 97
    98
COLLINS 13 24 29 30 54
    60 66 69 84 99 113
    114 117 120 133
COLVARD 47
COMPTON 19
CONE 52
CONN 76
COOK 62 124 127
COLLIDGE 71
COPINGER 5
COOPER 18 64 77 109 114
CORNWALLIS 141
COTTON 53 60 109 131
COURSON 71
COUSINS 84
COVINGTON 63
COWLES 20
COXE 68 128
CRABB 32 41 113 128
CRAFTON 100 104 105
CRAWFORD 4 5 7 8 9 12
    13 14 17 19 20 26
    30 31 34 36 46 55
    59 63 67 68 74 75
    76 77 78 79 89 85
    86 87 89 90 91 92
    95 98 99 100 101
    103 108 110 111 113
    114 118 126 127 128
    131 133 135
CREEMOR 1
CRISSMAN 134
CRITTENDON 8 74 84 118
CROOKSHANKS 75 77 101

CRUMP 88 97 140
CULBREATH 2 3 9 12
    18 20 21 43 50
    65 78 83 89 91
    92 116 124
CULPEPPER 21 68 131
    133 135
CUMMING(S) 76 78 107
    110 138
CUNNINGHAM 41
CURTIS 85

DABNEY 140
DALL 75
DANIEL 37 38 53
DANIELLY 89
DARBY 81 110
DARK 98
DARLEY 85
DARLING 25
DARSEY 56 81 123
DAUGHERTY 6 48
DAVIDSON 137
DAVIES 74
DAVIS 3 5 11 40 64
    66 74 75 76 79
    83 94 95 102
    108 109 116 122
    130 131 141
DAWSON 45 69 123
    125
DAY 47
DEAKINS 89
DEAN-DEANE 3 19
DEARING 130
deGRAFFENREID 3
DEMPSEY 88
DENHAM 13 26 40
DENNIS 1 106 120
    121
DENSON 125
DENT 8 10 12 17 34
    63 83 91 95
DEVORIE(?) 14
deYAMPORT 82
DILLON 12 70
DIVINE 45
DIXON 1 32 33 49 68
    143
DODSON 88
DOGGETT 99
DOOLY 40 63 70 107
DORSETT 39 77 78 79
    80 105

ORSEY 80
ORTCH 21 129
OUGHERTY 45 106
OUGLASS 1 75
OWNS 8 84
OYAL 57
OZIER 17 32 39 46 64
  67 114 120 129
RANE 10 36 62 63 66
  100 130
REW 6
RIVER 68 123
U BOSE 45 115 116
UCKWORTH 49
UDLEY 6
UNAWAY 103
UNHAM 12
UNN 4 26 27 32 33 47
  52 77 78 108 115
  134
URDAN 32
URGER 108
URKEE 73
UTCH 17
YSART 99

ADS 72
ADY 20
ARLY 138
DMONDSON 58 89
DWARDS 143
LAM 7
LBERT 24
LKINS 22
LLIOT 108
LLIS 12 18 33 52 60
  77 83
MERSON 69 70 129
NGLEMANN 12 13
NGLETT 63
NNOLDS 75
SPEY 83
UBANK(S) 16 38 97 113
VANS 7 14 31 49 63 65
  87 121
VERBY 9
WELL 139

FAISAN 9
FARRAR-FARRER 50 54 55
  56 60 83 85 86
FAWCETT 13
FEE 52
FELL 90

FENNILL 63
FERRALL-FERRELL 17 93
  106
FERRAR 55
FEW 4 8 15 40 41 50
  53 57 58 75 77 81
  82 91 101 107
FIELD 51
FINNEL 109
FINNEY 52 120
FITZSIMMONS 75
FLAKE 125
FLEMING 2 10 55 57 84
  96 97 98 106 109 132
FLETCHER 53
FLINT 14 54 62 91 106
FLORANCE 54
FLOURNOY 40 71 82 109
FLOYD 24
FORSYTH(E) 6 110
FOSTER 14 15 17 29 34
  90 91 95 102 103
  106 110 135
FOUNTAIN 96
FOX 43 46 49
FRAIL-FRALE-FREEL 31 33
  58 59 84
FRANKLIN 77
FRAZER 11
FUDGE 10 130
FULLER 11 20 45 66 79
  109 129
FURY 88 95

GAITHER 104
GALPHIN 26
GARDNER 2 32 74 77 79
  83 91 92 99
GARNETT 27 37 106 118
GARRETT 48 55
GARTRELL 33 65 91 124
GERALD 40
GERMANY 25 29 70 79 80
  88 97 98 109 110
  116 123 124
GIBSON 11 46 68 70 91
  105 123 125 139
GILBERT 5
GILL 51 118
GILMER 101 103
GILMOR(E) 75
GINDRAT 100
GOODE 136
GOODWIN 13
GOOLSBY 14

GRADY 2 51
GRAHAM 97
GRANT 66 125
GRAVES 31 64 67 93
  106 116
GRAY 47
GREATHOUSE 74 75
GREEN(E) 63 77 115
  127 135
GREENWOOD 3
GRIERSON 73
GRIFFIN 2 4 9 29 33
  39 45 63 81 89
  90 101 104 112
  118 120 122 124
  127 142
GRIGSBY 2
GRINAGE 1 2 4 14 51
  53 57 77 79 88
  108 141
GRUBBS 36
GUEDRON 69 130
GUEST 79
GUNBY 19 21 69 123
  130
GUY 133

HABERSHAM 3 4 5
HAIG 101
HALBERT 88
HALE 20
HALL 1 85 125
HAMILTON 3 4 7 13
  50 51 54 66 70
  77 114 120 123
  125 131 136 143
HAMLETT 3
HAMMOND 97
HAMPTON 11
HAND 130
HANDLEY 25 127
HANNON 89
HANSON 27
HARDEN 3 8 33 126
HARGRAVES 10 66
HARGROVE 76
HARKIN 100
HARRIS(S) 4 5 6 8
  14 15 28 31 51
  61 67 69 88 92
  117 121 123 124
  128 137
HARRISON 10 43 66
  122 124 137

HARVEY 106
HASTINGS 1
HATCHELL 21 22 129
HATCHER 77
HATTAWAY 33 93 100
HAWES 20
HAWKINS 9 71
HAWORTH 17
HAYNES 24 52 53 72 104
HAYNIE 7 42 55 78
HEARD 67 68 70 80 131
    132
HEATHECOTE 75
HEGGIE 21 69 89 108
    116 118 121
HEMPHILL 104
HENDERSON 43 74 86 87
HENRY 138
HESTON 1
HETH 2
HICKERSON 10
HICKS 63 64 65 115
HILL 19 20 93 124 127
    135
HILLARY 127
HINTON 11
HITT 130
HOBBY 13 125 127
HOBDAY 53
HODGE(S) 6   115
HODGENS 107
HOGE 24 79 92 123 142
HOGG 29
HOLDEN 74 75
HOLLAND 1 77
HOLLEMAN-HOLLIMAN 4 125
    129 130 136
HOLLIDAY 72
HOLLINGSWORTH 26
HOLLY 133
HOLT 139 141 142
HOPSON 51
HORN 72 108
HOUSTOUN 78
HOWARD 3 9 52 58 59 81
    87 90 91 95 114 116
    119 122 131
HOZICK 71
HUBERT 78
HUCHERSON 10
HUCHINGSON 21 44
HUDGINS 124
HUDNALL 72
HUDSON 69

HUGHES 8 9
HUME 55
HUNT 34 36 37 38 39 72
HURST 10 109
HUTCHINSON 110
HYNES 2

IVEY 49 107 136

JACKSON 8 13 52 60 92
    94 100 104 105
    114 126
JAMERSON 12 99
JARVIS-JERVIS 81
JELKS 17 20 88 98
JENKINS 19 54 81 83 114
JENNINGS 107
JOHNS 60 64 120
JOHNSON 1 16 20 47 57
    59 76 94
JOHNSTON 3 7 8 24 79 109
JONES 4 5 6 14 15 19 21
    23 25 26 27 37 38 42
    44 46 50 54 55 56 58
    60 66 67 68 69 70 79
    81 82 83 85 86 91 92
    93 95 96 97 98 101
    105 107 108 113 118
    119 122 123 124 126
    127 128 133 134 135
JORDAN 48
JOWELL 5 55 98

KEELING 135
KEITH 45 56 61 65 81 95
    126
KELLY 92
KENDRICK 12
KENNADEY 38
KENNEBREW- KINNEBREW .08
    134
KENNON-KINNON 90 112
KESSLER 61
KILLGORE 74 104
KILLINGSWORTH 63
KILPATRICK 134
KINDRICK 119
KING 61 65 77 90 117
KIRKPATRICK 134
KIRKWOOD 1
KNIGHT 62
KNOX 118
LAMAR 34 43 46 47 48 51
    53 67 69 76 87 100
    101 117 123 133 142

LAMBERT 139 140 141
LAMKIN 11 30 50 55
    62 68 69 90
LANGSTON 74 84 87
    100 102 109
    135
LANSDALE(DELL) 68
    69 135
LARKIN 102
LATHROP 25
LAURENCE 35
LAVARSH 139
LAWSON 55 127
LAZENBY 3 75 77 89
    112
LEAVER 90
LEDLOW 80 88
LEE 38 41 120
LEIGH 31 63 109 113
LEITH 38 60 112
LESLIE-LESLY 35 92
    124
LESQUIEUX 109
LEWIS 1 46 131 138
LILES 10
LINES 69
LING 40
LINN-LYNN 23 105
    127 142
LINVILLE 13
LITTLE 132
LLOYD 42
LOCKE 141
LOCKHART 105
LOCKLIN 51
LONG 73 97 99
LONGSTREET 69
LOVE 16
LOVELACE-LOVELESS
    11 17 86 107 119
LOVELL 29
LOWE 4 12 13 19 22
    24 26 33 34 36
    48 54 58 68 81
    85 91 92 96 116
    120 123
LUCAS 68
LUCKEY 12 13 58 89
LUKE 16 64
LYNCH 138
LYNES 126
LYON 14 97

MC BRIDE 3 5

MC CARDEL-MC CARDLE
    2 41
MC CARTY 1
MC CLUNG 78
MC CORD 99
MC CORKLE 142
MC CORMICK 74 102
MC COY 80 96
MC DANIEL 59
MC DONALD 6 61 95 98
    120 143
MC DUFFIE 41
MC EACHIN 91 92 95
MC ELWEE 16
MC FARLAND 39 40 95 98
    120 121 122
MC GAHEE 13
MC GAR 38 60
MC GEE 16
MC GINTY 23
MC GRUDER(MAGRUDER) 17
    30 36 43 46 48 57
    64 78 93 106 116
    122 126 131
MC HAMZIE 94
MC INTOSH 15
MC KAY(MC CAY) 54 100
MC KENZIE 103
MC KINNE(Y) 84 94 100
MC KISSICK 141
MC LAUGHLIN 50
MC LENDON 53
MC MUN 10
MC MURPHY 26
MC MURRELL 75
MC NAIR 55 64
MC NEAL 15
MC NEIL 8 9 18 30 34
    35 53 83 124
MC TYRE 75 135

MACKIE 75
MACOMB 56
MADDIRA 9
MADDOCK(S) 6 131 133
MADDOX 4 24 76 86
    90 115
MAGAHEE 65 90
MAHAN 1
MAHONEY 47
MALONE 17
MANES 42
MANTZ 135
MARBURY 24 51

MARCUS 51 78
MARSHALL 3 20 21 22 32
    38 48 49 53 55 60
    66 69 83 92 93 95
    107 108 111 112 113
    114 118 124 126 131
    132 133
MARTIN 13 17 18 34 42
    58 63 70 115 122
    125 143
MASSENGALE 64 68 70
    125 129
MAT(T)HEWS 5 83
MATHIS 24 25
MAULDEN 88
MAXWELL 24 53 72
MAYS-MAYES 74 132
MEADE 75
MEADORS 9
MEALING 117
MEARS 13
MEGAHEE 130
MELLOWN 26
MENDENHALL 82
MERIWETHER 4 14 35 50
    53 72 92 94 96 98
    100 110
MESSER 69
MESSINGER 111
MICON(?) 14
MIDDLETON 71 78 122
MILES 76
MILLER 13 41 46 64 93
MILLHOUSE 55
MILTON 96
MIMS 14 91 92 98
MINOR 29 33
MITCHELL 16 88
MONCRIEF 22 132
MONK 6 32 130
MONROE-MUNROE 7 16 143
MONTGOMERY 7 16 70 143
MOON 5 63 83
MOORE 1 5 10 13 26 28
    29 35 41 45 50 52
    53 54 58 84 88 89
    121 132 133 136 137
MORAN 8
MOREHEAD 29
MORGAN 25 126 133
MORRIS(S) 37 62 92 107
    121 141
MORTON 49
MOSELEY 68

MOSSMAN 54 79 96
MOTE 93
MOY 109
MURPHY 93
MURRAY-MURRY 58 65
    99 105 138 139
MURRELL 9 42
MYERS 15

NAPIER 13 14 23 24
    79 96 100 120
NAYLOR 73 74 77 78
NEAL 15 39 45 57
NEILSON 65 95
NELSON 10 82
NESBIT 65
NEWSOM(E) 61 63 64
    112
NIDAY 53
NIXON 1 2
NOE 79
NOLAND 95
NORMENT 11
NUNN 12

OATS-OATES 9 35
OFFUTT 26 61 62 85
    101 103 105
OLIVE 36 46 47 48
    56 59 75 78 94
    96 124
OLIVER 4
O'NEAL 33
OUVRAY-OUVRY 72 73

PACE 14 16 30 57 58
    94 104 105 109
    128 129
PAGE 38
PARHAM 32 99 135
PARKER 7 8 36
PARKES 96 119 120
    122
PARISH 85
PARIS-PARRIS 49 85
PASCHALL 14
PATTERSON 75 101 103
PATTON 78
PAUL 106 114 122 124
PAYNE 12 29
PEACOCK 75
PEARRE 42 61 62 80
    97 101 103 104
    115 116 125

PECK 62
PEEKE 30
PERKINS 74
PERRIAN 56
PERRY 68 121 130
PERRYMAN 30 32 47 60
    81 84 89 95
PERSONS 70
PETTIT 49 121
PHELPS 87 109
PHILLIPS 25 39
PHINIZY 60
PITTMAN 31 100
POAGE 8 9
POLLACK 130
POLLARD 126 131 132
POOL(E) 1 32
POPE 100 116
PORTER 41 58 67 75 121
    124 130
POUNDS 20 34 40 85 88
    101 115 120 122
POWELL 10 32 34 44 83
    94
POWERS 116
PRATHER 59
PRESCOATT 127
PRICE 138
PRINTUP 134
PRIOR 54 66 90

RADFORD 77
RAIFORD 15
RAMSEY 3 27 50 51 65
    83 84 89 119 120
    121 124 125
RANDOLPH 4 13 23 79
    96 121
RAVOT 55 127
RAWLS 22
RAY 26 27 32 41 57 73
    85 93 99 101 104 113
RAZOR 1
READ(E) 29 83
REED-REID 11 52 74 113
    121 128 129 132
REES 19 35 46 50 70
    105 107 108 114
    125
REESE 42
RLEVES 53
RENFROW 138
RENNOLDS 2
REYNOLDS 18 51 65 113
    117 119 121 129 134

RICHARDS 91
RICHARDSON 27 80
RICKETSON 74
RILEY 30
ROBERSON 116
ROBERTS 17 21 70 74
    90 95 96 104 108
    110 114 134
ROBERTSON 97 124
ROBEY 16
ROBINSON 14 103
ROCHELLE 17
ROGERS 115
ROSBOROUGH 49 76
ROSCOE 67
ROSS 4 8 14 40 43 54
    85 94 100
ROUSSEAU 79
ROXBURGH 139
ROZIER-ROZAR 88 93
RUSSELL 6 118 143
RUTHERFORD 141
RUTLEDGE 33
RYAN 100

SAMPLER 17
SAMPSON 11
SAMUEL 92 104 105
SANDERLIN 134
SANDERS 1 25 28 35 37
    40 51 53 58 80 90
    99 118 120 143
SANDERSON 11
SANDRICK 81
SATTERWHITE 27 47 110
SAVADGE-SAVAGE 29 39 77
SAXON 49
SCARBOROUGH 112
SCHICK 90 91
SCHLEY 121
SCOTT 12 15 18 40 66
    69 78 91 107 111
    118 124 136 141
SCRUGGS 2 19 64
SEARGEANT 38
SEAY 66 99 122
SELL 6 23 78
SESSOMS 90
SEWALL 12 86
SHACKLEFORD 2 24 29 52
    66 76 81 84 91 114
SHAW 42 76
SHEARER 20
SHEFFIELD 47 110

SHEFTALL 26
SHEPHARD 9 98 120
    121
SHIELDS 49 52 66 67
SHIPP 83
SHIVERS 117
SHORT 37 38 56 57 66
    93 124
SHUMATE 102 103 106
SIDWELL 78
SILVA 5
SIMMONS 12
SIMS-SIMMS 24 27 34
    40 51 52 56 80
    88 98
SINQUEFIELD 26 51 52
SKINNER 3 14 46 47
    61 75 84 95 116
    124
SLATON 35 36 85 96
SLATTER 82
SLAUGHTER 15 16 111
SLIGHT 6
SMALLEY 19 89
SMITH 7 36 44 45 48
    53 56 59 61 76
    85 86 87 91 98
    103 112 120 121
    130
SOMERWELL 8
SPAULDING 22 38 132
    137
SPIERS 6 68
SPIVY-SPIVEY 40 45
    111
STALLINGS 56 72 91
    92 95 106 114
    121 125
STANFORD 40 45 48 59
    66 68 69 77 84
    91 113 114 117
    134
STANTON 95
STAPLER 11 33 44 128
STARKE 40 58 65 91
    106 111
STEED 116 123
STEUBEN 138
STEVENSON 56
STEWART 2 13 52 56
STITH 93
STODDARD 115
STONE 13 15 72 123
STORY 64

STOVALL 22 132
STRONG 66
STROTHER 91
STUART 17 63 99
STUBBLEFIELD 73
STURGES-STURGIS 32 33
    37 72 73 93
SUDTHARD 1
SULLIVAN 34 38 42 62
    90 93 118
SUMTER 2
SUTHERLAND 19 20 77
SUTTON 41 128

TABOR 42
TANKERSLEY 16 34 64 92
    104 105 107 108
    109 114 126
TARVER 62
TATTNALL 97 99 143
TAYLOR 1 22
TELFAIR 54 77 78
    81 101 113 114 133
TERRILL 39
THOMAS 1 6 20 21 34
    85 95 98 108 110
    130
THOMERSON 2
THOMPSON 2 7 56 57 65
    99 103 130
THOMSON 1 6 23
THORNTON 83
TILLER 26
TIMMERMAN 50
TINDALL-ELL-ILL 10 12
    28 40 52 59 64 115
    118
TINSLEY 20 98 128
TODD 107
TOMKINS 68 69 135
TOMSON 141
TOOLE 41 46 97 102 115
TOOMBS 83
TRAMMELL 135
TRAMWELL 118
TRUEMAN 8
TUBMAN 59 60 83 97
TUCKER 117
TUDOR 116
TURNBULL 4
TURNER 12 16
TUSTREE 31
TWIGGS 119
TWINING 73

TWITTY 54
TYLER 52

UNDERWOOD 39 58 90 95
UPTON 17 34 50 52 101
    113 114

VAN DORLINDER 2
VANSANT 117
VAUGHN 1 44 48
VERNON 55 78
VICKERS 10
VINSON 68 126
WADE 135
WAGGONER 12
WAILES 73
WAINRIGHT 41
WALKER 12 26 32 33 35
    36 61 85 91 96 110
    143
WALL 47 53 100
WALLACE 7 16
WALTER 6
WALTON 3 10 14 23 33 35
    40 43 44 54 64 69
    77 80 92 95 99 100
    102 114 116
WARD 124
WARE 50 98 102 104 105
    107 112
WARREN 21 22 85 109 126
WASHINGTON 1 138 140
WATERMAN 95
WATKINS 49 50 54 63 71
    76 98 117
WATSON 4 11 21 54 72 76
    103 107 112 134
WAYNE 56 92 95
WEATHERBY 82
WEBSTER 2
WEDDERBURN 2
WEISSINGER 17
WELCH 118 138
WEST 17 104 111
WELBOURNE-WILBORN 86 87
    91 100 106 131
WELLS 30
WEST 17
WHEAT 33 87 88 89 123
WHEATLEY 7
WHEELER 125
WHITAKER 9 130
WHITCOMB 8 91 92 95 124
WHITE 1 6 9 10 14 15 39
    47 53 64 70 77 92 94
    110 111 114 135 143
WHITECOTTON 128
WHITEFIELD 48 134
WHITNEY 22
WHITTINGTON 120
WHITTON 89
WILEY-WYLEY 8 51 66
    82 132
WILKINS 18 38 42 48
    50 51 57 61 62
    63 89 90 92 103
    106 110 120 124
WILKINSON 116
WILLIAMS 17 37 46 55
    58 84 104 130
WILLIAMSON 5 97
WILLINGHAM 39 54 55
    64 66 74 82 104
    118
WILLIS 103
WIL(L)SON 12 49 52
    56 59 69 70 99
    109 122
WINFIELD 42
WINFREY 23 31 66 85
    101 113 114 136
WINGATE 128
WINN-WYNNE 25 28 51
WINSETT 58
WISEMAN 39
WISHER 16
WOOD(S) 2 18 34 43
    44 57 64 76 95
    106
WOODING 69 116 123
WOODRUFF 77 105
WOODWARD 58
WOOLRIDRIGE 56
WRIGHT 3 4 5 6 17 61
    70 71 77 79 89 106
    113 114 119 121
    127
WROE 16
WYATT 66
YARBOROUGH 1 5 19 66
    94 102 118 119 132
    133
YOUNG 5 14 32 64 99
    108 115 139
YOUNGBLOOD 26 27 39
    94 103
ZACHRY 33 66 72 116

www.ingramcontent.com/pod-product-compliance
Lightning Source LLC
Chambersburg PA
CBHW072336300426
44109CB00042B/1637